G000280193

Unlikely Rebels

THE GIFFORD GIRLS AND THE FIGHT FOR IRISH FREEDOM

ANNE CLARE

MERCIER PRESS

IRISH PUBLISHER – IRISH STORY

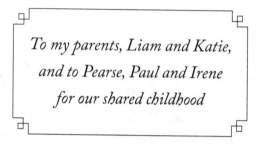

To my parents, Liam and Katie,
and to Pearse, Paul and Irene
for our shared childhood

MERCIER PRESS

Cork

www.mercierpress.ie

© Anne Clare, 2011

ISBN: 978 1 85635 712 8

10 9 8 7 6 5 4 3 2

A CIP record for this title is available from the British Library

This book is sold subject to the condition that it shall not, by way of trade or otherwise, be lent, resold, hired out or otherwise circulated without the publisher's prior consent in any form of binding or cover other than that in which it is published and without a similar condition including this condition being imposed on the subsequent purchaser.

No part of this publication may be reproduced or transmitted in any form or by any means, electronic or mechanical, including photocopying, recording or any information or retrieval system, without the prior permission of the publisher in writing.

Printed and bound in the EU.

CONTENTS

INTRODUCTION

It ought to have been a joyful occasion; there should have been flowers and music, wine and the laughter of family and friends. But there were none of these things: no pretty bridesmaids, no wedding cake, no speeches. And what speeches they would have been, with the bride's father a magnanimous solicitor, used to good company, and with intimates such as John B. Yeats and his sons. The groom's father, too, fraternised where talk was seasoned with wit and wisdom, for he was a papal count, a barrister and a fine-art connoisseur. As for the groom, what golden, happy words he would have used, a mystic poet with, perhaps paradoxically, a great gift of laughter and, most of all, a young man whose tender letters to her showed how much he loved his young bride.

So why were these nuptial pleasantries absent when Joseph Mary Plunkett married Grace Vandeleur Gifford on 3 May 1916? The venue itself was the least likely place to engender celebration of even the most sober kind. The marriage took place within the confines of the Catholic chapel in Kilmainham Gaol in Dublin, whose cold, grey walls had absorbed the sighs of Irish political prisoners for over 100 years. Illumination comprised candlelight, and the witnesses were British soldiers carrying bayonets. The British authorities might have allowed her sister, Nellie, a prisoner in the jail, to stand by her side, but Grace Gifford was not allowed even that comfort.[1] The only resemblance to an ordinary marriage ceremony was the age-old promise of fidelity spoken to the priest, but even that was macabre.

The words 'till death us do part' held a hollow ring for that young couple, who knew not only that there would be no married life or honeymoon, but that death by firing squad awaited the groom within a matter of hours, because he had been one of the seven signatories of the Proclamation of the Irish Republic at the General Post Office, Dublin, ten days before.

After the stark ceremony they were allowed ten minutes together, in Plunkett's cell, surrounded by British army personnel. A simple meal might have been provided. Instead, a bowl of gruel lay on a small table on the cell's stone floor. Grace recorded later that there was no spoon and, not surprisingly, the bowl was untouched.[2] This for a man whose family table was furnished with fine napery and crystal glasses.

No description of Grace Gifford on her wedding day is extant, except that recorded by the jeweller who sold her the ring on her fateful dash to the prison. He said that her eyes were red with weeping.[3]

There was a press notification of the wedding in Kilmainham Gaol in *The Irish Times*, and it read starkly: 'Plunkett and Gifford – May 3rd, 1916, at Dublin, Joseph Plunkett to Grace Gifford.'[4]

Thirteen words reflected aptly the paucity of the event. Yet, for all its starkness, even the Gothic horror of its setting, the ceremony at Kilmainham was, in fact, the wedding of the year. Daniel Maclise, the artist, has recorded in oils another politically significant wedding – that of the twelfth-century nuptials of the conquering Norman, Richard de Clare, Earl of Pembroke, known as Strongbow, to Eva McMurrough, daughter of the King of Leinster. Maclise saw the ceremony as symbolic of the death of Gaelic civilisation. The harpist's instrument is broken, and Strongbow's foot crushes some artefacts of early Irish art.[5] But if the artist's symbolism of the death of an old civilisation is valid, so too does the Plunkett–Gifford wedding symbolise, for all its wretchedness, the reawakening of Gaelic Ireland.

In that sense, it was the wedding of the year in 1916 – a sort of wedding and wake combined.

When all the executed had been buried, when the consequent War of Independence had been fought and partly won, and when the Irish Free State emerged from the Treaty of 1921, though only after the trauma of Civil War, southern Ireland began to settle down. The Irish Republic was not declared until 1948, and the generation who were born and grew up between those years were very aware of historical happenings. There were many mixed households, such as my own. We knew that our beloved grandfather, Christopher Walshe, had been regimental sergeant major of the Connaught Rangers during the First World War and that when he 'took the Saxon shilling' he was told by his brother Henry that he had disgraced his Fenian forebears: the brothers remained estranged for life.

When we hid under the stairs playing hide-and-seek, we knew that was where Great-Uncle James, who had been in the Ancient Order of Hibernians (AOH), had hidden a gun in 1916. We approached the vegetable shop of Paddy Spain in Sandwith Street with a certain awe, aware that this mild-mannered man, selling pot herbs and potatoes, and *always* with a bandaged hand, was reputed to have been involved in the attack on Oriel House, at the corner of Westland Row. His sister, Maggie, had been jailed in Kilmainham and had 'died of it' – the strange diagnosis of her neighbours.

There was mention of our maternal great-grandparents having met at the Foresters' Ball, he wearing their dashing uniform and she a green ball gown. There were uncles on the paternal side who had been in the Irish Republican Army (IRA) and aunts who had been in Cumann na mBan. We heard references to 'The Troubles', 'The Struggle', 'The Troubled Times' and 'The Movement'. Men were referred to as having been 'one of the boys', and this was an accolade. There was great talk of 'the Big Fella' and 'Mick', and my mother described how impressive Michael Collins was, walking in his IRA officer's uniform at the funeral of Thomas Ashe. We knew that our father, while still at school, had worked with Arthur Griffith on his paper *Sinn Féin*, and we absorbed all this when the hurts of Easter Week, the War of Independence and the Civil War were gradually fading in the huge effort to formulate a new nation.

It seemed the most natural thing in the world for me to take history at university. There, however, a rude cultural shock awaited, because a professor stood before me and I was informed by him, vis-à-vis the Great Famine:

1. The extent of the suffering tended to be overstated.
2. The help given by England tended to be understated.
3. *The Great Hunger* by Cecil Woodham Smith was not, we must remember, written by a professional historian.

It was a first taste of revisionism, and it led me to make a visit to Kilmainham Gaol. At that stage the Office of Public Works had handed over restoration of the disused jail to a group of voluntary workers, and guided tours were taking place. Perhaps that was the best place to learn Irish history, where much of it had happened.

It was a nostalgic visit. As a little girl, I had made visits to Aunt Kathleen (Power) who had a shop opposite the jail, and on these visits there had been playtime in the jail with the caretaker's daughter, Ita Stafford. The leaking roof over the main compound meant that small trees and shrubs had begun to seed themselves in the flagstone floor. We were warned about the dangers. The spiral staircase was *verboten*. We wondered at the Kilmainham Madonna painted by Grace Gifford, and an abiding childish memory was revulsion at the heavily encrusted cell doors, like a sort of wooden leprosy.

On my return as an adult, the encrustation was the least of many horrors. The whole place had fallen into advanced decay, but the voluntary workers were doing Trojan work in their spare time. It was the easiest thing in the world to set aside revisionists and happily associate with those who identified with the patriotic dead.

Women volunteers became guides, and men did physical work and acted as guides. There was a short training course, and then the new guide would take tours around the jail, pointing out such places as the cell where Charles Stewart Parnell had been detained, where Robert Emmet awaited his execution, the escape route of Ernie O'Malley, the execution yard, and the dungeon from which Anne Devlin emerged looking like an old woman at the age of twenty-five.

This was not book history: the records were there, the jail was there. Denial was impossible. This was history at source, not revised. It was, and is, at once an eerie and wonderful place. If I was the last guide there on a cold, winter's evening, I was glad to hear the great door close after me with its hollow, reverberating clang and to go back, unlike the unhappy political prisoners, to the comfort of a warm, welcoming home.

Of all the facts we gave the visitors, the story that most moved them was the wedding ceremony in May 1916. Everyone knew of the groom, Joseph Plunkett, but his bride, Grace Gifford, was, at best, a shadowy figure. She slipped quietly, tearfully, onto the stage of Irish history and just as quietly, having played her part, slipped back into the wings.

It was my good fortune to have met her niece, Maeve Donnelly, at the Dublin Society for the Prevention of Cruelty to Animals' committee meetings and to have been given, with other material, a sort of diary kept by her mother, Nellie Gifford-Donnelly.

The original intention for this book was merely to tell the story of Grace herself – to put a face on this sad bride. However, the Gifford papers revealed a whole family well worth recording. After one death at birth, there were six boys and six girls born to Frederick and Isabella Gifford. All the boys remained staunch Protestant unionists despite their Catholic baptisms. All the girls declared for Irish republicanism;

four of them became Catholic despite their Protestant baptisms, and two of them married signatories of the proclamation of Irish freedom. To trace their political significance, it is necessary to delve deeply into history and widely – to France, America, Canada and as far as Australia. Back in Dublin, where the Gifford parents settled and reared their family, two of the daughters afford us a very intimate account of a fairly typical Victorian ménage of the Protestant upper-class Ascendancy, as it then was in Ireland.

Essentially, this is the story of the Gifford daughters, who were, by virtue of their forebears and their training, most unlikely Irish rebels.

1

FOREBEARS

Frederick Gifford, the Catholic father of the Gifford rebels, married Isabella Julia Burton, a Protestant, on 27 April 1872 in the venue of her choice, the Church of Ireland parish church of St George, on the north side of Dublin. Though they differed in religion, both were unionists politically. Relatively little is known of Frederick's family, except what his name and faith imply, the details given on his marriage certificate and a few notes written in after years by his daughters Sidney (known as 'John') and Nellie.

The official details which Frederick gave on his marriage certificate were that he was a bachelor, 'of full age', pursuing a career as a land and law agent; that he lived at 8 Hardwicke Street, Dublin; and that his father, William Gifford, was a surgeon.[1] Family papers relate that both his (unmarried) parents died young, in County Tipperary, and that two maternal Catholic maiden aunts had raised him.[2] There is also an indication that his father, an aristocrat, left instructions and money to have his son educated in law, a process helped by the Solicitors' Benevolent Fund, but that he did not publicly acknowledge paternity. There was a rumour at the time, even more dramatic, that Frederick's mother was a daughter of Lord Edward Fitzgerald. The only other information can be inferred from heraldic sources, which confirm that the Norman Giffords came to Ireland in the twelfth century, along with their impressive family motto: 'I would rather die than be dishonoured.'

Owing to his being orphaned early with, apparently, neither siblings nor cousins, Frederick Gifford cuts a lonely figure, symbolic in a way of a man who seemed to be only nominally head of his household, who was for many years the only Catholic in a family of fourteen and who is buried alone in Deansgrange Cemetery, County Dublin. Surprisingly, though the more loved of the Gifford parents, he is the forgotten man. His fine tombstone, erected by Isabella, lies broken on his grave.

Isabella's details given in their marriage certificate include addresses at 7 Russell Place (near St George's church) and 'Innisfallen', Howth, a fine residence in its own grounds. There is one fleeting mention in family records that she escaped through a window to marry Frederick, perhaps because of family opposition to his Catholicism. She gave her father's profession as 'Clerk in Holy Orders', but it was the curate of St George's, R. Johnston, who married them. In fact, her father had died twenty years earlier.

Isabella's forebears, brothers Francis and Thomas Burton, came to County Clare in 1610. They were taking over land which had been violently seized from its lawful owners, though their own hands had not been bloodied in the process. They settled in a country that seemed subdued after the 'Flight of the Earls', and the people appeared to accept the Tudor and Stuart system of administration, based on the English model of shires and sheriffs, provincial presidents and lord justices, a system completely supportive of the fourteenth-century Statutes of Kilkenny and their denigration of the Irish. The Burton men were loyal to the legal obligations of those statutes, which forbade marriage to the Irish: their wives' recorded names show neither a Gráinne nor a Bridget among them. The sons of the earlier Burtons began to make their way in the world. Their line produced an eminent banker, an alderman, a mayor and an MP. Three of them became high sheriffs, including F. P. Burton, who took that office in 1751. His son Samuel married Hannah Mallet in

1808. They had four sons, including Robert Nathaniel Burton and Sir Frederick William Burton, who was an artist and Director of the National Gallery in London.

It was the second son, Robert Nathaniel, who married Emily Cole Hamilton Walsh and fathered her nine children, among them Isabella. Isabella's elder sisters, Hannah, Emily and Mary, remained unmarried and had enough money invested on which to live for some time. When faced with financial difficulties, they took up nursing to earn a living, Hannah eventually becoming a matron in an English hospital.

There is nothing in the family papers to indicate what became of Isabella's brothers, except for portraits taken in Buenos Aires and London, and references to their having been doctors. On the other hand, family papers, family word of mouth and church records inform us about the life of Isabella's father, Robert Nathaniel Burton, who was vicar of Borris, County Carlow, during the years of the Great Hunger.[3] He and the local parish priest used to give their breakfasts to the hungry. The vicar could read the Gaelic Bible from his time in Clare, and learned the Catholic rite for the dying – there were so many dying – so that if the priest was not available he could ease them into death with some dignity. Almost inevitably, he caught typhus and died in 1851. His brother, Sir Frederick Burton, financed the rearing of the vicar's children. He himself had been engaged to Margaret Stokes, an archaeologist, but when she caught smallpox her face became disfigured, and, according to Isabella, he jilted her. Isabella never forgave him for that.

Isabella's maternal line was more colourful.[4] Miss Emily Bisset, daughter of a wealthy Huguenot merchant, was her grandmother. Some Huguenots expelled from France had settled in America and felt themselves loyal Protestant subjects of the British Crown. They were, in fact, known as the United Empire Loyalists. When Britain lost the American War of Independence, these Huguenots fled northwards and were under the protection of the British army stationed at Halifax, Nova Scotia. The Bissets settled in their new North American home, Mr Bisset building his gold into the brickwork of his house (there being no banks).

When a young officer from Ireland, Captain Claude Cole Hamilton Walsh, whose mother was the Hon. C. Hamilton of Beltrim Castle, County Tyrone, met the fifteen-year-old Emily Bisset, they fell in love. He married her a year later, when she was sixteen, taking her back with him to his family home at Gortalowry House, Cookstown, County Tyrone. There Emily bore him twenty-three children, among them some sets of twins. Emily is reputed to have had red hair, which her great-grandchildren inherited, ungratefully. Claude was a boyhood friend of the Duke of Wellington and is reputed to have been on his staff at Waterloo, so it is not surprising to learn that the Iron Duke was godfather to one of Claude and Emily's sons.

Eventually, when there were still sixteen of his family unprovided for, Claude died. Emily sold her home, realised her other assets, chartered a ship, had the complete makings of a house put on board, purchased a year's supply of food, engaged governesses for the younger children and servants for the house and set sail for Australia. It is generally accepted that the only career for an upper-class girl in those days was wifehood, so perhaps Emily decided Australia was the best place to bring her unmarried daughters, since there was a great scarcity of marriageable women for the officers stationed there.

One of Emily's daughters, named after her, married Rev. Robert Nathaniel Burton, and they settled in Ireland. Their daughter Isabella mothered the six Gifford girls, all of whom, from this United Empire Loyalist background, played a determined part in Ireland's War of Independence, completely in contrast to the non-involvement of their brothers.

Isabella remained true to her upbringing, and, despite Frederick's Catholicism, she ignored the Catholic baptisms of the Gifford sons in accordance with the Palatine Pact, and reared their whole family, boys and girls, as Protestants.[5] The two parents still shared their political unionism, and, thanks to Nellie Gifford's notes and correspondence and detailed descriptions by 'John' Gifford, we get a very full picture of what it was like to grow up in Dublin in a privileged unionist household at the end of the nineteenth century.[6] But why were only the girls involved in the fight for Irish independence? The answer may have an economic element: to get a decent job in their day, being a Protestant unionist was a definite help; in fact it was almost obligatory. Even membership of a tennis club required a Protestant 'passport' at the time.

2

THE GIFFORD PARENTS

There is no picture in the Gifford family papers of the head of the family, Frederick. As one gets to know Isabella, one cannot imagine her lending herself to the popular photographic pose of the time: the husband sitting and the dutiful wife standing, hand on his shoulder, flanked by an aspidistra. Called the 'Guvnor' by the servants of the house, a more appropriate name for Frederick might have been 'The mistress's husband'. He seems to have been portly, at least in later years, and with an agreeable personality that made him an easy mixer. Nellie was his favourite child, and when she was a little girl he occasionally brought her with him about the country on his legal work – even as far as Donegal town, where they stayed in Hamilton's Hotel.[1]

Yet there was a certain remoteness in his relationship with his family. One Sunday morning he left his umbrella behind in church. One of the boys was sent to fetch it, but after a long time he came back, with no umbrella. Asked why he had been so long, he named the Protestant churches he had tried in the locality. He knew his father did not worship at St Philip's Church of Ireland with the rest of the family, but had no idea that it was Mass in Rathmines parish church that he attended.[2]

Although this indicates a distance between Frederick and his children, he was close to them in other ways. When one of them was put to bed for a misdemeanour, he would try to sneak up to the culprit with a piece of cake or some other delicacy, by way of consolation. Even so, though he was the more liked of the parents, Nellie was the only one who loved him unconditionally. The children tended to blame their mother, in fact, for any distancing they felt from their father.

Frederick never practised criminal law, which was considered not quite gentlemanly in those days. The two maternal Catholic aunts who reared him when his parents died, apprenticed their young nephew to a solicitor on the Liffey quays, James Swazy, whose offices were over Twigg & Brett, wine importers. He was working as an articled clerk when he married Isabella, but later changed to an office in the more prestigious Dawson Street.[3]

A lawyer in Ireland, particularly a land agent, could not have started at a more propitious time than the late nineteenth century. The big word in Ireland was 'land', and, in orbit around it, its various satellites bore the ugly names of 'rack rents', 'absentee landlords', 'potato blight', 'famine', 'evictions', 'cholera', 'emigration' and 'death'. Sir William Butler, one-time general in the British army, gives what may be presumed an unbiased account of an eviction he had seen: 'The thatched roofs were torn down and the earthen walls were battered in by crowbars: the screaming women, the half-naked children, the paralysed grandmother, the tottering grandfather, were hauled out.'[4]

After the Famine years, in 1879, with the memories of the Great Hunger still very much alive, Michael Davitt joined forces with Charles Stewart Parnell, the Home Ruler, to found the Land League. So effective was this leadership that within the working life of Frederick Gifford a huge upheaval of landownership took place in Ireland. Despite Frederick's distaste for eviction, his unionism precluded his support of republicanism. Gladstone's disestablishment of the Anglican Church in 1869 must have pleased Frederick, the Catholic. In the following year, Gladstone's first Land Act attempted, in a feeble way, to give some stability to tenants-at-will, by trying to give them some protection from unfair eviction, allowing them to borrow two-thirds of the cost of buying their land from the government and curbing exorbitant rents. Then there was the advent of Joseph Gillis Biggar, the grocer from the north of Ireland who, as an Irish nationalist MP, used obstructionism as a parliamentary weapon to delay the business of parliament in an attempt to force the British government to negotiate with the Irish nationalist MPs. He gummed up the 'mother of all parliaments' by deliberately droning on, even through the night, until, in 1881, the parliament was obliged to introduce 'closure of debate'. Never again was the Irish Parliamentary Party ignored, most especially when Parnell, their new leader, embraced more aggressive tactics.

The New Departure policy, which sought an amalgamation of parliamentary action and physical force to pursue the common ideals of land reform and self-government, was best expressed by Parnell's famous seven words to a tenant demonstration in Mayo in June 1880: 'Keep a firm grip on your homesteads.'[5] Huge crowds, menacingly quiet, gathered at evictions. Boulders were dropped from heights to hinder the approaching Royal Irish Constabulary (RIC). Then Parnell introduced another weapon – a psychological one – in his fight for the tenants, and the word 'boycott' entered English dictionaries: it meant 'to shun'. Captain Boycott, agent to Lord Erne, refused to acknowledge the bad harvests which made the tenants unable to pay rent and he evicted them. Parnell organised the total ostracising of Boycott by all. The land agent had to employ harvesters from the north of the country whose fees crippled him. Defeated, he fled.

Lawyers had particularly difficult transactions. The scope can be gauged by the £10 million authorised for tenant purchase under the Land Purchases Acts of 1885 and 1888. The legal professionals, including Frederick Gifford, were hands-on interpreters of the many Land Acts during the last quarter of the nineteenth century and the early twentieth century. There were added problems with all the statutes on land tenure. In the course of land sale and purchase, the conveyancing would have entailed scrutinising the title deeds, checking for squatter's title and fragmentation of property and noting rights of way, turbary rights and water rights. The late nineteenth-century land and law agent, however, had the additional headaches of acquiring knowledge of the many statutes passed on the subject of Irish land tenure down to the Redemption of Rent Act of 1891, the sixteen Land Acts passed between 1830 and 1891, the Supreme Court Rules of 1891 and the County Court Rules of 1890. Rules were issued under the Land Purchase Act of 1891, both in the Supreme Court and in the Land Commission; there were more rules pertaining to appeals to the Land Commission and from the Land Commission to the Courts of Appeal. Finally, there were also the rules under the Acts of 1860 and 1870.[6]

Nellie Gifford mentions her father's repeated visits to the Land Commission, but there are only a few glimpses seen of him at home with his family. He drew 'well enough', said Nellie, and sometimes 'broke out in cartoons' – as would his daughter Grace. He also made a small hobby of 'silverpoint', in which artistic discipline the artist used a silver pen on specially prepared paper. He was a fan of the then current musical success of Gilbert and Sullivan, and he sometimes used the adjective 'Gilbertian'. He could read the score of the comic operas and could play them on a six-sided or seven-sided concertina.

Frederick enjoyed an easy friendship with John B. Yeats, with whom he had in common not only art but also the law. Unlike his wife, he also enjoyed Sundays when the servants departed and he could go to the kitchen to warm his feet on the fender of the big range. He had a sense of fun and would, for instance, throw his handkerchief up at a cobweb on the high ceiling, to disapproving comments from Isabella. She was queen of the kitchen domain and resented his intrusion; the children confessed distaste for the kitchen when there were no servants there.

Frederick took an interest in gardening, bringing some plants over from England. One particular return from their two-month annual summer stay in Greystones, County Wicklow, was recalled by Nellie, because on their arrival home not only had the grass grown almost knee-high but the plants her father had put down before leaving were 'climbing and sprawling', and, most curious of all, low-growing, very red apples were in fruit. On biting the apples, the children discovered they were a new 'fruit' which they had never encountered before and which they were told were called 'tomatoes'.[7]

Frederick's daughter Sidney has left us a description of the smoking regalia of her father's bachelor days. A gentleman of that time would not smoke in the presence of ladies, so when he needed the solace of his tobacco Frederick would retire to another room and put on his smoking jacket. His outfit comprised not only the velvet embroidered jacket but also a velvet embroidered cap. His smoke finished, he discarded the allegedly polluted garments and put on his ordinary clothes to rejoin his womenfolk.[8] Nellie evocatively summed up her father as she saw him: 'He bore the vague, average hallmarks of what were called "the gentry" in Victorian times.'[9]

Isabella was six stone in weight when she married: a small, pretty, blonde, twenty-nine-year-old member of a strongly unionist and strongly Protestant Carlow family.[10] Her golden hair was pinned up but curled about the ears. Her portraits show attractive features, but there is little animation there. Her eyes look at the camera uncompromisingly, and her well-formed mouth is set in composure, not disclosing her reputedly excellent teeth.

There is no way a pen picture may be drawn to suggest that Isabella was a 'mumsie' type of mother. Phrases about her have survived to suggest instead that cuddles and kind words were in short supply but, it must be conceded, the social mores of Victorian upper-class Dublin might have regarded demonstrative motherly love as 'not quite the thing'. Perhaps it would be fairest to register first the pejoratives attached to her name, lingering long after her death, and then mention her undoubted virtues:

> Mother was not a port in a storm;
> rather she was a storm in a port.[11]

This antithetical summing-up by Isabella's daughter Nellie suggests a personality which might be called 'fractious' or 'difficult'. It was also observed that she was 'always carping' and 'easily ruffled'.[12] Most damning, perhaps, was her likely response to a childish query: the enquirer would be told not to ask stupid questions, or a reference would be made to 'hopeless ignorance':

> There was a pyrotechnic quality in her family that flared up at any ignorance or clumsiness which left us afraid to ask any questions. Though she seldom used many of her talents she was skilful in many arts. She could contrive a hat without effort, though she had never been taught anything but the elegancies of her times; a little French, Italian and German, water-colour painting. Her poetic fancy ran on the lines of Tennyson, a man of blameless character according to her information, and her sonnets had earned her the name of Sappho among her brothers.[13]

Artists, according to Isabella, came ready-made and instinctive, and anyone who kept steadily at a job, especially an artist, she termed, in a contemptuous voice, a slogger. It was observed that Isabella had little sense of humour, and even her grandchildren, though she never spoke crossly to them, saw her as *She Who Must Be Obeyed*.[14] One day this mother of twelve surviving children told one of her daughters, 'I never liked babies' – but they knew that without her telling them. When their nursemaid, Bridget Hamill, departed for her 'day off' after Sunday dinner, their mother had a distressed look because she would be burdened with them for the rest of the day. As to every other day, the norm was that they went out after breakfast with Bridget and went out again after a simple lunch of bread and butter, provided with bags of raisins and biscuits.

Isabella had defended Bridget Hamill when she was interviewing her as a nursemaid for the junior members of the family. Bridget's then employer, a publican, made disparaging remarks about her, but neither his trade nor his attitude pleased Isabella, so when he had finished his tirade she turned to Bridget and said, 'Call to Temple Villas and we will hear your side of the story.' Bridget obviously impressed her, and, happily for all of them, the girl became a loved employee and godmother of the youngest Gifford son, Edward.

Frederick and Isabella had met when they attended the College of Art in Kildare Street, then called the College of Design. Encouraging this artistic streak in her children, Isabella brought them each year to the Royal Hibernian Academy Opening Day and also took them (probably on the Bridget-less Sunday afternoons) to the National Gallery, the museum, concerts, any worthwhile art exhibition that was on, the circus and Dublin Zoo. She had sold some of her artistic work before her marriage and on one occasion felt confident enough to point out to John B. Yeats what she considered to be a flaw in one of his paintings.

Isabella did have her soft spots, and one of them was her Huguenot maternal grandmother, Emily Bisset, who chartered the ship for Australia. She appeared also to be close to Kate, her eldest daughter, and to have had a special liking for her second son, Liebert, though he seemed to be the least talented of her six boys.

As to the power structure in this family, a glance at their observance of the Palatine Pact shows who was the boss. This pact proposed that in 'mixed' marriages the boys follow their father's religion and the girls that of their mother. So the Gifford girls were all promptly baptised in Protestant churches with chosen godparents, but although the first three boys were baptised within a fortnight of birth, in Donnybrook Catholic church, there was a ragged pattern thereafter. Frederick Ernest was not baptised for almost a year and Edward Cecil for almost six months, with the very unusual situation of the officiating priest being his godfather and his nursemaid, Bridget Hamill, being his godmother. Anyhow Isabella brought them up from infancy, boys and girls, in her own faith. In fact, the census return of 1901 shows the whole house to have been Protestant, with the exceptions of Frederick and the servants. Isabella Gifford simply ignored her sons' Catholic baptisms. The Palatine Pact was eventually turned on its head in the Gifford household, with the boys remaining Protestant, true to their upbringing, but untrue to their baptisms, and four of the girls later choosing to convert to the faith of their father, in spite of their Protestant baptisms.[15]

Regarding their religious training, this daughter of a Church of Ireland vicar had a rigid procedure for Sunday devotions: each Sunday by 10.15 a.m. they had donned what the servants called 'church, chapel, go-to-meetin' clothes'. They were then marched to Sunday School, held in a hall built in the church grounds in Rathmines. The children sat in circles, according to age, girls on one side of the hall, boys on the other. Their teacher was described as thin, pale and elderly, dressed in voluminous black, with a heavy, beaded dolman. Her piety was old world and lacked appeal for the children. Like Isabella's three sisters, she was unmarried, the men they might have wed having been slain in pushing forward or defending the frontiers of the Empire to which they gave their loyalty.[16]

After Sunday School, which lasted for about an hour, they were sent to church, just as their mother and grown-up sisters and brothers were arriving. The Gifford pew was halfway up the aisle. The rector was an old army doctor, and the young Giffords, finding his sermons too long, had to be frequently poked into attention by their mother or by Kate. Church ended at 1 p.m. and one selected youngster went to dine with the parents (this changed each week).

The best clothes were worn to church, but the children's view of what was best often differed greatly from their mother's. This was especially true of Ada, who appears to have had a strong, youthful will. The children found Isabella's ideas of suitable headgear particularly unacceptable. On one occasion she bought Gabriel and Gerald what looked like postmen's caps. One winter, Nellie and Ada, the two girls closest in age, needed new hats, and Isabella decided to provide them with that year's fashion: 'boat hats', called familiarly 'boaters', which had an upturned brim and a delve in the crown going from fore to aft. Isabella considered them 'ladylike', but Ada, rated the most competent artist, drew a caricature of what they would look like in these 'nasty little Homburgs'.[17] An agonised 'confab' between the two intended martyrs sent Nellie to plead their case before their mother set out to make the purchase. She said she would make no promises. That was the voice of doom, and Isabella duly came back with a bag containing two of the hated hats – in fawn, which seemed to add insult to injury. Their red hair had been cut 'like boys', and she pulled the hats down on their heads with what was described as 'an antagonistic tug'.[18]

Suitably attired, the two young ladies walked sedately to their pew, hat elastic under chin, under their mother's watchful eye. As the service progressed, however, the elastic became increasingly uncomfortable and was quietly hitched up under their noses to ease the pressure so that the breath and prayers of these two young Christians wound their way heavenwards past a twin pair of elastic bands.

The reluctant boater-wearers waited for their chance, which came with the annual holiday in Greystones. They walked down to the breakwater, where the sea was deep, and whirled the hated hats into the water, as far as they could, gleefully watching the little boats riding the waves till they were so sopping with water that they sank.

They decided to accuse the blameless wind as the culprit which had 'unfortunately' snatched their hats from them, elastic and all.

Isabella tended to dress the children in pairs, by gender and in order of age, as can be seen not only in the story of the boaters but also in a charming studio portrait of Grace and Sidney, taken in R. Forbes' studio in Grafton Street, which shows two beautifully dressed little girls. Her own portraits show an artistic awareness in her personal dress, including in one picture a row of tiny bows placed perpendicularly to give herself height, and, in another, a lovely hand-crocheted over-bodice, probably made by herself. Her daughters seemed to display Isabella's good taste, even in their financially leaner years.

The portrait of Grace and Sidney

Isabella had very decided ideas about how any job should be done and was not shy when airing her opinions nor when seeing that they

27

were carried out according to her instructions. It was her custom to sit in the bay window of her bedroom each afternoon reading the Bible. One extremely hot summer's day, as she read, she watched with interest the construction of houses on the other side of Temple Villas. Tradesmen in those days generally dressed formally, wearing suits and sometimes black bowler hats. This, it was said, distinguished them from the unskilled. The workmen Isabella observed from her window were so dressed, despite the heat of the day. At last she could stand their assumed discomfort no longer and dispatched one of her sons into the city to buy straw hats for the men. When he came back, she sent a very embarrassed boy over to the builders with the hats and with the message that they were to 'put them on there and then'.[19] When the boy had delivered this peremptory order, he rushed away as quickly as he could, as the female, self-appointed Foreman of Works up in the bay window kept watch over some fumbling (and doubtless choice language) among the men, who eventually put on the hats – perhaps gratefully. It seemingly never entered Isabella's head that what she had done was unusually bossy.

It was from this window seat also that Isabella did the purchasing of the perishable foods for the household. She was regarded as 'a good handsel' by the dealer women, a superstition that if she was their first customer they would have luck for that day. So they brought their laden baskets, on foot, all the way from the city markets – huge wicker baskets with two handles, balanced on the head on a roll of cotton worn like a crown. The servants interviewed the dealer women first, in the basement kitchen, and then carried up plates containing samples of the fish, fruit and vegetables for sale. The three flights of stairs up to the adjudicator, Isabella, were often negotiated more than once before the judge in the bay window pronounced her decision as to the quality and price. So heavy were the great baskets that the good-natured Gifford servants used to help the dealers 'load up' on departure.[20]

Despite Isabella's criticism of her uncle, Sir Frederick Burton, for jilting Margaret Stokes, when he died his obituary notices lauded his distinguished career and this pleased Isabella. Lest her neighbours were unaware of the close connection between the artistic knight and the Temple Villas Giffords, on Sir Frederick's death Isabella dressed the children in black. It gave her the opportunity to explain, when questioned on their cause of mourning, that her uncle, Sir Frederick, the well-known artist, had died. She had to keep her end up in this well-heeled suburb, and if mournful garb for an uncle she hardly knew was the price to pay, then so be it. Perhaps, too, she remembered gratefully that it was his money that had reared her and her siblings after her heroic father had died.

3

Victorian Childhood

Frederick and Isabella did not, on their marriage, settle down in the residence where they spent the rest of their lives. They first set up home in Castle Avenue, Donnybrook, where Claude Frederick was born in 1874, their first child having died at birth. Catherine Anna, Liebert and Gerald Vere were also born at the same address. On their birth certificates Frederick was variously described as 'Solicitor's Apprentice', 'Land Agent' and 'Law Agent'.

The family's next move was to Cabra Road, where both Gabriel and Helen Ruth (always called 'Nellie') were born. In his career as a commercial artist, Gabriel was to use the nom de plume 'Brabazon', which took the last syllable of Cabra as its first syllable. On all the older children's birth certificates there was a column for who was present at the birth, and it had been filled in each case by the midwife's name but, in an oddly modern way, in Gabriel's case the words 'Father present at birth' were entered. There is a reference, in the detailed notes Nellie made, of the accommodation at Cabra being so cramped that two of the boys had to bed down in a nearby house, to reach which they ran across a field. Another move was obviously desirable, and the next home was on Palmerston Road. Ada Gertrude and Frederick Ernest were born there, but in 1884 Muriel Enid's place of birth is entered as Cowper Road. However, the twins, Grace Evelyn and Edward Cecil, were born in 1888 in the recollected childhood home of all of them, followed a year and a half later by the baby, Sidney. That home was at Temple Villas, Palmerston Road, Rathmines, a large house built to their specification.[1]

It is strange that in all Isabella's brood of twelve children not a single one of them was named for her mother, her father or any of her brothers or sisters, although there was both a Catherine and a Grace way back along the line. Furthermore, there is no indication of correspondence with, or exchanged visits between, Isabella and her sisters in England. It is mentioned that her brothers took degrees in Trinity College and entered professions, one in law and the others in medicine. Cousins do not float in and out of the remembered Gifford household scenes. In fact, the only cousins mentioned were two – both unnamed – who took part in the Boer War. One was killed in that conflict. His brother told Nellie about some of his duties. Normally a pleasant young man, who had been at school with her brothers, he told her they had been ordered to shoot down a defenceless, frightened old woman found in a farmhouse. Nellie was appalled.

To get a perspective of the social status of the Giffords and their standard of living in Temple Villas, the general living conditions in Dublin at the turn of the century must be recalled: they were wretched. There are many descriptions and statistics to support the dreadful picture: the death rate was higher than that of Calcutta. Fifteen thousand tenements in the fetid slums had been condemned, and two of them, four storeys high, collapsed, wounding and, in some cases, killing the occupants. Twenty thousand families lived in one-roomed accommodation, with sometimes four families living in the same room. For the human beings in these warrens, there was one water tap and one toilet in the yard of each house. A diet of milkless tea, bread and offal brought to the children a high incidence of rickets through lack of calcium, sore eyes through lack of vitamin C and stunted growth through inadequate food of any kind. Even the harshest winter could see them with no shoes and threadbare clothing. Sewage disposal and refuse collection were hopelessly poor; unpaved pathways were full of potholes. Tuberculosis was rampant, and so was despair.

Dublin employers of the unskilled gave another turn to the screw with unbelievably poor wages. While English immigrants such as Gerard Manley Hopkins were incredulous at the horror of it all, the Westminster Parliament was as concerned about the well-being of the conquered Irish race in Dublin as the Americans were of the native peoples in their country. The land situation in rural Ireland was slowly improving because of the Land Acts, but, from the Act of Union on, the capital city had deteriorated so much that it had not far to sink before reaching the nadir of 1913. To the wretched occupants of the tenements, the Gifford ten-roomed residence would have seemed a mansion.[2]

The house in Temple Villas had five bedrooms, a breakfast room – which doubled as a study for the school-goers, a dining room for the parents and a drawing room, strictly for visitors. At the top of the house was the nursery and a big bathroom, and in the red-tiled basement were the kitchen and scullery and a huge coalhouse. There was a system of bells for summoning the domestic staff.

The nursery under the rafters was where the nursemaid reigned supreme. She was, for most of the Giffords' childhood, Bridget Hamill from County Wexford, described lovingly and faithfully by Nellie in her later years. Bridget's stockings are worth recording. Their exuberance of colour might well have put Isabella off employing her, but, well aware of her nursery's numerical problem, Isabella chose to ignore her hosiery's riot of colour. Two pairs of Bridget's stockings are described by Nellie: one was knitted in half-inch bands of yellow, red and green; the second had a rainbow of bands in five different colours. Though Bridget was said to have eventually acquired a husband, a redcoat soldier from her home place, it is most unlikely that she intended, or indeed that the bizarre stockings effected, a military conquest. More likely she made a virtue of necessity and used the odds and ends of wool left over after knitting various gansies, deciding she might as well make use of the bits and pieces and knit them up, hotch-potch, as they came to hand. In any case, on a wage of ten shillings a week, 'all found', she could not afford to be wasteful.

The rest of Bridget's clothing was conventional, comprising a tight-fitted bodice buttoned down the front and an ankle-length dark skirt with a bustle at the back the size of a small pillow, on which her young charges liked to flop when they got the chance. The stockings were seen only when Bridget hitched her skirt while negotiating steps or when she sat at the nursery fire behind its mesh grid, toasting herself on cold days.

She is described as small, comfortable and blue-eyed, with a cheerful rosy face and her hair piled neatly on top of her head. She was also, unlike the desired feminine silhouette of the day, rather plump. So, on her 'day' off (the servants got one evening off every week and every Sunday after midday dinner), Bridget needed help in tightening her corset before 'walking out' with her redcoat soldier. The cords of her corset were put over the knob of her bedpost, and she strained till she had acquired the desired waist, watched by interested children.

Lest that ritual imply any laxness in discipline, it must be stated that this nursemaid extraordinaire was a born general, demanding strict obedience. The nursery grooming was meticulous. She made a game of their ablutions, three boys in the bath or two girls, or whatever combination of the under-eights she had in the nursery at any one time. Each became a vegetable – carrot, turnip or whatever – and as she scrubbed them briskly with soap and 'rinsed' them, she called them her 'Irish stew'. It was more difficult to make fun of hair-combing, especially for the long-haired girls, whose tangles she controlled with a 'rack', asking frequently as she combed the hair forward, working from the back: 'Is it forninst your forehead?' They were put, eldest first, sitting on the baize-covered nursery table for this operation. Eight of the children had red hair, three of the boys and all the girls except the baby, Sidney, a fact which mortified them and led street urchins to jeeringly call:

Red head, curly nob,
Put the kettle on the hob.

Despite the rough edges of their mother's personality, and despite her avowed dislike of babies, there is no doubt at all that if she considered that any of her daughters needed support, then she supported them 100 per cent. Thus, on hearing of the jibes about her children's red hair, she replied indignantly, 'Our Lord had red hair.' This biblical deduction may have been based on her perception of the great painters of the Renaissance, but the maid to whom she offered this defence of her children's russet locks was more scandalised than impressed. 'God forgive ye, ma'am,' she burst out, feeling it a sort of insult to the Son of God that He be declared a redhead.

'General Hamill', however, leading her little company, instructed them never to answer back, to walk with their 'toes out', two by two, except when they needed to make room for passers-by, when they formed a single file. On such outings, the custom was that the local nursemaids took the surname of their employer, so that the children from Temple Villas were led by 'Bridget Gifford'.

If Bridget brought the children to Palmerston Park, they happily climbed trees, ate edible berries and 'helped' the gardener. Palmerston Park was just down the road from home, enclosed by a tall wooden paling. It was mostly left to nature, but the gardener, a wily old war pensioner, said the 'best children', as a treat, would be allowed to collect the debris in the park for him to burn. There was great competition for this job.

Another, more interesting, destination was Portobello Barracks, where Bridget had her admirer and where the children were carried round on the shoulders of the 'chummies', as the redcoat soldiers were called, eye level with the gleaming helmets and weaponry hanging on the wall. Moreover, the soldiers gave them sweets.

There was a path beaten to the door of this barracks by young nursemaids wheeling bassinets. Incredibly, these young girls paid for the company of the soldiers – not for sexual favours but to be taught 'proper English'. They were from all parts of Ireland and were very likely frequently corrected by their employers, who spoke with the Rathmines' drawl. So the soldiers who were Irish were ignored and the girls sought their linguistic education from those born in Britain. They would have had Brummie, Yorkshire, Glaswegian, cockney and various other kinds of accents and idioms. It is an intriguing concept. Was a girl with lilting Cork cadences taught to say 'eeh bah gum', or was a girl from Derry initiated into the costermongers' dialect? However, from all the mingled (and mangled) consonants and vowels, even if the spoken English was not improved, little romances eventuated here and there, despite the fact that if a girl was caught 'keeping company' with a redcoat she stood a good chance of being dismissed 'on moral grounds'.

So, although the children were quite remote from their parents, being allowed only one at a time, once a week, to join them for dinner, they never lacked loving adult companionship. In 1963, when she was eighty-eight years of age, Nellie wrote, 'Whenever I am tired I close my eyes and rest my head in imagination, on the cosy, soft breast of the nurse of my childhood – Bridget … sitting in the most comfortable lap in the world.'[3]

Bridget was not a Victorian slave. Her word was law in the nursery, the little eyrie facing the back garden, and she was all things to all those in her care. She gave them the warmth, physical and psychological, that young children need to put down sound roots and to flourish. Apart from the bathing and hair-grooming, she fed them and put them to bed after they had knelt on the oilcloth floor, in their calico nightwear, to say their prayers.

There were three beds in the nursery: her own, one for the boys and one for the girls, as well as a cot for the baby. Bridget was comforter, disciplinarian and guardian and, on the side, sang rebel songs about 'Bold Robert Emmet' and Owen Roe O'Neill, as well as 'Those Eastern Waves', a song with innumerable verses. Her other cultural offering was a rich fund of stories. In their telling, unaware that she was doing so, Bridget used little Gaelic phrases and Irish ways of speaking English, frowned on by Isabella. Her particular bugbear was the past-perfect tense (for example, 'I was after …'). Just as Maud Gonne's French governess unconsciously taught anti-British sentiment to her young charges, so did Bridget, and some of the other Gifford servants, without realising it, passed on the deep resentments of a race never completely conquered, even after 700 years.

The servants, and Bridget in particular, gave the children little presents each Christmas out of their meagre means, 'unbeknownst to the misthress [*sic*]'.[4] One such present to Nellie, probably from Bridget, and remembered in detail over a lifetime, was a large yellow handkerchief. In the four corners were printed respectively a question, its answer and two curses:

> Did they dare, did they dare to slay Owen Roe O'Neill?
> Yes they slew him with poison whom they feared to meet with steel.
> May God wither up their hearts!
> May their blood cease to flow.

Finally, in the centre, were the words:

> May they walk in living hell who murdered Owen Roe.

It was definitely not a handkerchief for either Christmas or for a cold in the head. Nellie was in awe of it and had no way of knowing that the words were from a poem written by one of her own Protestant Ascendancy class, Thomas Davis, a leader of the Young Irelanders' abortive rebellion of the 1840s against England; neither did Nellie know that Owen Roe was the nephew of the Great O'Neill, hero of the Nine Years' War against Elizabeth I, who had given religious intolerance as a reason for his flight from Ireland in 1607.

William E. H. Lecky, in his *A History of England in the Eighteenth Century*, describes what he called 'the arrogance of a dominant minority' who, in the eighteenth century, not only excluded Catholics from a seat in parliament but even barred them from the public gallery, who flaunted the victories of the Boyne and Derry in tapestry and statuary, including a bust of the conquering King William, bearing an insulting diptych on Catholics (four-fifths of the citizenry) and whose toast on all occasions was 'to the glorious and immortal memory of William'.[5] They even celebrated, in Dublin, the discovery of the English gunpowder plot.

Most of all, however, they recalled, in triumphalist style, the memory of Owen Roe's rebellion of 1641, or, more particularly, its defeat: for the yearly commemoration, the lord lieutenant paraded to Christ Church in full state regalia where a sermon was preached on the defeat of the rebellion, at noon the great guns of Dublin Castle were fired, church bells were rung, and the day concluded with bonfires and illuminations. Though the official elaborate ceremony to celebrate his defeat no longer took place after the Irish parliament was abolished under the Act of Union, examples of the yellow handkerchief still fluttered defiantly here and there, around Ireland, or were folded reverently with the inherent promise 'next time, Owen Roe, or the next time again, or the time after that, we will win.' Bridget's rebellious piece of cotton was symbolic of latent resentment, biding its time. Meanwhile, Nellie, this little daughter of a unionist household, carefully put away her folded Christmas gift.

Tidiness and cleanliness were absolute musts in Bridget's nursery. The older children were trained to sweep the floor and to wash the babies' bottles. There was a bag of farthings from which one was extracted each week to reward the best child. There were certainly no expensive toys given to the children, but they made their own fun, typically placing each other, one at a time, in the centre of the tablecloth, which was then removed, its happy passenger carried noisily round the room until it was someone else's turn.

Isabella may have disliked Bridget's little Irish words and idioms, but there was no complaint about the training in etiquette. When the chosen child dined at the weekly dinner, one of the inflexible rules was that some dessert had to be left on one's plate, uneaten, for 'good manners'. Apparently the splitting of the atom can be compared to the efforts of the Gifford offspring to leave no more than a crumb on the plate. But it was left. 'General' Hamill had trained her soldiers well. To be so loved in recollection, as this paragon nursemaid was even after eighty years, was an achievement which few generals, if any, can have attained.

Another resident maid was Mary McKenna, a tall, limber girl with dark hair, very blue eyes and a friendly smile. She was the favourite daughter of a Howth fisherman. One Monday morning, clothes-washing day, Isabella came down, as usual, to see that everything was going well and to lend a hand. The clothes, which had already been washed in the scullery trough and boiled in a galvanised bath on the red-hot range, were then put in a primitive washing machine, a huge wooden tub on an iron stand, the door clamped tight to keep the suds from the floor. Normally Mary and the cook, Essie, who had to hand-turn this contraption for forty minutes, would be laughing and joking when Isabella arrived to give a few turns herself, but this particular morning Mary was helpless with crying. She shared a bedroom with Essie, and at 4 a.m. she had awoken from a dream that three strange men and one she knew had taken her dead father from the sea. Isabella tried to 'talk sense' to her gently but had to swallow her words a few hours later when Mary's mother came to report her husband's drowning exactly as dreamt.

John B. Yeats and his sons heard this story during one of their visits to the Gifford residence and, always attracted by the paranormal, were very interested in the realisation of Mary's dream. Of course there is nothing abnormal about a fisherman's family having subconscious, as well as conscious, fears about drowning, but the Yeats family's maid in London was a sister of Mary, and she also, they claimed, had this power.

Mary was very popular with the Gifford children, as was her mother, a handsome woman who wore a heavy black shawl. Under that shawl she always brought for them, all the way from Howth, a big soda cake packed with currants.

Essie was the third of the resident servants. She came from the outskirts of a large demesne in County Longford, and her details are listed in the 1901 census: 'Esther Connell, servant, born in Longford. Roman Catholic, aged 40, cannot read or write. Rank in household – cook and domestic servant.' To assess Essie's prowess as a cook one may turn to the 'Grace before Meals' said by Frederick Gifford in advance of an evening meal in the dining room of Temple Villas. He carved the joint while the housemaid stood waiting to take her and the cook's share down to the kitchen. Before she left, he said his 'Grace':

For what we are about to receive, the Lord make us thankful.
The Lord sent the meat but the Devil sent the Cook.

The housemaid suppressed her smile because Isabella patently disapproved. Essie had seventeen people to cater for, as well as casual staff. Though Isabella did the buying, it was Essie who prepared and cooked huge quantities of food. Six large white baker's loaves filled, each day, the crock in the scullery, which was the size of a porter barrel. The milkman came daily to Essie's kitchen too, and when he had filled a big jug for general use, a small jug was filled for the servants, free of charge: it was called 'the cat's tilly'. When a side of bacon was delivered, Essie would bone it herself and cut off rashers as required. As well as that, Essie helped with the housework and supervised the blending of the home-made polish in earthenware jars on the range – a mixture of beeswax and turpentine.

To illustrate the relative remoteness of the children's mother and the closeness they felt to the domestic staff, when young Gabriel took in the post one morning, seeing a letter addressed to 'The Lady of the House', he innocently asked if the letter was for Essie. She may not have been the world's greatest cook but, considering Isabella could only bake cakes and make desserts, it can be argued that Essie reared them all to healthy adulthood and, indeed, laid their physique for ripe old age.

The fact that Essie was illiterate, unlike the other servants, meant that the weekly magazine they all looked forward to, *The Princess Novelette*, a kind of Mills & Boon of Victoriana, had to be read to her. Essie was not shown in the 1911 census, the family by that time having largely dispersed.

More unusual than any of the resident servants, Ann, the charlady, came only at times such as Christmas, when the house needed a thorough cleaning. She took quiet pride in her work, and on each floor left a little square uncleaned, the size of a postage stamp – her hallmark to show, by contrast, the effectiveness of her labours. However, Ann was particularly 'fond of the bottle'. One day, when she was very drunk indeed, Isabella came down to the kitchen to find an amazing sight: one of the two oven doors was open, and the very intoxicated Ann was kneeling before it, rosary beads in hand, apparently confessing her sins, fortunately rather incoherently, to what she may have thought was the aperture of the confessional – or did she feel it was the fiery gate of hell?

Lastly there was Tom Coyne, the shoe-cleaner. He came each evening to clean fourteen pairs of shoes and was a particular favourite with the children, though sometimes they showed Bridget that he had not cleaned the backs of their shoes. Bridget would reply, 'A good soldier never looks behind.' Tom was shabby – 'threadbare' was the word used in Nellie's notes to describe his clothing – but kept himself scrupulously clean. This old man, still with the heart to sing despite a failing voice, made the long journey each night to Rathmines, in fair weather and foul, so he must have badly needed his lowly paid job.

Tom's one-time occupation had been music-hall artist, and he would regale them all with excerpts from the operas, including his favourite, 'The Heart Bowed Down by Weight of Woe'. There were three fingers missing from his right hand, but this did not prevent one of his singing mannerisms, to put his forefinger behind his ear as if listening to himself; another was pulling down his lips, as if to reach the low notes. This last trick sent the maids into fits of giggles, except Bridget, who was so impressed that she tried it, unsuccessfully, in singing her repertoire.

The Temple Villas servants gave credence to the old proverbial wisdom about the hand that rocks the cradle ruling the world. There was very little rocking done by either Isabella or Frederick. The servants and children lived in complete harmony with each other. In the nursery, there was much remembered laughter and few tears. The harshest discipline the children knew was an admonition by their nursemaid: 'Now then, none of your Andhrew Martins.'[6] Bridget had the gift – the dream of both teachers and parents alike – of moulding them with a perfect balance of love and discipline, and she held them effortlessly in the palm of her kindly, capable hands. It was severe competition for any mother, but especially for Isabella. In any event, in neither kitchen nor nursery was there heard anything unfit for children's ears from these daughters of the 'peasantry' – excepting perhaps the yellow handkerchief and the direful curses on the enemies of Owen Roe, and no one could ignore the fact that the past-perfect tense in English is not best expressed by 'I was after doin' it', even though this is a direct translation from the Gaelic *Bhios tar éis é a dhéanamh*.

It is clear why the Gifford children had happy memories of the servants in their home during their formative early years. It also seems clear that their mother, conscientious and well-meaning though her approach to rearing children may have been, missed out almost completely in capturing their hearts when they were small and vulnerable and most needed her love.

As described above, Nellie, the fifth child, has left us a marvellous description of her childhood which gives an insight into a typical Dublin household of the Ascendancy Protestant class in Victorian times. Her sister Sidney, who was to take the pen-name 'John Brennan' and who was always referred to thereafter as 'John', has also left her own account of that upbringing in her memoir, *The Years Flew By*. It is to Nellie's observant eye and excellent memory that we owe the mosaic of their early years; however, 'John' had the gift of analysis, and her description of the district in which they grew up is worth recording:

Our family home in Dublin was on the south side, in what was called a 'good residential district', which meant, in those days, a stronghold of British Imperialism. More than anything else the district resembled a waxworks museum. The people who surrounded us were lifelike but inanimate models of distinguished English people. It was a deadly atmosphere, in which any originality of thought or independence of action was regarded as eccentricity or lawlessness.[7] You have guessed it! This was Rathmines, butt of local humour for a couple of genera-tions because its residents seemed to typify the flunky Irishman: with their strange, synthetic English accent, their snobbery and their half-hearted desire to be a ruling caste. Rathmines was a phenomenon. It was not a racial group nor a political stronghold but a state of mind. Its people were castaways, wrecked by mischance on this island called Ireland and ever scanning the horizon for a ship that would take them and their families away to some of the other British colonies.

Sometimes Isabella's concern was 'keeping up with the Joneses', and such, in part at least, was the annual holiday in Greystones. This was considered so socially necessary in Rathmines that those who could not afford to go would pull down their blinds as camouflage and live in the back of the house during the summer months.

Greystones was largely owned by the Huguenot La Touche family, who shared the extremely evangelical inclination of another summer resident of Greystones, the mother of John Millington Synge.[8] Then a small fishing village, Greystones was slowly developing after the opening of the railway line from Dublin in 1850. There emerged a sort of unwritten law in Dublin which observed geographical distributions of holiday areas for Protestants, Catholics and Jews. The Protestants gravitated towards Greystones, partly because of the influence of the La Touche family and partly also because Wicklow (the 'Garden' of Ireland) was almost exclusively in the hands of Protestant landowners. Greystones was, as it were, one of their marine suburbs. Catholics, on the other hand – that is the few Catholics who could afford to go anywhere – tended to holiday in the marine townlands of north Dublin, especially Skerries, where the majority of the population was Catholic. Jews, who had already started to settle in houses near such areas as Clanbrassil Street and the South Circular Road, following escape from European pogroms, chose Bray as their holiday resort, as did some Catholics who lived south of the Liffey. Of course, the Dublin poor, which is to say the vast majority of its citizenry, had to be content with day trips to Dollymount or Merrion

Strands, partly spent picking and eating winkles as the protein to go with their unbuttered bread and bottles of cold tea.

Not so the Giffords. Though this summer migration was a very low-key version of her grandmother equipping the ship for Australia, one could never accuse Isabella of doing anything half-heartedly. A less sturdy being might have considered the transport of some seventeen people, with all their accoutrements, too daunting a plan. There is a description in Nellie's memoirs of their setting off for the yearly Greystones summer holidays: the little blonde Officer Commanding is standing at the top of the steps in Temple Villas, directing her troops. Her husband, her sons and the maids stagger down the steps with huge baskets laden with crockery, household utensils, clothes, bedding and food. The maids hated the holidays, and it is easy to see that even the going and the coming back were heavy chores; nevertheless, their shrewd young charges noted that when the coastguards started to call at the kitchen in the rented house at Greystones, the extra drudgery was forgotten as a bit of flirtation lightened the scene.

By accident rather than by design, the children were brought a little closer to their parents through the enforced proximity of a holiday by the sea. One could not fairly impute Isabella with a foisting off of their companionship by her appointment of Ellen as their 'bathing woman', who alternately coaxed and spurred even the most nervous to swim in the little cove where she, her sister and her son had bathing boxes. Ellen was queen of that cove and decided, first, if the sea was sufficiently calm for a child's limited strength. She observed the then popular theory that if you did not first 'wet your head' then the minute you stepped into the sea something fatal might happen – described as a 'contraction' or 'the blood rushin' to your head'.[9] So the bathers waded out till the water was waist-high, when they would pinch their nostrils to exclude the water and then dunk their heads. It was considered safest to dunk three times, and, though the children often objected loudly, Ellen was adamant. After this dunking ceremony, all but the strongest swimmers were given a lifebelt for deep water.

These belts were on ropes, which Ellen played out till she thought the wearers were in far enough. Their stay in the water depended on her mood. With two or three ropes in her hands, she ran up and down on the beach shouting directions to the pupils, who were sometimes out of hearing (or pretended to be) at the other end of the ropes. When she considered someone had been long enough in the water, that swimmer was dragged in ignominiously, despite protest. 'You've been in too long, so you have,' she would say when there were others waiting, because she did not encourage selfishness – or perhaps it was a ploy for more customers. The rope removed, it was back to the box to have the substantial bathing dress removed. The girls wore woollen bathing dresses, sometimes even stockings, and their long hair was held up by hairpins, three or four inches long, and squeezed into an elasticised waterproof cap. Properly dressed again, they emerged from their boxes, and the male watchers, young and old, stood at the cliff wall as the hair-combing began, calculating with much masculine humour how much of the 'bun' – the hair normally seen on the Sunday parade – was, in fact, genuine. Ellen, a sort of prototype of today's lifeguards, was very committed to the prowess of her swimmers, some of whom were second-generation customers, and she freely gave advice though, ironically, she could not swim herself. The Gifford girls graduated from her academy as strong swimmers. Mixed bathing was not allowed, but Frederick had his own way of teaching his sons to swim, like many a father before and after him. Ellen's rope was all right for the girls, but the boys were dunked unceremoniously by their father into the sea and had to swim, as if by second nature, but under his watchful eye.[10]

'The swimmin' woman' Ellen (and her boxes and ropes) were part of a departing nineteenth century, but the singing minstrels' show, which came from England, was looking towards the 1900s. The company erected a covered stage and introduced to the Greystones holidaymakers a new syncopated rhythm which preceded jazz.

Not the least of the Greystones delights for the children were the establishments that hired out horse-drawn vehicles by the hour, a half day or a full day. These 'chariots' ranged from the old-fashioned *vis-à-vis* (largely for the older generation who sat decorously opposite each other under parasols) to the wagonette, which could hold a fairly big picnic party. The favourite conveyance for the Gifford children, however, was a pony and trap which they were allowed to drive themselves. The 'pony' could be either a donkey or a jennet, and their favourite haunt was the Glen of the Downs.

For the Gifford children, these holidays were times of freedom and wandering over the countryside, finding *fraocháns* and wild strawberries in the fields about the house where they were staying, picking blackberries to make jam which was consumed while it was still warm, getting up at dawn in the chill air to pick mushrooms and then running back home to put them on the hob upside down, with a knob of butter, before eating them. There were days in the cove with Ellen, days taking turns at driving the trap, and days when they stood and listened to the strange new music coming from America via England.[11]

At the time the young Giffords were growing up, neither they, nor the grown-ups of their Protestant Ascendancy world, were aware of the first, faint signs of the weakening of the fabric of their society. They still held the jobs and offices, the privileges and status, much of the best land and all the great merchant houses. Those read like a roll call of the Victorian caste: Arnotts, Pims, Boyers, Kellets, Todd-Burns, Switzers, Brown and Thomas, Knowles, Eason, Elverys, Dockrells, Brookes Thomas, Sibthorpes and Findlaters. They enjoyed a trade monopoly on clothing, furniture, food, books, sports gear and building material. In Guinness' Brewery, a Catholic, no matter how excellent, could not become a No. 1 clerk. When a well-known coal-importing firm became unionised, it was discovered that there were two payrolls for the same work: Protestant employees were paid at a higher rate. Even the milk supply for the entire city was monopolised by Craigies, a Protestant Ascendancy family, except for a few small herds kept here and there.

The class cleft was particularly noticeable in Rathmines and Rathgar: the almost exclusively Protestant neighbours of the Giffords, in their fine, red-brick residences, had such occupations as surgeon, ship's captain, barrister, lieutenant colonel, professor of music and merchant. Their names were Fox, Phillips, Karmel, Stinger, Carleton, Harricks, Wallace, McNaught and Keohler. These were not the names of members of the old, dispossessed clans such as the Whelans, the Reillys, the Dalys and the MacDermotts, who, in fact, lived down the road in Plunkett's Cottages and were listed in the census as gardeners, labourers, charwomen, porters, messengers, a motor man, a packer, a stoker, a dressmaker and a coachman.[12] Almost exclusively listed as Catholics, many of them are shown as being illiterate. These two addresses, Palmerstown Road and Plunkett's Cottages, were a microcosm of Ireland. The descendants of the invaders had the power; the descendants of the dispossessed owned little or nothing.

Catholic Emancipation had been granted in 1829, but the slow process of educating Catholics towards upward mobility had only begun during the Giffords' childhood years. Symbolically speaking, the Gifford girls, like other Protestants down the years, eventually stepped outside their comfortable milieu and reached out a hand to the dispossessed, not only in Dublin but throughout the whole of Ireland.

4

GROWING UP

Eventually the time came when some of the young Giffords were cutting themselves off from Bridget's apron strings and being moved from the nursery to make way for newer arrivals. The games they played had become far more sophisticated than being carried around the nursery in the centre of a tablecloth. Now plays were being written and performed. Gabriel and Ada were the writers and producers of these dramas, and Gabriel later admitted that they gave their sister, Nellie, a number of roles from which she sustained minor cuts and bruises. In one of these plays, *The Vanishing Lady*, Nellie, placed on the top of a wardrobe in a basket, unfortunately fell off. Writing to her in the 1950s, Gabriel asked if she still had the scar where molten lead shot out of a bullet had landed on her foot. There were toy theatres too, constructed by Gabriel, and plays written especially for their cast. These three, Gabriel, Ada and Nellie, near in age, formed a close trio.

From about five years of age the Gifford children were assigned to a tutor, usually a girl of limited education. This lack of education was not important, however, since the tutor's presence was not so much educational as to free the nursery for the newer arrivals, to maintain the human assembly line, as it were, and, most of all, to keep the children occupied and out of their mother's household routine. So long as the tutor was quiet and reasonably well spoken, the children would be left in his or her hands. Once an unfortunate young male student from Trinity College took on the job as holiday work and faced half a dozen scowling youngsters who resented summer lessons. One day, when they were at their most difficult, he put his head in his hands and fled from the room, never to return.

The next stage in the children's early educational development was the choice of an establishment within easy walking distance of Temple Villas where the criterion for suitability was Isabella's assessment of how much the chosen Protestant ladies needed a boost to their limited means. Their whereabouts and availability she discovered at meetings of the Church of Ireland Missionary Society. The charitable nature of the appointment seemed to be paramount, the children's education perceived as an addendum.

The first such 'school' (they were all small private houses) consisted of the 'female teacher', her elderly father who had to be constrained in his garden chair with ropes and her alcoholic husband. Nellie described the teacher with compassion in later years as a 'poverty-stricken, distracted wife' who faced 'the desperate catastrophe she had to call her life'.[1] Her four pupils were allotted a small junk room which contained an old trunk full of travel books; the more popular ones, eagerly perused, were illustrated. The pupils were required to be able to recite biblical texts, but prompting seemed to be acceptable.

Either the grandfather or the husband had served in the British army, and this gave them points, as far as Isabella was concerned. As for the grandfather, he was tied up only when in the garden on fine days, presumably lest he should fall. The children were afraid of him, and he, they admitted later, of them. They did not tease him but stood at the back door looking out fearfully and hoping that the ropes that bound him were sound. There was no point in communicating their fears to their mother; they would have been told that it was all in their imagination.

The next educational experiment, as it might be called, was run by two ladies called 'the Miss Fitts'. Their house was about ten minutes' walk from Temple Villas, and the younger and more presentable of the two sisters interviewed prospective clients. Her 'aged' sister (for eight-year-olds this could have been anything from fifty upwards) was responsible for the 'teaching'. In this academy the children were locked in a room whose windows, overlooking the back garden, had heavy iron bars, leaving them no chance to get away. Their learning paraphernalia consisted of a few exercise books, a hymn book and a spelling book. In winter their room had a small, open fire on which the Miss Fitts occasionally boiled potatoes. When left alone, the children would 'test' the potatoes with the nibs of their pens. If the ink was not wholesome, at least it must not have been poisonous. There was, admittedly, an attempt at this school to teach 'writing', but the sad state of the older sister's hand, crippled with arthritis, set wobbly headlines, and, with the heedless cruelty of the young, the children deliberately copied the wobbles. Ernest was often kept in for making such copies. The Gifford children were taught neither history nor arithmetic but were given history and 'sums' to learn themselves. Often left alone in the locked room, they were unaware of whether their mentors were in or out of the house, although they could frequently hear the mumblings of an unseen man overhead. The end of that educational experience came one day when the snow lay heavily on the ground and the time for them to be released from their prison to make their way home was long overdue. Their mother, becoming anxious, set out to fetch them, and when she saw where they were being taught, that was the end of the Miss Fitts.

Outside of school, entrepreneurial skills began to emerge. The children had no chance, as children have nowadays, of offering to do gardening work or to deliver leaflets. But the human instinct to make money found expression, born of a chance remark made by their father. When he mentioned casually, 'That might be worth a few pence to old Hickey,' as he handled a book he had finished reading, he opened, to use Nellie's words:

... the door of Aladdin's Cave to us money-starved children. It was a heavenly idea, and so simple. When we had cleared out all the books we thought would not be missed, we turned our energies to other 'lines of goods' as the advertisements say. Our unpaid accomplices, the servants, thoroughly enjoyed it though 'Yiz'll be kilt' was their firm conviction. They never gave us away, however, and we kept strictly within the law, never stepping past things quite useless.[2]

Books considered thus unwanted having dried up, and facing a penniless future, there ensued the adventures of the boots and pheasants' feathers. Under the stairs in Temple Villas the footwear for all the family was housed. Discards were pushed towards the narrow end at the back and, thus ignored, accumulated a veneer of dust and even green mould. One of the young Gifford salespersons spotted an advertisement in a paper by somebody who actually wanted old boots and shoes. Their father sometimes received hampers of fruit or game from his country clients, and the children packed one of those hampers with the cleaned-up relics of abandoned footwear. The tram passed their door, but their entrepreneurial cunning showed itself in their decision to deceive any inquisitive observer as to what might be in the hamper. They stuck a few pheasant feathers into the wickerwork, leaving enough exposed to suggest that their burden contained game. Unfortunately, in those days, largish containers had to be left with the conductor. He was curious about the peculiar angles at which the feathers of these birds were protruding, so he pulled at one, and then another. They both came away far too easily. The young entrepreneurs took their hamper and dismounted at the next stop.

Christmas parties were sometimes given at Temple Villas for the children because Isabella considered that this was part of the required social pattern. One such party was recorded in detail by Nellie, partly because the guests included a little English boy and girl attending one of their schools, whose father was a 'neat' Englishman who was musically inclined. The Gifford children found their guests 'harmless', 'strange' and 'juiceless'. In Isabella's eyes, however, they were English and therefore beyond reproach. Her people had come to Ireland way back in the seventeenth century but, as far as she was concerned, to be English was a virtue in itself. It is interesting to see that, like their father's puzzlement as to the way English was spoken in England, so too were the children aware of a great gap between their accents and perception of things, and those of the British children. It was the old dilemma of the Anglo-Irish: the Gifford parents were unionists but though the young Giffords had, as yet, no political views, they still felt a distinct apartness from their English guests.

Isabella's flock was so extensive that her invitations were usually limited to children in the immediate neighbourhood. She excelled at preparing party dainties and even employed an entertainer. The piano being out of order on one occasion, she hired a music box with a handle so the children were all rather put out when the aforementioned little English girl, whose name was Nellie Watts, arrived with her violin and a musical score for a piano accompaniment by her father, who obviously intended to stay for the party. The children, who associated the piano with practising scales in a cold drawing room, were delighted with the music box, which required no skill, no respectful silence and no hypocritical applause. Everyone got a chance to turn the handle. It was a great success with all but the English father, who stood silently by. His daughter's violin and music sheets were quietly set aside.

The huge table was laden with food, fine china and a bonbonnière, which, like the cutlery, was solid silver. Isabella used a cookery book for party novelties, due caution being exercised not to disturb the digestions of excited children. One of these surprise dishes was poached egg on toast. It was, in fact, half a peach in a little blancmange, nesting on a bed of Madeira cake. The offended Englishman, perhaps short-sighted, but certainly a square peg in a round hole at a children's party, was at first taken in by the 'egg' and resented the children's laughter at the success of their mother's culinary ruse. A conjuror wound up the proceedings, and the violin went home with the little violinist, unused. Whatever about the guests, Nellie and her siblings enjoyed the well-planned evening, but Isabella had to pacify Mr Watts, who felt insulted by being offered a false poached egg. This was a new, more relaxed aspect of Isabella's personality.

A little further along the road to maturity came the advent of *The Magazine*. This private endeavour appeared periodically, its editions governed by such eventualities, all unpleasant, as days too wet to go out, or measles, or some other catastrophe keeping them housebound. Once under way, however, even when the sun shone again or the spots vanished, the publication was completed. Its riches were written in old exercise books, and every edition had a new name. Ada was the genius behind their inception, with Gabriel as assistant editor. Only one edition survived into Nellie's middle years, and she describes it as bearing the proud name of *The Barrel Organ*. Isabella had contributed a poem to one edition, and John B. Yeats and his sons were often pursued, when they dropped in for a chat with Frederick Gifford, to contribute 'stuff'. To the children, stuff was stuff, and they had no way of knowing that these contributions embraced one of Ireland's greatest painters and, many would argue, its greatest poet. These editorial gems contained poems, pictures, short stories, caricatures, 'jokes' and a serial that picked up the threads in each issue with the curious, unchanging words 'Now abaht that snake …' There were lampoons on neighbours and visiting tradesmen, but never anything like that about the servants; they were family. *The Barrel Organ*, which eventually disappeared, had a sketch of the head and shoulders of an Aran islander wearing a cap and signed by Jack B. Yeats. Yeats wrote the name 'Mícháil' under it.[3] A radio commentator in later years reflected during a programme that John Millington Synge, who went to the Aran Islands on W. B. Yeats' advice, learned Gaelic from an islander called Mícháil. Had she sold this little impromptu sketch, drawn from memory, the world of art would have had another small masterpiece and Nellie some much-needed cash during some of her poorer years.

The sons of Frederick and Isabella, when they had graduated, if such is the word, from the various impecunious ladies' establishments, went on to more conventional academies. A Mrs Harden's Dames School on Ormond Road is mentioned by Gabriel. He refers also to St Andrew's School and seems to have preferred it to the High School, which was then in Harcourt Street, on the site of what is now An Garda Síochána headquarters.

Claude, Gerald Vere and Gabriel are listed in the High School address book. They were among the earliest pupils at the school, which opened in 1870. One of Gerald's classmates was W. B. Yeats.[4] Gabriel reflected, in later years, that although he found the Irish Protestant schools 'slovenly' (he meant, presumably, rather loosely organised) they had distinct advantages over the British system and the Irish Catholic system, both of which 'moulded' the pupils too much for his liking. Moreover, his Protestant Irish schools did not insist on compulsory games, which was apparently a bonus for him because he wore glasses. In fact, despite the pejorative adjective he used in his correspondence with Nellie, he made a spirited defence of the Anglo-Irish Protestant community which their educational system produced and cited names such as Hamilton, Boyle, Berkeley, Burke and Wellington. What he did not observe, however, was that most Irish Protestant schoolboys in those days were almost guaranteed careers in a commerce which was almost exclusively in the hands of their co-religionists. This was also the case with state offices under the Crown, which were the prerogative of the same elite. The Catholic schools, whose students he saw being 'moulded', were trying to retrieve their people from the scholastic barrenness of the Penal Laws.

Kate, perhaps because she was the oldest girl, was the only one of the Gifford daughters to receive a full third-level education. She went to Alexandra College, which, in 1880, was the first women's college to prepare its girls for degrees at the Royal University, where she took an Honours BA in languages. The Catholic girls' colleges later followed this development. Kate mixed socially with her peers at venues such as the tennis club, but her sisters, who followed her to Alexandra, never settled happily there. Nellie described it as 'the gilt-edged Alexandra School in Earlsfort Terrace'.[5] It was, in fact, where the gilt-edged Hilton Hotel now stands, opposite what was then the Royal College and which until recently housed some departments of University College, Dublin, and is now the National Concert Hall. The school was, Nellie says, run on 'the conventional pattern of topnotch schools', but to Nellie and her sisters, Sidney and Ada, it was 'a seat of misery'.[6] Ada did not make a big impression because, Nellie defensively argues, she was not 'a pretty little thing', but she was, nevertheless, even in adolescence, witty, a cartoonist and a clever storyteller. She was not dressed 'tastefully', and that did not help on her first day. What's more, being a year apart in age, the sisters were separated, so they were no support for one another. The only subject in which they seemed to shine was poetry, where their father's Gilbertian love of rhyme had been transmitted to them, as well as their mother's poetic prowess.

In her reminiscences, Nellie recalls that there were some really attractive girls at Alexandra but that:

> ... bone of their bone was the strongest snobbery I have ever come across. It was kneaded into them from their earliest days ... They surrounded you the first day asking 'what's your father?' If he had a profession, then you were accepted and since ours was a lawyer, we passed that hurdle. Not so lucky were the very nicely-dressed children of a fashionable draper of Grafton Street, and others, also drapers, of Georges Street.[7]

The Lord Lieutenant's children attended the school and were, Nellie recalled, 'the recipients of the slavish attention of the headmistress'.[8] However, when one of the drapers' children indulged in trivial horseplay and was being corrected in front of the other children, a reference was made to 'little shopkeepers' children', with an added comment that such was all you could expect from them. The next day their mother told the headmistress what she thought of such denigration and withdrew her children from the school.

Even worse was Nellie's description of the 'Clergymen's Daughters' School'. In retrospect, their treatment angered Nellie more than that of the drapers' daughters, perhaps because of her maternal grandfather, the Rev. Robert Nathaniel Burton. She observed that they came from warm, rural backgrounds but that after a few months at this offshoot of Alexandra College they showed an obvious deterioration in their appearance. Their grooming worsened, and chapped hands told of an unsuitable diet or poor heating, or both. They were accommodated in a large grey house next to the school, paid for by some form of subsidy. Even their food and the way it was served was demeaning:

> Their luncheon consisted of thick chunks of white bakers loaf. This was thrown in an open laundry basket and dumped in the hall. The children came and just took a piece and went to the playground to eat it, as other children displayed dainties beside them. I always felt sorry for them and noted that they herded together looking shabbily dressed and unloved.[9]

It might be thought that Nellie and Ada took a rather subjective, sour view of this educational experience, but Sidney, who came after them, is equally graphic and condemnatory. She described scathingly the very moulding that Gabriel abhorred:

There the children were not educated at all – they were just processed
so as to manufacture English children of the upper classes. You were
trained to look down upon the people of Ireland and all other countries as 'natives'. Every language but English was 'a jargon' and so you
spoke all foreign languages with a Mayfair accent to show how much
you held them in contempt ... History was 'a rubber stamp' whose
chief or only content was lists of English monarchs, along with their
battles, conquests, dates of birth and dates of death. As for Irish history – whenever I hear anyone saying 'Who Fears to Speak of '98?'
I feel that a great many of our generation could have answered that
question by saying 'Every single teacher in the school where I was
taught.' It was a well-kept secret in my school that we lived in Ireland,
or had any history of our own at all.[10]

A particularly unpleasant aspect of the college for Sidney was the
snobbery of both staff and pupils. She reiterates what Nellie also
despised. On her first day she was subjected to the customary inter-
rogation by her classmates to gauge her admissibility to their elite
companionship. There were three determining criteria: her father's
profession, where she lived and where she spent her holidays. The
legal profession and Temple Villas passed muster. Greystones was
suitably select and suggested no lack of wealth, which would have
been the kiss of death, socially speaking. Pulling down the blinds
and retreating to the back of the house would have merited a very
low grade with these strict social judges. The final requirement of the
inquisition was to describe one's coat of arms. Having vaulted the
other hurdles, Sidney went along with this 'test', while despising it.
She would not be patronised. Deciding that 'coat of arms' probably
meant 'family crest', she described an embossed design on the doors
of a safe in her father's office. 'Ours is a lion and a unicorn,' she said.
Other past pupils have spoken of this aspect of Alexandra, but not
Kate, perhaps because she was more scholarly than her sisters.

Nellie was removed from Alexandra College in her early teens and promoted within the household to a rank equivalent to Junior Assistant Housekeeper, given such tasks as supervising the larder and helping to host both her mother's formal 'at homes' and her father's much less formal entertainment of his evening guests. There were three pantries at Temple Villas: one off the scullery for the servants, one for the family's food (for which Nellie possessed the key) and one for the fine china and cut glass.

One of Nellie's duties was to 'cut the rashers'. Each morning, she laid the side of bacon, skin side down, on the table to carve out the ribs and slices. These rashers were then given to Essie, the cook. Nellie also had to make the coffee, called 'drip' coffee – and it was slow to prepare. Ground coffee was packed into a strainer in the lid of the coffee pot. Boiling water was then poured onto the coffee, and it was left standing on the great kitchen range to keep it warm. She also made the butter pats and graduated into cake-making and desserts. She loved the friendly atmosphere in the kitchen and happily, for the time being, settled into her post, the purpose of which seemed to be to lighten Essie's load.

Nellie ruefully reflected over the years that she was taken from school sooner than the others because she was considered to have less ability. The remembered remark of one of the servants, possibly trying to echo Isabella, was 'Miss Nellie, you're very dull of apprehension.'[11] It rankled. Nellie argued that she gave her attention only to what attracted her, and that approach does not, admittedly, lead to a rounded education. There were certainly no sighs from her when she said goodbye to Alexandra as she had found its class consciousness particularly unacceptable and recalled that the students were not so much taught there as allotted material to learn themselves.

Nellie has left us a detailed description of her mother's afternoon receptions. The drawing room was locked except on visiting days and held the grandest furnishings of the house. The Gifford children had rarely, if ever, been inside the sanctum of the drawing room until their teenage years. The missionaries of the Church of Ireland, where the Giffords had their pew, brought back from their missions beautiful treasures of fine workmanship, carved and painted figurines, which stood on the mantelpiece and on a small table inside the door. The treasured ornaments had been bought by Isabella at missionary sales, and the mantelpiece and table containing them were dusted only by Nellie.

There was a silver salver in the hall on which callers placed their visiting cards. On these were embossed their names and addresses and, in a lower corner, the hours and days on which *they* would be 'at home' – usually 2 p.m. to 4 p.m. An order would have been sent up to the nursery forbidding 'games' during these hours and asking that the children be kept quiet. The receptions were held twice a month in winter but less often in summer. Bridget kept the nursery as quiet as possible on these occasions. The children could not see the hall from the high landing, but they could hear the knocks on the door and knew that the maid was dressed up for the occasion in black, with a white cap, apron and cuffs. Each caller, almost all matrons with grown-up, or growing-up, offspring, were representatives of their families. Their own visiting card was carried in a neat, often valuable, card case. They also deposited a separate card for each grown-up member of their family.

The guests knew the protocol. They stayed just long enough, as a rule, to sip a cup of tea, with a small slice of cake or a scone. The conversation had to do with their private affairs, mostly about their children and especially about their young sons. The room in which they chatted was a display area, swept and cleaned by the servants after their departure for the next visiting day and then locked.

Nellie's other duty was to hand round tea to the guests, a task, she argued, not as simple as it sounded. Victorian dresses covered even the instep, and these heavy, flowing skirts had to be negotiated carefully.

A minute cup of tea was brought to the visitor, and she was offered the options of cream and lump sugar, the latter supplied with a pair of tongs. On a second trip the choice of cake or scone was made.

The guests were usually dressed in dolmans, short, padded capes which reached below the waist and were decorated with jet beads. There was a slit on each side for the arms. A de rigueur bonnet was perched on top of the head, held by narrow ribbons and festooned with a veil, through which Nellie was often kissed. She was not expected to converse with the guests unless spoken to. However, she did hear snippets of conversation which obviously intrigued her, and one, which she found appalling, helped to shape her attitude to life. A visitor was describing where her teenage son had been drafted with his regiment: 'It's called The White Man's Grave.' To Nellie, the woman seemed to say this with a smirk, as if she were describing a trip to the circus. Nellie knew the lad, because he had been at school with one of her brothers. She remembered him as pleasant, socially easy, a singer of Percy French's songs. He was tall and well built, with just a little of the shyness of youth. Why, she thought, should a young lad just finished school have to face death in some outlandish place? He did, in fact, find his death in service, but even before that Nellie resolved that, if ever she could, she would prevent such a fate in a far-off land for her young contemporaries. She was realistic enough, however, to realise her relative powerlessness to change things.

Other similar conversations irked her. Everyone seemed to have someone at war. Some of the boys saw getting away from the High School, St Andrew's and the other boys' schools as an adventure. Such schools were supplying likely crops of recruits for the officer class. One particular description of training especially nauseated her. The training yard, she was told, was flooded with blood – or what looked like blood – to condition the young men to war.

A cousin returned from the Boer War regaled them with war stories in a conversational way. His family was not poor, but neither were they very well off, and this, rather than any empirical zeal, was often the reason why young men enlisted. Nellie found it difficult to accept his descriptions of cold-blooded deeds, including the brutal killing of defenceless people. She was particularly horrified at the killing of an old woman at her home: she had not been taught at Alexandra College that, just as you cannot make omelettes without cracking eggs, so you do not build an empire without cracking heads. Tudor and Cromwellian savagery in Ireland had not been on the school curriculum. Nellie knew, however, that this young man was telling the truth. He had been given orders, and those orders could not be questioned. Nellie made a vow that no one would ever make her stand idly by if someone's home, or their life, was threatened.

In a much lighter vein were the visits of the Yeats family to Frederick Gifford. John B. Yeats had been a barrister but enjoyed little success and instead explored his artistic gifts. He took a studio on the South Circular Road, and Temple Villas was a halfway house between the studio and the Yeats' residence in Dundrum. They visited frequently; sometimes John B. was on his own and sometimes he was accompanied by one of his sons, Jack or William, or by both of them. They were entertained in the dining room and, though this room was not as precious as Isabella's drawing room, nevertheless the number of the children allowed to fraternise with these visitors was controlled.

Nellie paints a cosy scene: the two senior men are smoking pipes. There is a warm coal fire and a decanter of whiskey on the table. Because it is winter, she has brought lemon and boiling water to make 'hot toddy'. She puts a spoon in each of the big cut-glass tumblers so that the hot water will not crack the crystal, and she has provided scones and small cakes. The lawyer and the artist have both law and art in common. They swap memories of legal incidents. Frederick rises to fill his guests' glasses, and Willie wanders over to the sideboard to take some grapes. Nellie, meanwhile, waits for her chance to ask Jack for a contribution to the magazine produced by the young Giffords. He never refuses. But she gets more than that for her culinary care of them. She is about to learn the art of back-scratching and that corruption lurks everywhere: as well as their magazine, the accomplished Giffords also ran the family Bedlam Sketching Club and invited the Yeats visitors to judge their competitions. Nellie's unique approach to this activity, given that she had no talent, was to cover her blank paper with pencil, then smudging it all over with her thumb to produce large areas of differing greys, finally taking a rubber to create curved shapes here and there; the resulting whirls of grey and white she would call *Sunset on the Lake* or something equally vague. She knew she was the least accomplished artist in the family. Why, then, was she awarded a prize by these, her talented judges? Sultana scones and hot toddy are the answer. Her brothers and sisters, fellow competitors in the Bedlam Sketching Club, withdrew, and it collapsed. They could sketch, they said, but they could not bake. When Sidney Gifford met John B. Yeats years afterwards in New York where he had settled, he enquired after 'the cook'. She thought at first he meant Essie, but it turned out that he was still remembering Nellie and her scones.[12]

Sidney also recalled her father's visitors and remembered John B. Yeats as a brilliant conversationalist, with charm and kindliness lighting up the flow of words in his pleasant speaking voice. She remembered too his absent-mindedness, thinking he was in his own house and stuffing keys left lying about into his pockets.[13] Frederick must have missed this agreeable companionship when John B. went to America in 1908.

The young people had their visitors also. Gerald Vere, who was studying law, sometimes brought Eustace and Ambrose Lane, Lady Gregory's nephews, home to dinner. They might stay the night at Temple Villas because even if they were only a little late, their mother would lock them out – despite their both being delicate. Their brother, Hugh Lane, was away in London, they said, collecting pictures to sell. Their Gifford friends were unimpressed: painting pictures would have interested them, but not buying and selling them. Their visitors quickly realised that telling funny stories would make them popular at Temple Villas, and one of them, feeling inadequate at this social grace, kept a notebook of jokes which he consulted discreetly. Muriel, going through a tomboy stage, grabbed the notebook as the unfortunate amateur comic was scanning it under the table. It contained a list of his friends and, opposite their names, 'suitable' jokes. It was an obvious precaution given that Isabella was so conservative. Another contemporary of her brothers wrote poems to Nellie, but they too disappeared in time.

The children loved the 'downstairs' visitors, their father's as well as their own. Their mother's drawing-room dolman-gowned guests were less loved than endured.[14]

5

INTO THE WORLD

Visiting is a two-way business, however, and the teenage Giffords, as well as entertaining in their home, also paid calls. There are a few descriptions of their being introduced to the social world. On a rather tattered page of *The Monitor*, an old early twentieth-century periodical, there is an article by Nell (Eileen) Gay, a member of a well-known republican family. The title, 'The Pretty Ladies', sets the tone of the article, written about four of the Gifford girls: Nellie, Muriel, Grace and 'John'.[1] When Sidney started writing in her teens, while still at Alexandra, she decided, perhaps correctly, that an obviously Protestant sort of name, and the name of a *girl* at that, would not get her very far in republican journalism. She told Jack White, editor of *The Irish Times*, that when she left Alexandra College (about 1905) she signed her very first effort in journalism for Arthur Griffith's *Sinn Féin* with the name 'John Brennan' because she thought 'it sounded like a strong Wexford farmer'.[2] From then on, except for official papers, she always signed herself 'John', and that was what the family called her thereafter.

Eileen Gay's article eulogised the girls' charms, writing that their dress was both beautiful and 'quaint' – an interesting word. The Giffords chose fabrics like velvet and flowing silk and sometimes made their own clothes. Another, more robust description comes from a relation of Maeve Donnelly, Nellie's daughter. He informed Maeve in a letter, 'They were a rather wild, attractive lot; could have been on the stage.'³ The *Monitor* article describes the girls' entrance to the Sinn Féin rooms, all tastefully dressed: 'they were like a bouquet of flowers.'⁴

One of the houses they visited was that of District Justice Reddin on the north side of the city, where they were likely to meet people of artistic, literary and political bent. Another literary salon was in the home of George Russell (Æ), a gentle, tall, humorous man and a visionary poet. At his Sunday 'open house' evenings, the Gifford teenagers were made very welcome, partly because of their first appearance there. While in London, young Frederick Ernest Gifford had been befriended by Sylvia Lynd, the wife of the essayist Robert Lynd, who described himself in the London *Times* as 'a Protestant Ulster nationalist'.⁵ Sylvia introduced her mother, Nora F. Dryhurst, to Ernest, and she arranged for his attendance with his sisters at Æ's salon. She persuaded the young Giffords to dress in costume for the visit and introduced them under the Celtic names of Deirdre, Fionnuala, Gráinne and Cúchulainn. They had walked to Rathgar, where Æ lived, wearing these theatrical costumes, evoking much interest on the way. To their embarrassment, they found the other guests in normal attire. This alone could have earned them the description of being a little wild and suitable for stage careers. However, it endeared them to their host, Æ, and during later visits to his home they met Count Casimir Markievicz and his wife, Constance Markievicz, James Stephens, Padraic Colum, Sarah Purser (a distant Gifford relative), the Yeats family and Maud Gonne. This was all a far cry from mother's 'at home' visitors, and these teenagers were made very welcome at Æ's and wherever they went.⁶

Other members of the family were going out into the world, however, in a more real sense. The shadowy Liebert, second son of Frederick and Isabella, had left home by the time of the taking of the 1901 census, when he was twenty-five years of age. His was a strange name, rather musical and Norman, and its choice was equally unusual. At his birth, the name was familiar to Isabella as the trade name of some household commodity. She fancied the sound of it, and, alone among her sons, he received at baptism only one first name.[7] He joined the British Merchant Navy and sought Canadian citizenship.

Edward Cecil, Grace's twin went to America and there seems to have been little if any contact between either him or Liebert with the family over the years. A letter was delivered one day to Temple Villas with an apologetic note from the Rathmines post office.[8] The franked stamp indicated a date ten years past. The letter had fallen behind a grid and had lain there till some reconstruction work on the office was being done. It was from one of the absent boys, Liebert or Edward Cecil, but it is unclear which one. Other than this letter, the two seemed to fade from the family history books. Neither Nellie nor 'John' say much of them in their family records.

The eldest boy, Claude Frederick, went into his father's legal office. Frederick had left the Bachelor's Walk address, and, in 1895, Frederick Gifford & Son operated at 46 Dawson Street. In 1901, Frederick Gifford & Claude Gifford are at 5 Dawson Street, and in 1906 they have moved to No. 16 where they stayed until 1913. The last listing, for Claude only, is 1913.[9] By that time his father was seventy-seven. Later, Claude is listed as Lieutenant Claude F. Gifford, 50th Battalion Canadian Overseas Expeditionary Force. By Easter Week 1916, however, the Claude Gifford family home was in Baggot Street, not very far from where Commandant de Valera was holding Bolands Mills and still nearer to the little Irish Volunteer outpost at Clanwilliam House.

The third Gifford boy, Gerald Vere, had also studied law. He had just done his finals in 1901 when he contracted meningitis and died unexpectedly, aged twenty-three. The family, and especially his mother, were devastated.

Gabriel, the fourth son, took up the study of art, which brought him to London and fraternisation with W. B. Yeats. The poet wrote a poem (lost unfortunately) about their walks in London parks. Gabriel's next move was to America, where he made his living as a commercial artist. He married there and had a daughter, Geraldine, called after Gerald perhaps. His letters show him to be a good family man, but with a decided distaste for both Irish Ireland and Catholic Ireland, in whose faith he had been baptised.

Frederick Ernest, to give him his full name, was the ninth child of Frederick and Isabella. While art, the armed services and the law had provided careers for his brothers, it was decided to make Ernest an electrical engineer, even though he, too, had artistic leanings. It was a sensible choice, in that electricity was obviously an increasingly important source of power. He was placed for his training with an electrical firm in Kildare and, since his work was often at night, his social life was minimal. The firm moved to Rawmarsh, Yorkshire, and later to London. Ernest moved with them. Here too his work inhibited social relaxation so that he had to make a determined effort to find himself an outlet for his leisure time. He discovered a sort of literary club in London, and it was there that he met Sylvia, the wife of Robert Lynd. The warm-hearted girl had observed a tall, red-haired young man, standing shyly and alone at his first meeting. She welcomed him and introduced him to her mother, Nora Dryhurst, whose husband was director of the London Museum and who was herself a journalist and a sort of collector of nationalist causes: the young Indian movement, Young Egyptians, Young Irelanders – they were all grist to the mill of her enthusiasm. She seemed unaware that Ernest might not have had any anti-loyalist feelings, and there is a brief, mind-boggling reference to her attempt to do Irish step-dancing with Indians and Egyptians who wanted their countries to be free of English power and English influence. During these attempts at multi-racial Irish step-dancing they were 'like wooden figures', and there was much laughter at their attempts to keep the feet in perpetual motion and the torso in statuesque immobility.

Ernest was invited to Nora Dryhurst's London home, and she was delighted to hear of his talented family. She learned of Liebert and Edward Cecil, who had gone off to America; of Claude, who was partner in his father's legal firm; of Muriel who was still in Dublin; of Kate, who had got her degree; of Nellie, who was housekeeping at home; of Gabriel, Grace and Ada, all of whom hoped to make a career in art; and also of his youngest sister, who had left school and wanted to be a journalist. He showed her an article by 'John' published in Arthur Griffith's *Sinn Féin* and some pictures too, including a reproduction of a painting by William Orpen of Grace, a student at the Slade School of Art. Nora Dryhurst's interest in the colourful careers of Ernest's brothers and sisters led to her friendship with the whole family, to her introducing them to Æ ... and to two doomed marriages.[10]

The girls were also making their way in the world. Because she was over twenty, Kate was allowed to read the newspapers, denied to the younger ones for fear of corruption. She drew Nellie's attention to a government advertisement in the press announcing a new scheme of training, which was to produce at its conclusion 'An Itinerant Cookery Instructress under the Department of Agriculture and Technical Instruction for Ireland' to teach all over Ireland. This grandiose title was soon to be reduced to 'The Cookin' Woman' by its rural female students. Its training centre was at 20–21 Kildare Street, Dublin, and it was called the Irish Training School of Domestic Economy.[11] In fact, the course was in 'household management' and included both laundry and dressmaking. Kate pointed out that the paper suggested taking a 'trial course' and thought this was an excellent opportunity for Nellie. Nellie raced off to her amused father to coax the required £1 entrance fee from him because she had no pocket money at that stage. She acquitted herself well at the Kildare Street interview, but she herself remarked, wryly, that several family strings had to be pulled for her to be admitted to the course. Unionist strings would have been almost standard, as they were with practically every post apart from the most menial. Nellie learned that she would require a white apron, that the course would last for six weeks and that, as surprised as she was joyful, she would then be a salaried lady.

Once qualified, Nellie had to provide herself with all her own cooking paraphernalia, and, since her lessons were sometimes held in vacated schools or even sheds (one shared with a sheep shearer), she had to bring not only her pots and saucepans, ingredients and implements, but also a collapsible table. She often had upwards of twenty girls and women in her classes, and the six-week course actually lasted for twelve weeks because it was deemed that a continuous six weeks would be too demanding for the students. She would alternate one group with another, spreading the lessons over twelve weeks in all.

She hired a pony and cart, or donkey and cart – whichever was available – to bring all the gear from venue to venue, including the *pièce de resistance*, which was called a 'mistress' stove, of reputedly American origin. One English inspector expressed horror when he saw 'the stable' as he called the shed in which Nellie at that point was teaching, but the young domestic scientist piously (and perhaps not very appropriately) mentioned in defence the most famous stable in the world.

Another difficulty for Nellie when she was working away from Dublin was accommodation. The 'big houses', owned almost exclusively by Nellie's own class, would never take boarders, so she was obliged to take accommodation in cottages, varying from the very comfortable to the cold and damp. She and her fellow instructors had been warned in their training how to test for a damp bed: on their first night in a bed, in which there was usually placed an earthenware hot-water bottle, they were to insert a mirror between the sheets. If the mirror became misted, the bedclothes were dangerously damp. Nellie solved one such situation by spreading the bedclothes out to dry at the fire and sleeping in a bare but dry bed, wrapped in her warm dressing gown. One cottager with whom she stayed economised (as most of them did) by using dripping instead of butter on the bread. The dog in the house thrived gratefully on the 'drippinged' bread that Nellie slipped to him.[12]

Such discomforts she took in her stride, considering her sheltered upbringing. She has left behind an indication of her affection for these Irish country folk in both a fairly excruciating poem, technically speaking (though full of warmth), and a very beautiful and moving short story. It was a love story on both sides for rural Ireland and Nellie Gifford. The country people were reincarnations of her beloved nurse, Bridget Hamill, and she had no difficulty in loving them. She played her violin for their set dances in the evenings, and we get a marvellous glimpse of her 'goings on' from Patrick Galligan, Thomastown, Kilbeg, County Meath, interviewed in his own home on 12 November 1970, when he was seventy-four years of age:

There's a bit of history attached to this house that I live in. It was built for a man called Denis Creevan and was finished around 1904 or 1905. There was a cookery class started in the parish, cookery and domestic economy and all to this. The lady that was sent to us was a Miss Gifford and she turned out in later years to be [a sister of] the lady that was the maid, the bride and the widow the one day. She was married to the 1916 leader [Joseph] Thomas [sic] Plunkett.

Well, she left this house and went to lodge above in Dunne's of Marvelstown. The reason that she had come to this house was that it was hard to get any place to stop at the time. She was stopping in Kells, I suppose. Father Clavin was after coming here and he was anxious to get some place for her so he got on to the Creevans to know if they could keep her. Julia Creevan stopped with her and she slept above here in this room. But anyway she left because Paddy Creevan was reported for keeping lodgers in a county council cottage.

She remained in Dunne's for some time. But she was a grand person. I remember her well, I used to be a young fellow there doing jobs in the evening for Mrs Dunne and getting my dinner into that. But, anyway, there was nothing for her only Irish tradition, all about Ireland. One thing she longed for turned out to be the cause of her misfortune here, and got her out of the parish. She wanted to see an Irish wake.

Well, there were two old Lynch brothers, Pat and Farrell. Farrell was a process server. Pat was a good old character but he died and didn't she get around Michael Dunne and Dan to bring her to the wake – they were going to the wake and she would go with them. She went in, so she did, and she heard the songs, cut the tobacco … Mrs Dunne wasn't to have heard anything about it because at that time, do you see, it was a terrible crime for a young one to go to a wake. No women were allowed at wakes, only the immediate friends. Well, it reached Fr Clavin's ears and didn't he go up the next day and got on to Mrs Dunne about her and, sure Mrs Dunne didn't know anything about her going to the wake. What kind of a character would she be that would go out at that time of night? With the result that Mrs Dunne got rid of her. She had [another] sister who got married to Tom MacDonagh. Her son is a district justice.[13]

Nellie not only attended a wake and learned the local ballads during her 'cookin' woman' career, but she also had several ballads written about herself, her charm and her beauty. She liked Limerick least of her venues and most enjoyed County Meath. On one train journey, she carried a Persian kitten Isabella had given her for one of her Meath friends who particularly wanted a 'Dublin' cat. It was closeted in a basket, and the fear was that the ticket collector would deem it against the by-laws and banish it to the luggage compartment. An animated discussion ensued. Dogs were forbidden but did this cover cats too? The consensus was that the less these officials knew, the better, and since the kitten at this stage was heaving in the basket and causing it to creak, as well as emitting a faint *miaow*, the whole carriage collaborated, and when the collector arrived they fussed and carried out various acoustic diversionary tactics – coughing, laughing and talking – and all this put him off the scent. When he had safely departed, and when all the windows and doors had been closed, it was thought that the Persian needed air and exercise, and the released kitten happily spent the rest of the journey wandering across the laps and shoulders of the passengers and even perched on top of a man's hat until Nellie's station meant necessary captivity in the basket once again. Before that, in her chat with a fellow passenger, when Nellie asked who was minding her children at home, the answer was that they were being looked after by 'the boy' (the hired help) and that she had every confidence in him: 'That fella,' she said 'could mind mice at a crossroads.'[14]

It was usual to have a helping woman who gave a hand with cleaning the demonstration venues and setting up the equipment. One of these helpers came to Nellie with a tale of woe: her son had broken the 'weddin' present' – a pot oven. This was a major loss in a cottage household, and Nellie promised to replace it on her next trip to Dublin. The helper would have been 'touchy' at any hint of charity, to use Nellie's expression, and so she was asked to do something in return, to keep the balance even – a mini cooperative as it were.

Grace often went to Broadstone Station in Dublin to 'see Nellie off', and on this occasion went with her on her, so far, fruitless search for the required pot oven, which, she was told, was out of date and, if there was one in Dublin, she would most likely get it in Moore Street. When they arrived there, Nellie left her bags with Grace and went off to the recommended shop. On her return, complete with pot oven, she found Grace in conversation with an elderly lady. It was Nora

Dryhurst. They had never met her before but she had simply walked over to Grace and said, 'You must be Ernest Gifford's sister Grace. He showed me sketches of you in London.'[15]

By 1911, all the boys had left Temple Villas, but not all the girls. Nellie was surprised, on one of her early visits home from Meath, to find that her sisters were actually receiving pocket money, something she had never enjoyed, despite her housekeeping role. Grace showed a definite artistic flair which had motivated her parents to arrange for her to study at the Metropolitan School of Art in Dublin and, later, on the advice of Sir William Orpen, at the Slade in London, where she was a pupil of his. It was there, in 1907, when she was nineteen years of age, that she sat for him for the portrait, a copy of which was shown by Ernest to Nora Dryhurst and which Orpen had called, somewhat prophetically, *The Spirit of Young Ireland*. He seemed to have supplied some of the jewellery she wears in the picture – she referred afterwards, jocosely, to her 'necklace of rosary beads'. Grace spent a year at the Slade before returning to Dublin in 1908. Meanwhile, Muriel had tried nursing but found the actuality far more demanding than her idealised concept of it had been and she had not, as yet, replaced it with anything else. 'John' was beginning to make her way, not very lucratively, in the field of freelance journalism. Ada was experiencing a little friction with her mother, and, just as Kate had initiated Nellie into her career as rural instructress, so too Nellie now supplied the money for the fare to America where Ada wanted to exploit her undoubted artistic talent as a way of living. By the end of that year Ada had made the move to America. She kept in touch intermittently, but never returned to Ireland.

That left only Kate and, in the Victorian Age, the eldest almost automatically became her mother's household aide-de-camp and, in the case of large families, a surrogate mother to the younger ones. Such was the case with Kate Gifford. Gabriel, Nellie and Ada, the trio in the middle of the family, and only half a dozen years or so

Kate's junior, sometimes saw her on a seniority pinnacle, remote from their childhood and their world. This sense of otherness most probably evolved from the fact that Bridget Hamill, in her nursery eyrie under the roof, had only a clutter of juniors at a time. Kate had well left babyhood by the time they were weaned, and she had graduated to dining full-time with their parents, not just once a week. Another factor which, perhaps, also set her apart was that she was the best-educated girl of the family. Some time after her graduation from the Royal University in 1898, she went to Germany and taught English, recalling later a noticeboard in the hall of the establishment where she taught. It set out the names and nationalities of the language teachers: there was just one odd one out. The French, Spanish and Italian teachers all hailed from a town in the country whose language they taught, but for the teaching of English, where one might expect an English name and city, there appeared instead 'Miss Kate Gifford, Dublin, Ireland'. Her German students had no problem with this.[16]

Kate was never considered beautiful. Apart from her strong features, dark-haired Irish beauties were the conceived stereotype of Irish good looks in her youth. Fairly tall, the blue-eyed Kate had the most uncompromising red hair of them all – her brothers called it 'carroty' – and she had a high colour, which did not help. Despite all this, there is evidence that in Germany her hair received much admiration.

In 1957, six months before she died at the age of eighty-two, Kate went over all her papers. She decided to destroy a great bundle of correspondence consisting largely of letters from her parents during the German sojourn of their eldest daughter. The letters must have been a comfort to the young teacher in a Germany that was very different from that of today. There were no shoals of Irish students doing sabbaticals or taking summer jobs, no Irish bars for fraternisation. Kate had only the loving letters from Temple Villas, starting with the familiar salutation 'My dear Kate' and ending with a parental benediction. Who else would keep a bundle of letters for sixty years right through all that lay before her: a return from Germany, an insurrection, a civil war and imprisonment in Kilmainham Gaol?

Frederick and Isabella have been seen as somewhat distant from their sons and daughters in their childhood years, but they must have worried when Kate was away, and how that worry, which is another name for love, must have been read by Kate between the lines of that bundle of letters, treasured over the long, long years.[17]

6

REVIVING AN OLD CULTURE

The Gifford daughters still living in Ireland, Nellie, Grace, Kate, Muriel and 'John', were becoming increasingly part of a social metamorphosis, an extraordinary phenomenon. Slowly, almost imperceptibly, coming from several spheres of interest, from all walks of life and from everywhere in Ireland, there was a hankering after and a groping towards things Irish. The 'hidden Ireland' of the writer Daniel Corkery was being revealed, and Dark Rosaleen (*Róisín Dubh*) of the poet James Clarence Mangan was awakening from her slumbers. The folk memory held many appalling images in its *béal oidis* (oral tradition), ballads, poems and even on its yellow handkerchiefs – not figments of the imagination but facts, corroborated by annals and reputable historians down the years. In fact, Pádraig Pearse was to declare Ireland's independence 'In the name of God and of the *dead generations*.'

Though the movement to which the Giffords became committed was essentially a twentieth-century phenomenon, there had been repeated movements, armed and unarmed, to rescue Gaelic Ireland from the cultural extinction envisaged by her conquerors. 'John' was the first of Isabella's daughters to engage in this Irish Ireland, though the threads from which were woven the fabric of Gifford republicanism were there long before the Irish Ireland movement impinged on their adult lives. There were Bridget's ballads and poems, the knowledge that their grandfather, the Rev. Robert Nathaniel

Burton, had died helping famine victims, their father's stories of harrowing evictions during the Land War and their fraternisation with the servants who were anti-British. In fact many anti-British hands were rocking many cradles all over the Empire – because the servants were nearly always members of the conquered races. Then, too, there was the Gifford friendship with intellectuals such as Æ and James Stephens, as well as a questioning reaction to their mother's determined stand regarding England's superiority. Lastly, there was a distinctive withdrawal, recorded by 'John' and Nellie, but quite probably felt by their sisters too, from a voracious empire whose militant colonialism engorged greedily the lives of many of their brothers' young classmates, leaving their womenfolk without fathers, brothers, husbands and sons.

It was curious that not one of the Gifford boys was even remotely touched by Irish patriotism. Their sister 'John' described them as a mixture of Fabian socialists and half-hearted unionists who remained so perhaps because they knew that those who did not conform to this political belief would be ostracised in the tennis club. There was also the further danger of career exclusion. Anyway, the three who went off to the wars were excluded geographically as well as ideologically, while Gerald Vere lay buried in Mount Jerome and Ernest showed no interest whatever in the national movement; nor did Gabriel, even when he went to America where the Gaelic movement was almost a *sine qua non* for mixing in Irish-American society and even though Ada, with whom he had always been close, was very much involved with her compatriots there. Gabriel contributed one curious little offering to Irish history, however. He did a sketch, pencil on paper, of his brother-in-law, Thomas MacDonagh, on 27 July 1912.

The Gifford sisters made up for this lack of interest. They were in the thick of the new phenomenon. Their father Frederick expressed the disbelief of fathers everywhere when, if one or other of them stayed at home in the evening, he asked bemusedly whether they were ill or if anything was the matter.

On a not-untypical day, the poet Seumas O'Sullivan invited them to the Martello Tower at Sandycove where he, Oliver St John Gogarty and Arthur Griffith were having a holiday. Griffith, normally shy and even asocial, was relaxed and happy as he rowed the lady guests around Scotsman's Bay. In return, when they were staying in a farmhouse in Avoca, County Wicklow, they invited O'Sullivan and Griffith down for a visit. Griffith was delighted with the ten-year-old son of the farm because he knew so much Irish history, and, on his return to Dublin, he sent the boy a copy of John Mitchel's *Jail Journal*, one of the great classics of Irish republicanism.[1]

Evenings might be spent at céilís or at the Abbey Theatre. 'John's' description of the Abbey in those early days makes it sound like a village hall. They knew many in the audience: the Yeats family, those they had met in District Justice Reddin's home and the home of Æ, and those who were becoming known to them through 'John's' political writings. In fact, if a non-acquaintance arrived, it was unusual. They bought seats in the cheaper 'pit', but if they wanted to talk during the interval to someone who had a seat in the grander stalls, they simply lifted the dividing rope and settled down beside the friend.

'John' was contributing to an Ireland which had already, for some time, been seeking its cultural roots. Douglas Hyde, who was later to become the first *uachtarán* (president) of the twenty-six-county Free State, found a deep interest in the Irish language; Bunting and Joyce rescued the old Irish music; the interest of Petrie, Stokes, Wilde and Burton lay in the archaeological stone treasures of Ireland's ancient past; Lady Augusta Gregory, excited by the resurrected tales of Celtic mythology, wanted to immortalise them in a national theatre, while W. B. Yeats' aim was to enshrine them in his plays and verse. This was all going on while the china teacups tinkled delicately during afternoon 'at homes' such as those of Isabella Gifford. Anglo-Irish ladies still basked in the belief that they had a civilising influence on a conquered race close enough to barbarism and at best fit only to be their servants. But other descendants of those who had ruthlessly created the Anglo-Irish Protestant state were questioning the superiority theory on which their arrogance and domination had been based. The people whom their forebears had savagely conquered had a language with both the clarity of inflected speech and an embarrassment of riches in descriptive vocabulary, as any student of Gaelic literature will know.

As well as the Anglo-Irish devotees (who also included Edward Martyn, George Moore and Æ), native scholars such as Eugene O'Curry, Father Peadar Ó Laoghaire and Father Dineen were also painstakingly conserving, in grammatical and dictionary form, the old language – the vessel of all that had been Ireland, good and bad, before the predatory invasions. John O'Donovan's *Grammar of the Irish Language* and *Annals of the Four Masters* were milestones. Eugene O'Curry, a native Irish speaker from County Clare, with no formal education, had inspired Petrie, Stokes, Todd and others with his extraordinary knowledge of ancient Irish civilisation. The newly established Catholic University of Dublin appointed him to the Chair of Archaeology and Irish Literature. His essays on Tara and on Irish round towers were world acclaimed, and he opened doors to the study of the history, literature and laws of his people.

A list of 'Celtic' societies which were established during the nineteenth century will give some idea of the depth and scope of interest of the time's Gaelic reawakening: the Ossianic Society, the Iberno-Celtic Society, the Gaelic Union, the Ulster Gaelic Society, the Gaelic League, the Society for the Preservation of the Irish Language. The Gaelic League increased from forty-three branches in 1897 to 600 in 1904, with a membership of 50,000. Some of the other organisations could be seen as dilettante groups, interested in old language treasures and lost artefacts. However, as the century progressed the aims shifted towards language rehabilitation, and entwined inextricably with these newer groups were political as well as linguistic yearnings, despite the misgivings of a few.

Added to all this, at a non-scholarly level, young people were joining the Gaelic Athletic Association to play Gaelic football and hurling. They no longer needed to subject themselves to the almost inevitable racial blackballing at local tennis clubs by the Planter classes. Céilís were held in church halls, at crossroads and in kitchens, with jigs, reels, the 'High Caul Cap' and 'The Walls of Limerick'.

The Gifford sisters were very much part of this Celtic buzz. Nellie Gifford has left her own description of the movement:

> Nothing distinctively Irish was too small or too vast for the sweeping enthusiasm of the Gaels of this period. Funds were raised by Irish concerts, and songs written to sing at them. Many of these were comic songs with a sting in them for the anti-Irish men or women. Learning Gaelic was stiff going, especially to scholars who had been working all day, so these night classes generally finished with an Irish dance … Irish girls induced sometimes reluctant boyfriends to these dances, hoping by easy stages to coax them to learn the language. Everyone was anxious to teach any visitor the various Irish dance steps …
>
> An Englishman visiting Ireland about twenty-five years ago found a great, an almost feverish, activity all over the country for for-warding the use of Gaelic. Those pioneers for the language realised that, after all, it was the great poverty of the Irish that was the first greatest stumbling block to putting the Gaelic language back in Ire-land. And so with an enthusiasm and amount of self-sacrifice they shouldered, not merely the language question, but the whole structure of Irish life which was at that time a badly-copied form of an out-of-date English model.[2]

As well as all this, the dancing Celtic feet were not only active at the céilí. On the sports fields too they were happily used in the national games of hurling, football, rounders, camogie and handball under the aegis of the Gaelic Athletic Association, which flourished and spread its activities to every parish in Ireland. With that native-games ethos came also its language, music, song, 'Buy Irish' campaign and, above all, political independence.[3]

Maud Clare, who was a member of Cumann na mBan (the Women's Association), described the enthusiasm:

> You would get up in the morning and think 'what will I do for Ireland today? Will they ask me to carry a dispatch? Will I go to the Irish class tonight?' It was exciting – a dream we all had about a free Ireland and an Irish Ireland – our own again.[4]

'John' Gifford described The O'Rahilly, head of his old Kerry clan and later a founding member of the Irish Volunteers, when he returned from America a wealthy man:

> The O'Rahilly made himself the employee of his country and no wage-earner ever served a master so diligently and incessantly as this head of a kingdom ... He was well-known in every part of Ireland for driving his own *gluaisteán*, as he called his car ... on behalf of the Gaelic League, Sinn Féin and the Irish Industrial Revival.[5]

Other descriptions of this gradual change in ordinary Irish society, as well as in some pockets of the intellectual Anglo-Irish class, cover such phenomena as the street meetings to educate the people as to what was going on and also the encouragement of Irish industry, which found chief expression in *Aonach na Nollaig*, a Christmas fair held in the Rotunda in Dublin, at which goods of Irish manufacture only were sold. The language classes, debating societies, concerts and distribution of pamphlets were all directed towards an Ireland increasingly aware of its past and planning its future.

A very human reflection on the Irish Ireland movement, after it had developed an armed faction and spilled over into the War of Independence, came from one member of Cumann na mBan when describing how she came to be involved. Eileen Walsh's eldest brother, Phillip, who had bought her first piano for his young sister, was in the IRA, and an English sniper's bullet was to cost him his life in Dublin's **North King** Street during the 1916 Rising. Eileen was only sixteen when it happened, but she joined Cumann na mBan so that she could carry guns for 'the boys'. 'We did that to help the movement,' she said, 'and in my case to remember Phillip. We used to go to céilís too, but that was to meet the fellas.'[6] And who would deny that tentative courtships and romantic attachments, as well as military alliances, have their place in the future of an embryonic nation, even though that nation was, as yet, still a dream in Irish minds.

7

THE MIGHTY PEN

Young journalist 'John Brennan' became a part of what was, effectively, a propaganda machine for the early enthusiasts of the movement. Words being traditionally mightier than swords, the plethora of nationalist written and oral matter worked its formative qualities on the minds of some of those not yet converted.

In 1891, the first bilingual Irish–English weekly paper had been launched by the Gaelic League, but there had been, for more than 100 years, pro-Irish literature in English. The 1848 rebellion of the Young Irelanders, while sparse on physical confrontation, had been rich in words – in prose, poems and ballads – many of which were being recalled in Ireland in the early decades of the twentieth century. People were beginning to feel, indeed, 'A Nation Once Again', in Thomas Davis' famous words. After the aborted rising of Robert Emmet in 1803, his speech from the dock had been quickly circulated. It was now reprinted. The Ascendancy literary awakening, led by Hyde, Gregory, Yeats and Synge, was also subtly and unconsciously feeding Irish nationalist aspirations. In America, the septuagenarian Fenian, John Devoy, in *The Gaelic American*, and Patrick Ford, in his *Irish World*, were proposing new directions for Irish politics. At home there were old reliables such as the pro-Redmond *Freeman's Journal* and saucy newcomers such as the magazine *Bean na hÉireann* (*Woman of Ireland*), familiarly called *The Bean* (pronounced *ban*) and published by Inghínidhe na hÉireann (Daughters of Ireland) under the editorship of Helena Molony, lifelong friend of 'John' Gifford. It was a monthly magazine that circulated freely in Ireland and in the USA, and discussed matters of social and national interest. It was called 'the women's magazine which men read' and attracted contributions from Stephens, Æ, Griffith, Markievicz, Colum, Plunkett, Sir Roger Casement, Katharine Tynan and Maud Gonne (all unpaid, like its staff). 'John' Gifford was an enthusiastic contributor, as well as a member of the editorial staff.

Katharine Tynan submitted a serial in which an English officer was to marry the girlfriend of his foe – a gallant United Irishman who had been fatally wounded in the fight for Irish freedom – but the editor of *Bean na hÉireann* rewrote the ending, reviving the dying United Irishman and whisking him off, pale but alive, to claim his bride from the English enemy.[1] In the 1908 Christmas number, Susan Mitchell's anti-conscription ballad about the Irish boy in Carrick workhouse who was conscripted into Her Majesty's army, 'for the glory of the Empire', appeared. In the same issue, Padraic Colum's anti-English play *The Saxon Shilling* was also published, and, nurturing the same enlistment antipathy, in a later issue of November 1910 Arthur Griffith also argued against conscription:

> The strength of England lies in her armed forces. Guns and battle-ships are useless to a nation which cannot procure men of courage and intelligence to work them ... Without a large Irish contingent in the British army that army would be of no more use in serious warfare than an armed police.

The Boer War had erupted in 1899, and the Irish republican media vociferously supported the Boers and rejected any conscription in Ireland to fight these farmers who, like themselves, wanted a republic. On the one hand, there was this anti-conscription propaganda in the Irish Ireland press, but on the other there was also *The Irish Times*, the *Irish Independent* and the evening papers lauding the Irish Parliamentary Party of John Redmond, the aims of the British Empire and its need to conscript in Ireland.

Even a short list of further Irish Ireland publications gives some idea of the flood of anti-English propaganda:

The Leader (editor D. P. Moran)

The Gaelic Athlete

The Irish Felon

The Irish Penny Journal

The Nation

The Irish Review (editors Professor Heuston and Joseph Plunkett [suppressed])

An Claidheamh Soluis (editor Pádraig Pearse)

A secret detective report from Dublin Castle on another republican paper, *The Spark*, named as its owner and editor respectively Máire Perolz of 10 North Great Georges Street and Countess Markievicz of 49B Leinster Road, Rathmines (both friends of the Giffords). The Irish Ireland press was being watched.

A whole hive of weekly publications, however, was ready and willing to sting, like wasps, the imperial lion: *Nationality*, *Republic*, *Honesty*, *Volunteer*, *Hibernian*. Their proprietor was J. J. Walsh of 26 Blessington Street, and their printer was the Gaelic Press, Upper Liffey Street, which was raided and destroyed some years later, on 24 March 1916. The editor of *The Spark*, Ed Dalton, in a scathing editorial of 2 April 1916, described as an atrocity the raiding of the Gaelic Press by 'an armed deputation of forty Defenders of the Rights of Small Nationalities'. Having hurled this piece of irony (the alleged reason for Britain's entering the First World War), Dalton pointed out that the raid concerned yet another nationalist paper, *The Gael* – not one of J. J. Walsh's but one also printed by the Gaelic Press. Dalton argued that if anyone should be arrested then it should be the editor: the printer had been merely doing his job.[2] In the same issue, a letter from J. J. Walsh appeared in which he described how the printing machinery had been destroyed by 'the military tyrants' from Dublin Castle and both type and print matter confiscated, including some issues of *The Spark*. Walsh set up a fund to help the Gaelic Press, then almost ruined.[3]

The advertisements in *The Spark* make typical Irish Ireland reading. A céilí is advertised for Óglaigh na hÉireann (Dublin Brigade) at 25 Parnell Square; Domhnall Ua Buachalla advertises bilingually his Luciana bicycles; Gleeson's of O'Connell Street are 'the pioneer Irish goods only store'; the Hon. Secretary of the Sinn Féin Bank, Alderman T. Kelly, seeks subscriptions; Whelan & Son of Ormond Quay offer green, white and orange badges at one penny each. *The Spark* itself cost a halfpenny.[4]

It was Griffith's newspapers, *The United Irishman* and *Sinn Féin* (before he modified his republican stance), which, more than any other publication, swung opinion in Ireland towards national freedom. Griffith was in full, unmodified republican flight when these words of his appeared in his issue of 13 July 1908: 'Let us renounce the disastrous policy of making the parliament House of England the arena of the Irish struggle. Let us make the dissolution of the British Empire our immediate object.'

Catering for the other extreme, the Ascendancy elite, were two publications. One was *Irish Society and Social Review* (price one penny), founded in 1887 and covering, to use its own phraseology, 'Balls, Parties, At Homes, etc.'. It also covered society weddings where minute details included not only the people, the church, the residence, clothing and flowers, but also the gifts (some in the luxury class) given to the several bridesmaids. *The Irish Figaro*, owned and edited by Ramsay Colles, concentrated more on Dublin Castle, vice-regal personalities and general Anglo-Irish 'hangers-on'. However, it was not above taking a snipe at republicans. In fact, its chief claim to fame, in a résumé of Irish Ireland propaganda and counter-propaganda, is an incident that followed a derogatory reference in one of its editorials to Maud Gonne (who had herself been a one-time habitué of Anglo-Irish social gatherings): Arthur Griffith went into the newspaper office and vigorously whipped the editor. It was a most uncharacteristic act of violence from the mild-mannered founder of Sinn Féin and earned him ten days in jail, because he would not pay the fine imposed by law.

Other nationalist publications included James Connolly's *Irish Worker* and (after its suppression) the resurrected *Workers' Republic*. James Connolly used editorial manipulation in his *Workers' Republic* to extract wage rises, to recruit for his Irish Citizen Army, to extend greetings to workers in all nations and to keep alive the spirit of Irish nationalism. An editorial of the suppressed *Irish Worker* flung the following challenge to Westminster:

> If you leave us at liberty we will kill your recruiting, save our poor boys from your slaughterhouses, and blast your hopes of Empire. If you strike at, imprison or kill us, out of our prisons or graves we will still evoke a spirit that will thwart you and mayhap rise a force that will destroy you.

The Irish Ireland periodicals, newspapers, news-sheets and pamphlets had much in common: an almost complete lack of funding, plenty of material from unpaid journalists – ranging from mediocre to excellent – and an enormous drive to say their republican or separatist piece in defiance of the ruling power; one might say that they were daring the British authorities to close them down – a matter in which they sometimes obliged. *The Irish People*, mouthpiece of the Fenians, suffered a punitive raid of its premises and destruction of its plant in Parliament Street, Dublin.

'John Brennan' established her name firmly as a republican writer during these years, not only in *Bean na hÉireann*, but also in Seán Mac Diarmada's *Irish Freedom* and in Griffith's *Sinn Féin*. The quality of her work is obvious, especially in the engaging and informative *The Years Flew By*, but the remarkable aspect of it was that she was a young woman leaving the unionist island of Rathmines and swimming fearlessly in the turbulent waters of Irish republicanism. She was unable to share the happiness of her success with her parents, who were not pleased with what they could grasp of any of their daughters' involvement with this new movement, and the more explicit republicanism expressed by 'John' would have appalled them.

The Gifford daughters were also attracted to the Irish Ireland stage. They had behind them their childhood experiences of the early dramas of Ada and Gabriel and of Gabriel's home-made toy theatres. Now they became involved not merely as onlookers but as prompters, bit-part actors and providers of 'things' (props) in a few of the many amateur and semi-professional performances in Dublin City. Dublin was awash, you might say, with such entertainments, though there was nothing amateurish about the last-formed of these pre-Rising companies – at least as far as its well-equipped little theatre in Hardwicke Street was concerned. This group, which called itself the Irish Theatre, was set up in 1914 by Joseph Plunkett, Thomas MacDonagh, Edward Martyn and Jack MacDonagh. The theatre, which included dressing rooms, was provided by Joseph's mother, Countess Plunkett, and, in the typical, multi-faceted Irish Ireland fashion, on the floor beneath the theatre the sisters of W. B. Yeats, Lily and Lolly, were producing exquisite, miscellaneous items of Celtic-embroidered linen.

The Irish Theatre's aims were the production of Irish plays other than peasant plays, plays in the Irish language and foreign masterpieces. Grace Gifford had no acting ability, but she helped out with the scenery. 'John' was a devotee and supporter of the Irish

Theatre productions and assisted with the props. Nellie got 'bit' parts in the company's plays. She has left us a glimpse of her future brother-in-law, Joseph Plunkett, playing the part of a wandering poet and being excellent in it. His melodious voice, she said, spoke the opening lines of the play – 'How beautiful the Volga looks tonight' – but, when not on stage, he sat quietly looking on and saying little; during that period he was far from well and his lungs were causing him trouble.[5]

Nellie also described a first night at which she was confronted with a typewriter for the first time in her life. She was supposed to clackety-clack on the keyboard to appear to be recording the words of an actor. That was all right until she came to the end of the carriage. Not knowing what to do, she sat there, consumed with embarrassment, and had to let the actor continue his dialogue unaccompanied.[6]

It was undoubtedly their love of Irish that inspired the tutor Thomas MacDonagh and his pupil Joseph Plunkett to go out on a limb to produce Gaelic-speaking plays. Plunkett amicably disagreed with the other directors of the Irish Theatre when they chose Swedish writer August Strindberg's *Easter* for production and so he resigned from the group. Despite the execution of Thomas MacDonagh after the 1916 Rising, the Irish Theatre continued on under John MacDonagh, Thomas' brother, and Edward Martyn.

At the Gaiety Theatre in Dublin, during a production by Count Markievicz of George Bernard Shaw's *The Devil's Disciple*, it was considered a 'fun' thing to get a walk-on part. So 'John' Gifford and her friend Máire Perolz got themselves two minor roles. The play being about the American War of Independence, the Count had the bright idea of casting his pro-English 'Castle' acquaintances as the English soldiers while Constance supplied actors for the rebels from her republican cronies. One theatre critic said that the scuffles on stage were very realistic.[7]

Concerts must also be included in any Irish Ireland survey. Moore's melodies, the poetic rhetoric of Thomas Davis and the Young

Irelanders, harps, fiddles and bagpipes were featured, and young heroes such as Teddy O'Neill were enshrined in melodic verse. They were all part of the musical agenda. Dancers obliged with jigs, reels and hornpipes. Often a *tableau vivant* would feature Dark Rosaleen or Éire and Her Four Daughters (the four provinces). The participants' gowns were Gaelicised with Celtic embroidery. In one, Countess Markievicz featured, in full armour, as Joan of Arc. The Gifford girls also took part. Muriel's long red hair was suitably dramatic for her to be Queen Maeve, and 'John' became Robert Emmet's housekeeper, Anne Devlin. Less elitist than drama, these concerts were very often the soul food of those whose families had clung on to life through famine and evictions and uprisings. The stuff of these concerts reflected and nurtured the affective, emotional nature of their political thinking and prepared them for the 1916 Rising. What they saw, heard and felt was deeply rooted in truth. No one needed to spell out for them what had happened to their forebears. They had heard it all in their *béal oideas* and in their songs and ballads.

Susan Mitchell's aforementioned anti-conscription ballad, a great favourite at concerts and céilís, sums up the ironic rejection of Britain's recruitment posters for manning its armies with Irishmen. It is about a boy from Carrick who 'took the Saxon shilling':

> He didn't see much glory and he didn't get much good.
> In most unrighteous places he freely shed his blood.
> The best years of his manhood he spent across the foam.
> But when they had no use for him they up and sent him home.
> He has bullets in his right arm and bullets in his leg,
> So he had no *grá* for working, nor had he leave to beg.
> The peelers have their eye on him – twice he's been in gaol.
> By now he's in the workhouse. Glory be to God![8]

Audiences sang the last sentence with much gusto.

The Irish Ireland movement was in flood, veering towards a situation where it would, at last, burst its restraints. The daughters of Frederick and Isabella Gifford, in defiance of their upbringing, were very much part of the whole dramatic change.

8

DARKER DUBLIN

Apart from the plays, concerts, céilís, Gaelic games and a feisty republican press, there was a very much darker side to the Dublin of the early twentieth century, and this increasingly became the concern of those involved in the Irish Ireland movement, including the Gifford sisters. James Connolly's daughter Nora described Dublin's housing conditions, which she observed while electioneering for the Labour Party in Townsend Street in December 1910: 'I went up pitch black stairs, my feet slipping and squelching in the filth on them; some wide, some of them with steps missing. And the smell … the smell!'[1]

The hopelessly inadequate sewage and limited water supply caused horrific conditions. The one water closet in a yard, clogged and stinking, was supposed to take away the waste. Instead, ordure (human and animal) built up in the small courtyards and was removed by a sanitary cart once a week – in theory at least. Winter found shivering children in inadequate clothes and with little in their stomachs. Their bodies and immune systems were deprived of proper nourishment, and their bare feet were blue with the cold and wet. Most of the ruling class had moved out to the salubrious suburbs such as Rathmines and Rathgar, ridding themselves of the stench and infectious danger of abject poverty. The Irish who lived in the little villages around the city, such as Coolock, Blanchardstown, Lucan and Tallaght, were the lucky ones. Their cottages were infinitely superior to the rat-infested city slums where death from fever and starvation was endemic.

A law was passed in Britain, in 1906, to feed those school-going children who were in want. No such law was passed for Ireland, where the situation was infinitely worse, despite several attempts made by the Irish MPs at Westminster. The only thing to be said in its favour, from the Irish Irelanders' point of view, was that this neglect recruited new supporters for their policy. A native government, the argument ran, could not possibly be so indifferent to its wretched poor.

The Giffords became involved when Maud Gonne MacBride (the beloved muse of W. B. Yeats, one of the founding members of Inghínidhe na hÉireann (INE) and estranged wife of Major John MacBride), returned from France. Seeing the horror of the Dublin poor, she proposed to get school meals for the starving children through the munificence of the Dublin Corporation. 'John' Gifford, by then a member of Inghínidhe na hÉireann, described Maud Gonne MacBride's deep warm-heartedness, which had been greatly moved by the pitiful children on the Dublin streets. She saw them not only barefoot and hungry, but also wearing buttonless hand-me-down coats kept closed by their own cold hands or by a large safety pin. One virtue of the Ascendancy elite having moved out to new suburbs with their own town councils, was that Dublin Corporation's members were now more likely to be tradespeople and merchants. They agreed with Inghínidhe to strike a rate for school meals, but their legal advisers told them they could not do so without the determinedly withheld Westminster permission. Maud Gonne MacBride went ahead anyway, without official help, and with other members of Inghínidhe formed the Ladies School Dinner Committee (LSDC). Canon Kavanagh, parish priest of one of the most deprived Dublin parishes, St Audeon's, asked her to supply meals to his school's children. She and the Canon had been friends since the time she had been part of the Ladies Committee for the

Patriotic Children's Treat, which had organised a picnic for deprived Irish children in Drumcondra to counter that provided officially to honour Queen Victoria on her visit to Ireland in 1900.

Maud Gonne MacBride spent several weeks in Ireland in the autumn of 1910, and during this time 250 children were served hot stew with potato and beans by herself, Hanna Sheehy Skeffington, Countess Markievicz, Helena Molony, Kathleen Clarke (wife of Thomas Clarke), Helen Laird and Muriel, Nellie, Grace and 'John' Gifford.[2] The Patriotic Children's Treat had been a one-off children's party timed to coincide with the Queen's visit; the LSDC's meals, vital for health, were sustained for as long as possible.

Most of the children had never tasted beans before, and they were a special favourite. School attendance improved, and Fr Thomas Keane, another nationalist priest, asked the LSDC's help for his school in John's Lane. The children's meals were served on great trestle tables in the school yard, and the volunteer caterers worked hard at cooking, washing up and raising funds to buy the ingredients.

Meanwhile, the Sisters of the Holy Faith, founded by Margaret Aylward, ran three 'poor schools' – one in Temple Bar (one room in which they had all their fifty pupils), one in Little Strand Street and a third in the Coombe. At these schools, food, books and clothing were provided.[3] Margaret Alyward's Catholic charity schools received help from some Protestant sympathisers, who were as aware as she was of the dire lives her pupils led. Their aim was not proselytism.

On Nellie's first visit to St Audeon's she noticed what she thought were little bundles of wet rags left to dry around the fire, but then discovered that the teacher allowed the very smallest toddlers to lie there, where they often fell asleep. Their mothers were using the school as a kind of crèche while they went out to work or to seek it.[4] Many of the children had no underwear. This fact was brought to the attention of an appalled Canon Kavanagh when one of them inadvertently exposed her bare bottom. The very next day he arrived with what were described as red woollen garments, mostly too big. But, as Nellie Gifford wrote in her notes, the kind man had been generous in good faith. It is a cheerful, comforting thought with which to leave the wretchedness of it all – scrawny little tummies full of warm food and cold little bottoms clothed against the winter in voluminous red flannel.[5]

Despite the moving description Nellie has left us of St Audeon's, she did not put as much work into the school meals as did her sisters, because of her absence on work in County Meath. She cut her political teeth, as it were, in 'Meath of the Pastures', where she spent most of her years as a domestic economy instructress.

At Sandymount, Countess Plunkett was also feeding the hungry, and there were other such kindnesses around the city. The work of these women was a great help, but the enormity of the problem required state aid. Westminster had turned its back once again on the suffering in Ireland. Its callousness was not forgotten, a repeat of the Famine laissez-faire, and this time there was the added insult of the comparative care of the parliament for London's poor, enshrined in legislation.

The Irish MPs at Westminster were a motley lot. Some parliamentarians were mere lickspittles, dressed up in the required customary garb of the day – frock coats and tall silk hats; some were in politics with an eye to whatever was the equivalent of today's brown envelopes and Ansbacher accounts; but others were gutsy participants, opposing a parliamentary system where empirical needs were satiated at the expense of the colonies.

All the Giffords would have been aware in their childhood, from the talk amongst their father's friends at Temple Villas, of such parliamentary personalities as Parnell, Butt, Biggar and Davitt. But it was a contemporary MP, Laurence Ginnell, the Member for Meath, whom Nellie Gifford most admired, particularly for his very practical approach. His legal booklet, *The Brehon Laws*, recorded the fact that, while the land of the old Gaelic clan was communal, the *maighin digona*, or farmhouse and attached small garden, was a sanctuary for the family unit, protected by law – roughly the equivalent of an Englishman's home being his castle.

Ginnell, as well as being an MP, was also a barrister of the Middle Temple in London and took the unusual step, for a barrister, of also becoming a sort of highwayman and cattle rustler. His method was to watch carefully the movements of the RIC, his sworn enemies, and to enter a field as remote as possible, under cover of darkness, to drive the cattle onto the road. The field was then ploughed, leaving it unfit for grazing, and notices were pinned to the cow's horns, bearing such messages as:

The land is for the people
and the road is for us.

or

Blessed are the cattle drivers
for they shall inherit the land.

He acquired a committed following, none more keen than Nellie and 'John', who became infected with Nellie's enthusiasm. Both Nellie and 'John' also supported Ginnell's Dublin demonstrations in 1911, joined by their sister Grace, protesting against the visit of Edward VII. In time, after 1916, Ginnell became known at Westminster, with a mixture of toleration and affection, as 'the member for Ireland'. The Meath designation was not big enough to encompass his activities. During the ensuing struggle between England and Ireland, the pockets in the tails of his regulation parliamentary frock coat became a sort of illicit mailbag, carrying messages to and from imprisoned rebels.[6]

The next Irish figure in the political limelight with whom Nellie and 'John' associated, this time actively, was James Larkin, especially on one historic occasion which put Nellie in considerable danger but for which her personal courage is rarely credited. This giant of a man, six feet four inches in height, who had escaped from the Liverpool slums, had a leonine head to crown his stature and a heart that felt a deep, abiding compassion for the exploited manual workers of his day – often unfettered slaves of unscrupulous masters. With the fabled Larkin compassion went an iron will and a *modus operandi* in which courage and determination were the driving forces. His character was forged in an extremely harsh childhood, and his statue in O'Connell Street has perfectly caught the man. Hands outstretched, a mob orator, he could mould the mood and the actions of huge crowds, captured in the web of his impassioned words. None knew more than he the sour fruits of exploitation. When only seven years of age, he was already working in the slums of Liverpool, to which city his parents had emigrated from Newry. He was apprenticed two years later to a decorator, and at eleven became an engineer's apprentice. When Larkin was fourteen, his father died, and things got even worse: he had to fight to keep starvation at bay. Caught as a stowaway with ten others on a ship bound for Buenos Aires, they were badly treated by the ship's captain, who demanded excessive labour and gave them poor food. The young Larkin organised a strike. It was three 'firsts' for him: his first strike, his first success (ultimately) and his first imprisonment for his stand. His confinement for one night, in irons, in the ship's hold, with just a drink of water and a swarm of rats for company, was a remembered nightmare.

Later, in Liverpool, Larkin founded the National Union of Dock Labourers and, back in Ireland in 1909, he tried to instil his courage into the poorest and least skilled of the workers, the dockers. They were already doing strenuous work for ten hours a day, barefoot and barebacked in a hold with dust-polluted air, dodging trolleys which were a danger to life and limb, especially to exhausted men. Their required output was approximately 100 tons of cargo a day, but that was not enough for their employers, and by an unfair system of bonuses their output was hiked to 200 tons a day. Even the strongest tottered at the end of three days, knowing all too well that there were dozens lining the quays to take their place. Added to this, their exploiters entered into an unholy franchise with publicans: the men were paid in the pubs only, where they were required, if they did not want to lose their pitiful jobs, to spend some of this sweated money. In return, the publicans paid a divvy to the bosses. After a day of curses, physical violence and the ever-present fear of losing their precious jobs, all too often the exhausted men spent money on drink which was needed to put bread on the family table.

James Larkin met this exploitation with his own brand of militant, fearless trade unionism. His method, facing the employers in unbending confrontation, using the strike weapon and involving other workers in any given strike, became known as Larkinism. He was a zealot and said himself that he was 'fighting a holy war'.[7] He was operating in a slumland which was physically rotting at its core. The putrid tenements actually collapsed in places, their decaying walls no longer able to sustain the structure of a roof, maiming, killing and entombing some of their wretched inhabitants.

On 26 August 1913, the tramway workers, whose employer was William Martin Murphy, had gone on strike and had abandoned their trams on the streets. Murphy was reassured by Dublin Castle that the RIC, the Dublin Metropolitan Police (DMP) and even the British army of occupation would support him in a confrontation with the trade unionists. At a strike meeting in Beresford Place, the DMP arrested Larkin on a charge of 'seditious conspiracy, of disturbing the peace and raising discontent and hatred among certain classes of His Majesty's subjects, of inciting hatred and contempt of the government, and of inciting murder'. Though he was released on bail, the magistrate, Swift (a shareholder in Murphy's Tramway Company), issued a proclamation as the DMP had asked him to, that banned a meeting arranged by Larkin for Sackville Street (now O'Connell Street), Dublin, on 31 August. Typically defiant, Larkin burned the ban and swore that he would speak in Sackville Street as arranged.

During that weekend the Dublin streets saw bloody confrontations and even death. Seán O'Casey, the playwright and a member of the Irish Citizen Army, went to pay his respects to one of the victims, a fellow trade unionist, young James Nolan, as he lay in his coffin. In *Drums Under the Window*, O'Casey described the scene:

> There he was asprawl under a snowy sheet, looking like a mask on a totem pole, one eye gone, the other askew, the nose cracked at the bridge and bent sideways: the forehead and cheek royal purple: from a distance it looked like a fading iris on a wide patch of snow. The mighty baton![8]

On his release from custody, Larkin had taken refuge in the Markievicz residence in Rathmines, a house which was habitually a refuge for the poor, for nationalists and for artistic friends. The Count lived there when he returned from looking after his estates in his native Poland, and, though among his wife's many friends James Larkin was not a favourite of his, nevertheless he went along with a scheme to throw the watching authorities off the scent, which enabled Larkin to go to Sackville Street as promised. The Countess gave a big party, allegedly for her husband's friends to celebrate his return from Poland, and the place was full of lights, laughter and music – not at all a venue where one would expect to find a socialist hideaway. The bohemian revelry was not what the authorities associated with Larkin, so the DMP withdrew.

But there was another problem: how to get the six-foot-four Larkin to the main street of the city and past the watchful DMP. The plan required first that a young student from the College of Science, Gussie McGrath, go to the Imperial Hotel in Sackville Street (opposite the General Post Office and owned by William Martin Murphy), to book a balconied front room for a Protestant clergyman, the Rev. Donnelly, who would be brought there by his niece. The niece was necessary because the reverend clergyman had to be deaf – his Liverpudlian accent would give him away otherwise – and this obliged his 'niece' to do all the talking. He would have to stoop to conceal his giveaway height.

Nellie Gifford was chosen to act as the niece because, owing to her absence in Meath, she was unknown to the DMP. The balcony outside the room would be Larkin's platform. A frock coat belonging to the Count, glasses to shorten his long nose, black hair powdered grey and a grey beard and whiskers completed the disguise. The stage was set. The uncle and his niece arrived in a cab and were admitted to the hotel, Nellie doing the talking.

When Larkin found the window of his room impeded by flowerpots, he flew out and into another room, tearing away at his false beard and whiskers to the astonishment of hotel guests. The arrangement had been that he was to signal to Nellie when he was ready to speak so that she could slip away. But in the charge to another room he forgot, and the police took her into custody.[9] As Larkin began to address the assembled crowd there was a triumphant roar from the packed street. He had kept his promise, even though he was not allowed to say very much before the DMP stormed his 'platform' – but what he said did not matter. What mattered was his moral victory. For her courageous and very necessary part, Nellie Gifford is given little or no credit. At best she is referred to as 'Miss Gifford, a schoolteacher'. A newspaper cutting among her papers credited 'Miss Helena Molony' with her role, and even the excellent *Life of James Larkin* by Donal Nevin accords her sister, Sidney Gifford, the honour of being the Rev. Donnelly's 'niece'.

Cameras recorded the devastation of the scene in Sackville Street. The frenzied police, over 300 of them, wielded their batons indiscriminately. The pictures are reminiscent of those we see of the Russian Revolution and the batoning of nationalists by the Royal Ulster Constabulary at Drumcree in Northern Ireland in 1996. To move was to invite a baton blow. Some lay on the streets, especially in Prince's Street, which had been blocked. Constance Markievicz was injured by a baton.[10] The hospitals were overcrowded with the injured, both policemen and strikers. That Sunday was international news, and Larkin's name became a byword worldwide.

William Martin Murphy's reaction was swift: the following Wednesday, 3 September, he chaired a meeting of some 400 employers who decided to lock out from employment any member of Larkin's Irish Transport and General Workers' Union. Appalling misery followed. Despite food ships sent by the British Trades Union Congress, and in spite of the efforts of the food kitchen in Liberty Hall, the lock-out by Murphy and his Federated Union of Employers broke the strike. The agonised men had to watch the hunger of their families. Many intellectuals railed against the employers, including Joseph Plunkett, W. B. Yeats, the Sheehy Skeffingtons, Thomas MacDonagh, Pádraig Pearse and George Bernard Shaw. It was the Giffords' old friend from their teenage debut, George Russell (Æ), who gave voice most strongly in his criticism of the employers. In his famous open letter, he addressed them with cutting vituperation:

> You determined deliberately, in cold anger, to starve out one-third of the population of this city, to break the manhood of the men by the sight of the suffering of their wives, and the hunger of their children.
>
> We read in the dark ages of the rack and the thumb screw. But these iniquities were hidden and concealed from the knowledge of men, in dungeons and torture chambers ... It remained for the twentieth century and the capital city of Ireland to see an oligarchy of four

hundred masters deciding openly on starving one hundred thousand people and refusing to consider any solution except that fixed by their pride.[11]

The workers, the intellectuals and Larkin lost that battle, but they were not to lose the war that lay ahead. The strike triggered off the formation of two bodies that brought enormous changes to Ireland. Larkin's sense of nationalism played second fiddle to his deep and abiding pity for the poor – but it surfaced now and then. In his presidential address to the Irish Trade Union conference at City Hall on 1 June 1914, he said, 'I claim we have the opportunity given us of achieving much in the future of our beloved country, to work and live for, and if needs be die to win back, in the words of Erin's greatest living poet, for Cathleen Ní Houlihan, her four beautiful fields.'

Larkin left Ireland for America in 1914, but his 'failed' general strike had a domino effect on the fate of Cathleen and her fields. To harness the bitter antagonism of the Dublin workers, the Irish Citizen Army was founded on 19 November 1913, initially to protect the workers from the DMP. Jack White, a former officer of the British army and son of Field Marshal Sir George White, trained and drilled this new Irish 'army' of two companies, 500 men and inadequate weaponry, whose aims, defensive or otherwise, were both socialist and republican. Its membership dwindled gradually as want increased and the desperate men went back to work, but Larkin, with James Connolly's committed support, was determined that it should not be allowed to die. It acquired a constitution and a flag: 'The Plough and The Stars'. A successful recruiting drive brought in new members, including Countess Markievicz.

As a result of her part in the Imperial Hotel drama, Nellie Gifford was dismissed from her post in County Meath. She had always intimated that a certain amount of 'pull' (Protestant and unionist) had got her the job, and these two categories now quickly rejected her.[12]

She came back to Dublin, and, not long afterwards, this daughter of the Ascendancy class in Ireland donned the uniform of the Citizen Army and stepped out with the dockers and labourers of Dublin. Nellie was the only one of the Temple Villas sisters to join what was an armed force of the Irish Ireland movement, though she was seen as a 'field cook', rather than a soldier. Her mother's thoughts on the matter may well be imagined.

9

INTRODUCTIONS

It is the way of things that as young people who share a common dream meet each other, many romances will result. Such was the case with the Irish Ireland movement. Moreover, there can have been no pre-revolutionary country where women played a greater part than Ireland in those years. So it was hardly surprising that two of the Gifford daughters found romance through the movement.

Pádraig Pearse had acquired for his boarding school a fine old building standing on its own grounds, Cullenswood House on Oakley Road, Ranelagh, and invited Nora Dryhurst to a celebratory open day in 1911. Poets and writers knew Mrs Dryhurst well and had often availed of her kindness and hospitality. She had taken Ernest Gifford's sisters under her wing and brought Muriel, Grace and 'John' along for the occasion. It was a lovely summer's afternoon, and Mrs Dryhurst and the three girls were greeted on the steps by Pádraig and Willie Pearse, Thomas MacDonagh and Joseph Plunkett. 'Now I want you to fall in love with these girls and marry them' was her humorous introduction.[1] Two of the men obliged her: Thomas married Muriel, and Joseph married Grace – a good score for a matchmaker. It was typical of MacDonagh's ease of manner that he came down to the sisters, arms outstretched, and said it would be difficult to choose in such company.[2] Gracious it was, but tongue-in-cheek, because very soon he was a kilted visitor to Temple Villas, courting Muriel and scandalising the West British neighbourhood with his traditional Gaelic dress.

In fact, his choice was immediate and mutual, though Muriel was not his first love. The legendary MacDonagh charm had not been in cold storage up to then, and the young ladies he escorted were a great source of interest for his pupils at St Enda's. One such lady, fleetingly mentioned, was called Veronica. A name that stayed the course a good deal longer belonged to Mary Maguire. Mary had been at boarding school at the Sacred Heart Convent at Blumenthal in Holland, along with Rose Fitzgerald, who married Joseph Kennedy and gave birth to John Fitzgerald Kennedy. Mary's career was less dramatic. She became headmistress of St Ita's (established as an equivalent girls' school when Pearse moved his boys to Rathfarnham) and married Padraic Colum the poet, a friend of MacDonagh and Pearse.

The pupils sensed more than a passing affair when this red-haired young lady appeared on the scene. Muriel Gifford, who had also had a previous, mild romantic attachment, was described poetically in an article of 1917 in *The Monitor* as fairly tall with a roseleaf complexion, dark eyes and masses of Titian hair, coiled in plaits and held in place by a bandeau. The Romeo of these tragic lovers was of average height, had dark, crisp hair, grey eyes and great personal charisma, which was eventually to charm Isabella, despite his Catholicism, his politics and even despite his kilt and matching brat (a traditional short cloak) and Tara brooch. But then this *was* an aspiring professor coming to court her daughter. Besides, it became obvious that the two families had much in common. Both *matresfamilias* came from Protestant backgrounds, though Thomas' mother, Mary Parker, had converted to Catholicism when she was still in her teens, before she met Joe MacDonagh. The children of both households 'published' a family bulletin, and, like the Giffords, the MacDonagh offspring also staged plays. Another parallel was that two of Thomas' brothers joined the British army. Furthermore, Thomas had spent some time abroad studying art, and – an odd little likeness – he, like Bridget Hamill, was given to quoting St Columcille.

There was also, however, much that was utterly dissimilar in their upbringing. Mary MacDonagh, though a daughter of an immigrant compositor of Greek at the Trinity College Press, taught her Cloughjordan students Irish songs – with an eye out for the inspector, of course, whose appearance would cut short such un-English activity which was enough to merit a reprimand or even dismissal. When the MacDonagh parents moved to Cloughjordan in County Tipperary they were the first Catholics ever to teach there and, even more extraordinarily, young men (some of them moustached) from their previous posting followed the MacDonaghs to complete their national-school education during the winter months. They financed themselves with summer jobs and had their lunch, not in the school yard with the children, but across the way in Bowles, a pub where they could have a pint and a sandwich. Such was the need and greed for education among those who had been denied it for so long.[3] There is one thing certain – the anglicising jingle proposed by Britain for the schools it financed in Ireland would not have been given the breath of life in the school run by Joe and Mary MacDonagh. It ran:

I thank the goodness and the grace that on my birth have smiled
and made me in these Christian days a happy English child.

Instead, they taught where they could, and especially to their sons, the stuff of Irish Ireland. Joe's ancestors in Roscommon were reputed to have faced Sir Richard Bingham's Tudor savagery at Ballymote Castle.[4] So we find their descendant, the young Thomas, home for the holidays from Rockwell College, singing that rousing Gaelic ballad 'Aililiu na Gamhna' at a concert in Moneygall. A happy child – but definitely not an English one.

MacDonagh's love affair with Muriel progressed against lessening opposition, and with much enthusiasm by the leading players. They saw each other almost daily during their courtship, and when he could not come, three, and even four, letters would arrive.[5] In those days, when you posted a letter in Dublin for a Dublin address it reached its destination in a matter of hours. When he was expected and the doorbell rang, Muriel would fly to the door to greet and embrace him.[6] She was still a Protestant when they married on 3 January 1912. Because it was a 'mixed' marriage, it was a low-key affair in the little temporary chapel waiting to be replaced by the Church of the Holy Name which stands today on Beechwood Avenue. There was no best man or bridesmaid, but Pádraig Pearse was to be witness. Unfortunately, Pearse failed to appear, and a man cutting a hedge stood in for him. Informality was the order of the day.[7]

By now MacDonagh was lecturing in English in University College, Dublin, and their marriage was a happy one.[8] Their first child, Donagh, was born later that year on 12 November at Temple Villas, like his aunts Grace and 'John' and his uncle Edward Cecil. Barbara, Muriel and Thomas' daughter, was born three years after that. In one of life's strange vagaries, when Donagh was born he was christened at the Church of the Three Patrons in Rathgar, and who should drop in to pray before cycling into the city but Pearse, who knew nothing of the christening. The delighted father came up to him with the greeting, 'Well, you got here in time for the christening anyhow.'[9]

The romance between Joseph Plunkett and Grace Gifford was not as instant as that between her sister Muriel and Thomas MacDonagh, but they were meeting at the MacDonagh house on Orwell Road and at various Irish Ireland activities. He was, as usual, doing a balancing act between his enormous *grá* for life and indifferent health. To understand this extraordinary young man, who was to become the great, tragic love of Grace's life, it is essential to learn of his background.

His mother, Josephine Cranny, was the daughter of a very wealthy father who owned whole stretches of first-class residences, especially in the now elitist Dublin 4 area. Their home was a nucleus building of what is today Muckross Park Dominican College, the name deriving from the Cranny's Kerry origins. Though an heiress, the young Josephine had been a sort of personal assistant to her mother, answerable to her beck and call. Marriage to her first cousin, George Noble Plunkett, may have been a welcome release. There were many suitors from the time she was sixteen, though her father's reaction to these early 'offers' was to place her as a boarder in a school run by the Sacred Heart Convent nuns at Roehampton, south-west of London, for a year. In fact she was twenty-seven, to George's thirty-three, when they married. It was an arranged union, an effort to conserve the property, to 'keep it in the family'. There had always been a great affection between the two young cousins, and the papal title 'Count' may well have swung the balance in George's favour. Josephine brought to the marriage a commendable skill as a singer, pianist, violinist and flautist, as well as property on Marlborough Road, Donnybrook, and the prospect of much more. In turn, George brought to the union family property on Belgrave Road in Rathmines, a well-earned reputation as a fine-art connoisseur and a wide reading expressed in an enormous appetite for books, especially books about Ireland; in fact their housing requirements eventually spilled over from his library.[10] He brought something else to the marriage, less tangible but very important: a kindly disposition, although, uncharacteristically, he shared a deep dislike, with others, of W. B. Yeats. Recently a grandson, remembering his grandfather, described him as 'a sweet and gentle dote'.[11] In Dublin parlance, this is the vocabulary of merit and love.

On the American leg of their worldwide honeymoon, the couple met legendary Irish patriots John Boyle O'Reilly, John Devoy and Jeremiah O'Donovan Rossa. On returning to Dublin, they set up home at 26 Upper Fitzwilliam Street which was to remain their town residence until their children were grown up.

In 1866, the Count was called to the bar, but he did not practise as a lawyer. Even before his appointment as Curator of the National Museum his interests were politics, journalism, learned societies, fine art and books; he himself wrote a highly regarded monograph on the work of Sandro Botticelli. When he eventually took up his duties as curator of the museum, he was classed as a higher civil servant and, as such, was required to attend the yearly state levee when the viceroy came, a duty that was an affront to the Count's nationalism. He had to wear the requisite black velvet embossed jacket with cut steel buttons, knee breeches of flannel-lined white satin, silk stockings with laced clocks, and buckled patent-leather shoes. At balls the wives were expected to wear a train. It was important to be seen on these occasions, but the Plunketts were wealthy enough to sometimes ignore such need, and the Count's post was not a sinecure but one gained on merit.[12]

This is not to say that they did no entertaining. In fact, every year the residents of the very upper-class Merrion and Fitzwilliam enclaves gave 'dances', and Josephine was not wanting as a hostess. An afternoon children's party would be followed by an adult dance and a cold supper, with professional musicians (violinist and pianist) who provided music until six the next morning. The repertoire included waltzes, lancers, gallops and the Boston. About 150 guests danced through the small hours, and 'almost all' the young men in uniform disappeared, on active service, between one year and the next.[13] Josephine's parties were on a more lavish scale than those of Isabella Gifford, but then the Plunkett children's parties had no fake poached eggs and no hurdy-gurdy. You can't have everything in this life.

Joseph Plunkett was reared by a strict disciplinarian. To illustrate this point, and to furnish an odd little coincidence between the Plunkett and Gifford households, the story of Biddy, who nursed Joseph and his siblings, is apt. From their babyhood, Biddy washed, ironed, sang patriotic songs and took them to play in Fitzwilliam

Square. Apart from the similarity of her name and occupation with those of Bridget Hamill, she also knitted socks (though not striped). On returning from a stay in Paris, Countess Plunkett considered that Biddy had become too familiar and dismissed her summarily, to the grief of her young charges.

In the matter of holidays, however, the Plunketts were in a class of their own. Greystones was enough to get the Gifford girls past the snobbery of their peers, but the Countess thought nothing of bringing the whole family to spend the summer in St-Malo in Brittany, or Knokke in Belgium. One year she hired a canal boat to transport them all, with furniture, to Tuam. Nearer home, a house in Firhouse was rented for three summers, from which they could come and go to Upper Fitzwilliam Street. That house was called 'Charleville', and the whole family used to stand at the gate and vigorously boo a neighbouring driver of a two-ponied trap because she whipped the ponies unmercifully.[14] Finally, the Count bought Kilternan village (complete with abbey) in County Dublin, and again they moved freely between Fitzwilliam Street and Kilternan, where they had cows, dogs and horses and also huge greenhouses with grapes and peaches.[15]

Like Isabella Gifford, the Countess was a study in contrasts. She had been reared by her mother never to look at servants when speaking to them – though it was suggested that this arose partly from fear, the teenage Josephine having been scared of giving orders to those much her senior. In any event, to her credit she eventually tried to take on management of her estate. A grandson remembered her climbing a roof to assess damage. 'No shame in getting your hands dirty,' she would say, 'never be ashamed of it.'[16]

The eldest child of the marriage, Joseph Mary Patrick Plunkett, to give him his full name, was ill from infancy, a misfortune attributed to his parents being cousins. Early pleurisy and pneumonia developed into glandular tuberculosis, but his physique and eager mind were at war with his recurring illness. Paradoxically, his body was that of a vigorous young man, as testified by his sister Geraldine.

From 1900, when he was thirteen years of age, he was schooled, as his father had been, by the Jesuits in Belvedere College, but, on an apparent impulse, perhaps because she had been happy at her English boarding school, the Countess placed her three boys, Joseph, George and Jack, in Weybridge boarding school in England. Joseph and George were later sent to Stonyhurst College to take a two-year philosophy course. They joined the officer training corps there, went on manoeuvres on Salisbury Plain and said, if anything, that this experience increased their sense of nationalism.[17] England was training Ireland's future rebels!

The Plunkett daughters did not receive the same educational care as their brothers, an approach typical of the day. Allowed to sit in on their brothers' lessons with tutors, a few terms at the Sacred Heart schools in Leeson Street and at Mount Anville comprised their formal education. But they also had access to their father's huge store of books, which was their Stonyhurst, and they emerged well educated.

Irish winters had such a poor effect on Joseph's condition that his mother took him to Paris, where he studied under the Marists at Passy. He also wintered in Italy, Sicily and Malta and spent some time with his sister in Algiers where, apart from learning Arabic, he indulged in both dancing and skating. In fact, while there in 1911, his skating was considered so skilful that he was offered a job as instructor at the largest skating rink in Cairo and was youthfully tempted by the magnificent white uniform that went with the job. Sartorially speaking he was never a dandy but, nevertheless, had suits 'of good cloth, worn carelessly'.[18]

After the War of Independence, when the Free State was established, portraits of the executed leaders of 1916 were displayed on school walls. What the students saw of Joseph Plunkett – always called Joseph Mary Plunkett – was a schoolboyish face in pince-nez amongst the group of Proclamation signatories. There was no way of knowing then that most pictures of his adult life had been deliberately destroyed when he set out with a false passport to join Sir Roger Casement in Germany and that this old photograph seemed to have been superimposed, not very flatteringly, on the official portrait of the other signatories.

Nellie Gifford, who obviously regarded him as her favourite brother-in-law, said:

> Data is a cold affair, for the Professors. History will be cold on the warm, human motive that impelled them [the Irish rebels] towards their target, or the odd kinks, loves and capabilities – all in short that make the man live on. Ignoring these endearing little items leaves the subject on the dissecting table for all time … Joe was a very devout Catholic and a minor mystic and a minor poet. He himself would be the last to say otherwise … He inherited a weakened physique that housed a courageous and generous personality. Whenever there was a bit of fun, as at the amateur theatricals held in a hall owned by his mother, he was keenly attracted. Above all he was always interested. Any topic carrying your own particular slant gained his eager attention, his quiet attention, as if he must lean a little out of the chatting circle, retiring (from it) and relishing (your slant) to the full. He was bigger than his memory will probably be.[19]

Dr Theo McWeeney said of him, 'he had rather untidy, silky hair … his bright darting eyes lit up his face. His hands were long and delicate, graceful hands. He was a man who spoke quickly, gaily, full of enthusiasms … He had an interior life of a great intensity.'[20]

Joseph Plunkett's sense of humour was puckish. In Algiers, on losing a broken piece of Celtic jewellery in the sand, he remarked, 'That will give food for thought if an archaeologist finds it some day.' When very young, his party piece was to sit on a chair, quite still, arms rigidly at his side, and let his dextrous feet do a spirited jig or reel to the Irish music.

Joseph Plunkett had fallen in love before meeting Grace Gifford. The girl was Columba O'Carroll, daughter of a doctor in the Fitzwilliam area. Her family disapproved because of her young suitor's ill-health, but the romance inspired a very beautiful poem in *The Circle and the Sword*, the collection of his work selected and seen through publication by Thomas MacDonagh while Joseph was in Algiers in 1911. His poem about his first, youthful love was written to Columba (his 'dove'):

> White dove of the wild dark eyes
> Faint silver flutes are calling
> From the night where the star mists rise
> And fireflies falling
> Tremble in starry wise,
> Is it you they are calling?[21]

The two young men, Thomas the senior by nine years, met when the Countess sought a tutor to teach Joseph Irish. They took to each other instantly, sharing a love of literature and an abiding sense of nationalism; the people of the Donegal Gaeltacht, where they studied Irish, recalled them proudly and affectionately. Thomas and Joseph also shared an irreverent nickname for Pearse. They felt his inspirational dream for Ireland was not well served by his occasional impracticality and referred to him affectionately as 'Pop' – 'Poor Old Pearse'. Despite that, he inspired them. His dream for Ireland was theirs too.

Joseph lived for two and a half years with his sister Geraldine in one of the Plunkett houses on Marlborough Road, Donnybrook. Since he was not well after his return from Algiers, it was felt that this arrangement was desirable for his full recovery. She was very fond of him, her eldest brother, and also very much aware of his wide-ranging interests, which included motorbikes, art, the wireless, wine, playing the violin, poetry and the study of mysticism. He had even found time, in 1906/07, to design the Irish postage stamp which depicted a neat, Celtic cross. It was sometimes found postmarked on envelopes beside Edward VII stamps, cocking a snook at the monarch, as it were, because it was, at that time, unofficial. It appeared again in blue and black or green and black around Easter Week 1916. Later it became an official stamp of a free Ireland.

Among Plunkett's favourite mystics was the irrepressible woman-before-her-time St Teresa of Ávila. They had much in common, Joseph Plunkett and Teresa Sánchez de Cepeda y Ahumada, a young Irish rebel and the first woman doctor of the Catholic Church: both from wealthy backgrounds, both suffering ill health, which they determinedly ignored, both much travelled, both as much at home with the practical side of life as with its spiritual dimension, both humorous and warmly human, both determined to change that which they saw as wrong.

The 'Columba verse' indicates how the young poet set about expressing his love for his lady. But it is his poem where he tries to express his love for Christ that is best remembered. He is the supreme pantheist: everything in nature reminds him of his Redeemer: flowers, stars, skies, birds, rocks and trees:

I see his blood upon the rose
and in the stars the glory of his eyes.
His body gleams amid eternal snows,
his tears fall from the skies.

If it is true that we are known by our friends, then the goodly company who constituted Joseph's mind-companions, including not only Teresa of Ávila but also St Thomas More, St Francis and St

John of the Cross, stamp him with a certain greatness which would have benefited his country eventually had he lived. It is sometimes said that he was already dying before his execution, but he had recovered repeatedly from such attacks. Another visit to a warmer climate might once more have restored his health, and, besides, by 1916 penicillin was little more than a decade around the corner.

For all that, this frail revolutionary did a lot of living in a short space of time: missions to Germany and America, and an insurrection, of which he was Director of Military Operations. Time may have been running out for Joseph Plunkett, but he grasped the passing hours and defied his mortality. No leader, however physically robust, could have managed more in the short time left to him.

10

A QUESTION OF GUNS

The céilís, concerts, drama, Gaelic sport and Irish classes and romances were largely convivial, social aspects of the Irish Ireland dream, yet, distinct from that, with the borders inevitably blurring at times, were the starker features of what was evolving around the country. 'John' Gifford wrote of the men and women involved: 'Some were in Sinn Féin; others in the Irish Republican Brotherhood; others in Inghínidhe na hÉireann. Still more were in the ranks of the Gaelic League or the GAA. Within a few years these scattered groups had coalesced, and an Irish revolutionary force was in being.'[1]

These were obvious milestones on the road to rebellion. After 1913 it became obvious that the influence of the republican press, the bitterness engendered by the lock-out strike and the consequent formation of the Citizen Army were slanting events closer to armed confrontation. At the same time, the unionists in the northern counties, reacting to the 'threat' of John Redmond's dream of Home Rule for Ireland, decided to arm. Apart from private purchases from Germany of arms and ammunition by wealthy unionists, £100,000 – a huge sum in those days – was subscribed to buy the arms that were smuggled into Larne, County Antrim, in April 1914. The importers deliberately cut off public communications on the day of the arms arrival, and, in a convoy of motor cars, 35,000 rifles and five million rounds of ammunition were distributed across Ulster. No police stopped the convoy, though what they did was illegal. The Royal Irish

Constabulary, the Conservative Party, the unionist Ulster landlords – none of them wanted Home Rule either, and this illegal army had their tacit support. Even more significantly, the British army officers in the Curragh, County Kildare, mutinied and refused to march against the Ulster Volunteer Force (UVF). They resigned their commissions rather than oppose those they perceived to be friends.

They were to have no such misgivings when the nationalists in the south proceeded to arm. In fact, the UVF did the south of Ireland militants a favour: they pointed the way. Three months later, in July 1914, a nationalist Protestant, Erskine Childers, lent his yacht, *The Asgard*, to enable the importation into Howth Harbour, County Dublin, of a much humbler cargo than that at Larne. The subscribers of the purchase price of £1,500, in comparison with the north of Ireland's £100,000, were fellow Anglo-Irish Protestants: Sir Roger Casement, the Honourable Mary Spring Rice (a daughter of Lord Monteagle and sister of a British ambassador), Alice Stopford Green (later a senator in Seanad Éireann) and a Captain Berkeley. In all 1,500 rifles were bought, of which 900 came on *The Asgard*. That figure made the purchase price approximately £1 per rifle, so it is obvious they were not the best rifles in the world. One might even wonder if they were not relics of the Napoleonic wars. No matter how it is viewed, numerically or qualitatively, this was David confronting Goliath. Apart from the £100,000 UVF importation, the republicans also faced the weaponry of the three official armed agencies supporting unionists, north and south. On one small island there were now nine 'armies':

1. the British army of occupation (armed)
2. the Royal Irish Constabulary (armed)
3. the Dublin Metropolitan Police (armed)
4. the Ulster Volunteer Force (armed)

On the republican side, minimally or not at all armed:

5. the Irish Republican Brotherhood (IRB)
6. Na Fianna (a sort of boy-scout nationalist movement set up in Dublin in 1909 by Bulmer Hobson and Countess Markievicz among others)
7. the Irish Citizen Army (ICA)
8. the Hibernian Rifles (a small, exclusively Catholic militia based in Dublin)
9. the Irish Volunteer Force (which included the IRB)

Goliath had far superior numbers and equipment. David had 700 years of resentment, a dream of freedom and, of course, 1,500 weapons worth approximately £1 each. It is interesting to contrast the smooth, unopposed importation passage of the huge UVF purchase at Larne with that at Howth, where the gunrunners were almost entirely without transport. The Fianna had brought along a small horse and cart and a trek cart – a very narrow, short, covered cart, manually powered. In a photograph of them running along with their quaint wagonette, it looks like a mobile fruit stall from the Moore Street market. There were also some bicycles, whose crossbars neatly accommodated a rifle, and the rest were just hidden under jackets. While all this compares pathetically with the Larne fleet of cars, headlights ablaze to illuminate the scene, nevertheless the Fianna's arrangements were adequate for the delivery, and the strange little wagon proved very useful, taking a major stash of the rifles. Darrell Figgis and Conor O'Brien had been involved in the purchase of the guns at Antwerp. Childers' wife, Molly, in the yacht, was to wear a crimson garment as a signal to the waiting party, which included Mary Spring Rice, Gordon Shephard (an English friend of Childers) and two fishermen from Tory Island.

Also at Howth that day was Cathal Brugha with a group of his

IRB men to guard the shipment. Another group of approximately 800 Irish Volunteers had allegedly made a routine march from Fairview to arrive 'coincidentally' at Howth. On the way back to the city with their haul they were stopped in the Raheny-Clontarf area by W. A. Harrel, Assistant Commissioner of the DMP, backed up by a large contingent of Scottish Borderers. He demanded surrender of the arms, but Bulmer Hobson, who was in charge of the delivery, refused. Hobson left Thomas MacDonagh and Darrell Figgis to argue with the Assistant Commissioner while he slipped away to move his men quietly and quickly through fields and round the backs of houses, each carrying rifles. A word of pity may be allowed W. A. Harrel: the man was only doing his duty and he was confronted by two of the ablest talkers in the movement. MacDonagh, the persuasive university lecturer, a wordsmith by profession, and Figgis, a worthy debater in any company, used their 'blarney' to give time to the fleeing convoy. In the event, only nineteen rifles were lost. It was an occasion for glee, but unfortunately the day was to end on a tragic note. Dubliners, having heard of the successful manoeuvre, jeered the Scottish Borderers as they marched back to barracks along the Liffey quays. Hasty tempers combined with tired, irate, trigger-happy soldiers, left three people dead: the first casualties, it could be said, of the War of Independence, unarmed and shot without trial.

Superintendent Brangan, in charge of a contingent of the DMP who had been ordered to Howth, was brought before a tribunal which accused him, because he was Irish, of turning a blind eye to the dispersal of the guns. He was summarily dismissed and deprived of his pension rights. On appeal, his conviction was quashed and his job and pension restored.[2]

Some Howth residents were given weapons to store. They were instructed to keep the weapons oiled and serviceable. One such 'minder' was Molly Brohoon, who eventually went on the run.[3]

Another very different episode took place the following year, edging Ireland towards use of those imported arms. Words can undoubtedly be weapons, and never were they more so than when Pádraig Pearse stood before those assembled in Glasnevin Cemetery, in 1915, at the interment of the old Fenian Jeremiah O'Donovan Rossa, whose remains had been brought from America. It was, at least partly, an orchestrated exercise in emotional political blackmail, and the conductor was Thomas MacDonagh. The occasion had all the ingredients for drama: one of the revered, though defeated, 'Bold Fenian Men', O'Donovan Rossa, had been brought home for burial in his native land. There was dignity and a reverence for the old warrior in the thousands who lined the route and in the marching feet representing every Irish Ireland ideology and every organisation, however insignificant, involved in the movement.

If the funeral itself was impressive, Pearse's oration at the grave was electrifying. Even the cadence of his words was intrinsically dramatic, and the concluding triad rang out unforgettably in the hushed air, challenging the might of England with its simple thirteen words:

The fools, the fools, the fools: they have left us our Fenian dead.

Pearse, the poet and dreamer, who was certainly no Sarsfield militarily speaking, mesmerised his listeners with his monosyllabic challenge. It was a defining day in Irish history.[4]

Reaction around the city was divided, as in the Gifford household: the daughters deeply moved and involved, their mother indignant at such fuss about a *Fenian* and their father feeling, perhaps, a little uneasy about the future.

11

ENTER CUPID
BEARING ARROWS

There has been little enough mention so far of the young woman who called herself Grace Vandeleur Gifford. The 'Vandeleur' was included as a sort of pride in her ancestor, John Vandeleur, who had started the Ralahine Commune experiment in County Clare to improve the lot of his tenants. Her Orpen portrait – as *The Spirit of Young Ireland* – shows a very attractive young woman. Nellie described Grace as pretty; certainly she makes a delightful child study in the studio photo with 'John', and Orpen's portrait in oils is arresting.[1] Her niece Maeve said that her face was striking rather than pretty. Of medium height, Grace had tawny red hair and brown eyes.[2] Both she and Muriel represented the quiet side of the Giffords, wedged as they were between the irrepressibles: Gabriel, Ada and Nellie on the one side and the feisty 'John', their junior, on the other. Grace had a quirky sense of humour and so marked a talent in art that her parents agreed to Orpen's advice that she continue her art studies in London.

Her first meeting with Joseph Plunkett did not develop romantically with anything like the immediacy of the courtship that led to the marriage of her sister to MacDonagh. In their case there were many reasons which would have intruded: for one thing, Plunkett's debilitating tuberculosis resulted in his being away for a year after they were introduced. Furthermore, he was entirely dependent on his mother's munificence, and, while she spared no money on his winter health trips abroad, and though he was dressed in the best of clothes (however carelessly worn) and had use of her car and the wherewithal to indulge his numerous interests, this young man in his late twenties, highly educated and highly intelligent, had no career as such.

After his return from Algiers, Joseph and Grace continued to meet frequently at the MacDonagh home and at the various theatrical and other social gatherings of the movement. It seems, however, that it was the publication of yet another nationalist paper that quickened their friendship. This one, *The Irish Review*, started off as a more intellectual approach to Irish problems. Professor Houston launched it in 1911, along with James Stephens, Thomas MacDonagh and Padraic Colum. Colum took on the editorship for 1912/13 and Plunkett then became editor, when he had to save it from financial ruin. The contributors to this publication read like a roll-call of intellectuals: Joseph Campbell, Lord Dunsany, Darrell Figgis, Arthur Griffith, Professor Mary Hayden, Winifred Mabel Letts, Francis Sheehy Skeffington, Pádraig Pearse, John B. Yeats, Standish O'Grady, Professor Eoin MacNeill and Sir Roger Casement.[3]

Its stated (tongue-in-cheek) policy in the first issue was 'non-party and non-political': 'we will try to deal with them [current politics] with as little partiality and as little bias as is good for people in earnest to have.'

Soon, however, being very much in earnest about nationalism, they became as nationalist, though using different terminology, as the republican press. During the 1913 Dublin lock-out strike, Plunkett, born into wealth, vehemently took the side of the workers in his paper. In fact, this strike, with its attendant misery, was a great motivating force in his increased commitment to the movement and precipitated the IRB into helping to found the Irish Volunteers in 1913, in a reaction to the part played by Dublin Castle in breaking the strike.

An article in *The Irish Review* by Plunkett's friend, Sir Roger

Casement, suggested the raising of a volunteer force to defend Ireland's neutrality in the event of war. There was also an article in Pádraig Pearse's Gaelic League journal on the same subject by Eoin MacNeill, a founder of the League and Professor of Irish in UCD. It was called 'The North Began'. These articles prompted the IRB to arrange a meeting for 13 November 1913, at the Rotunda in Parnell Square. The numbers who turned up greatly exceeded expectations and required an overflow room, but, though this numerical success seemed impressive, it soon became clear that the members of this new force, the Irish Volunteers, did not speak with one voice. The one unifying factor was resentment that Westminster had deferred to the northern unionists, whose Ulster Volunteers had been allowed their arms importation without interference. Having conceded that unity of spirit, there was trilateral thinking in the ranks of these southern Volunteers from day one.

On the outbreak of the First World War, John Redmond was to recruit 27,000 of his followers to join the British army as a sort of bribe to force the implementation of Home Rule. He called his group 'the National Volunteers'. A second grouping represented a sort of middle-of-the-road philosophy, questioning the deferral of Home Rule, deploring the unchallenged ease with which the Ulster Volunteers had established themselves and feeling, however vaguely, that it would not be a bad idea for them to arm. They retained the original title of the Irish Volunteers. Eoin MacNeill, one of the moderates, was appointed leader of the Irish Volunteers. They resented the official handling of the lock-out strike and indifference to the starvation and appalling misery of the Irish poor.[4] A third loosely structured entity, and the most extreme politically, was made up of members of the Irish Volunteers and guided, often behind the scenes, by the IRB. They were heirs to the armed separatism of the Fenians and included Thomas Clarke, who had survived the imprisonment meted out to captured Fenians, unlike others, with his sanity intact. This group also included The O'Rahilly, Bulmer Hobson, Pádraig Pearse, Thomas MacDonagh and Joseph Plunkett.

Those who joined the British army from Ulster sought and received a specially named Ulster Regiment with appropriate regimental regalia and insignia. Redmond sought the same for his National Volunteers but was refused, despite the fact that a recruiting poster appeared with Redmond in the stance of the famous Lord Kitchener original, finger pointed at the viewer and bearing the words 'Join an Irish regiment today'.

In all this hurly-burly, in the November 1914 issue of *The Irish Review*, Plunkett observed, 'Our entire staff has for some time past been working full time and overtime (if such a thing is possible) in the Irish Volunteer organisation.' This issue also published a rejection of John Redmond's pledge to commit the Irish Volunteers to fight for Britain in the First World War. The rejection was formally couched in the form of a manifesto, signed by twenty men, whose names included five of the later signatories of the Proclamation of the Irish Republic. This edition also published 'Twenty Plain Facts for Irishmen', the last two of which read:

19. The Union Jack is the symbol of the Act of Union of 1800, by which the Irish nation was deprived of her last rights and liberties.
20. The Irish Nation Lives.

No wonder the police confiscated as many copies as they could. This confiscation almost closed the paper, which staggered on a little while longer only through the pumping in of Plunkett money.[5] While it lasted, however, Grace Gifford had found her true métier. She helped with the newspaper's layout and also contributed some of her delicate, subtle cartoons. A clever one of actors Micheál Mac Liammóir and Maureen Delaney appeared, and the confiscated issue featured her caricature of the Irish writer, George Moore.

Working together on *The Irish Review*, its last young editor and the young caricaturist, both in their twenties, began to find each other very congenial company.

An example of one of Grace's cartoons

12

NELLIE'S BURRA

Some sympathy must be allowed Frederick and Isabella Gifford. It was bearable to have a republican professor as a son-in-law, particularly since he had been offered a post and a house in University College, Galway, at £1,000 per annum (an offer MacDonagh refused); it was allowable that another republican, son of a wealthy papal count, should come courting; even 'John's' republican journalism might be borne – after all, she was hobnobbing with some of the Protestant intellectuals her parents knew, and, anyhow, it was unlikely that her parents ever read the journals in which her work appeared.

Nellie's involvement with James Larkin, however, was something else. They were unlikely, to say the least, to subscribe to Larkin's own assessment that he was fighting 'a holy war' or others' assessment that he was a visionary seeking dignity for the poorest or that he would obtain a very special niche in the folklore of Dublin. They read, in fact, in the establishment press, that he was leader of 'the rabble'. Nellie herself summed up the predicament: 'Poor mother, she was like a hen who had hatched out ducklings.'[1] To put it another way, they were unlikely rebels, these Gifford girls.

Though Nellie lost her job as a result of her involvement with Larkin's Bloody Sunday, she was never a lady to sit around doing nothing and was soon immersed in a very different sphere of the movement. Her role in helping Larkin to keep his promise to address the workers in Sackville Street had been carried out fearlessly and effectively. Her next involvement with the movement, however, came from her own initiative and that of her friends Helena Molony (also a member of the Citizen Army) and Máire Perolz.

From 1914 on, both in England and in Ireland, conscription was the word of the day. Anti-conscriptionism, even in the earlier Boer War, had been very much a feature of Irish nationalism. The Boers had been making a determined fight, but British recruiting sergeants scoured Irish towns and villages to lure Irishmen into their army. Anti-recruitment propaganda declared that obstruction of this recruitment was for Ireland's honour and a help to the Boers struggling against their common enemy. Inghínidhe na hÉireann had been active anti-recruitment workers, and some lady enthusiasts even went into pubs (not socially acceptable at that time) and, under the watchful antagonism of the recruiting sergeant, handed out anti-recruitment literature.

The Great War, however, needed far more recruits than the war against the Boer farmers. Nellie Gifford, remembering all the lost Anglo-Irish friends and relatives of her tender years who had fought Britain's battles abroad, sometimes with fatal results, entered the anti-recruitment arena with fervour. To use her own words: 'I, so to speak, "took fire" and made plans in my mind to avert this horror for Ireland.'[2] Nellie may have been attracted to James Connolly's 'army' because of her admiration for Countess Markievicz and her experiences of the abjectness of Dublin's poor at St Audoen's, but there was also the moral divide between an army of aggression and one seeking freedom.

One Sunday she arranged to meet Helena Molony and Máire Perolz outside Liberty Hall. They had been invited to the Reddin house on the north side of Dublin, one of whose sons was a student at Pádraig Pearse's School, St Enda's. It was a house set in fields and boasted a small theatre for entertainment. A banquet would round off the evening. All the guests were going to be very much in favour of an Irish Ireland.

Before they started out, however, Nellie, who had been too busy on anti-recruitment work to see the daily papers, asked the others for news about the feared conscription for Ireland. 'It's all right,' she was told, 'we're not called.' She was pleased and bought a paper to read the good news, but the wording of the report worried her: Ireland was excluded – but what about Irishmen living in Britain? Helena Molony suggested that the only way to deal with that was to have an Irish MP ask a question in the House of Commons. The parliament, however, sat on Tuesday, in two days' time. The Irish MPs had already left for England – all but one, Alfie Byrne. Nellie insisted that they should contact him; his home was quite near Amiens Street Station (now Connolly Station), just around the corner from Liberty Hall.

They found Alfie had left to visit a friend before taking the boat for Holyhead. Undaunted, the three ladies set out for his friend's house. There they learned that he had gone on to another house, and they just missed him there too. They decided to go back to his home and wait. The MP himself answered the door. At first he thought they were on feminist business (to which he also gave his support), but when they put their plan to him he immediately agreed and on the Tuesday asked, in the House of Commons, if conscription applied to Irishmen living in Britain. Asking the question, recorded in Hansard, was enough. It was a signal for an influx of Irishmen from all over Britain back to Ireland.

Some of the men who returned found jobs through Nellie Gifford's employment agency, which was her next move in opposing recruitment for the British army, and among them was Michael Collins.[3] There were three faces to the ubiquitous recruiting drives in Ireland: the trams and several public places were plastered with posters of brave Irishmen wearing khaki and going off to fight for 'poor little Catholic Belgium'; there was 'the gallantry of the Irish' – propaganda which deceived few and irritated many; and there were also the wives of those serving in the British army who were not going to rock the boat that provided them with a welcome income. Added to all this there were the employers – the vast majority of them Anglo-Irish – who actually had leaflets printed after any unsuccessful recruiting drive. The wording was brief: 'Your country needs you; we don't.'[4] The message was clear: if their employees did not enlist, they were to be made unemployed and their jobs could easily be filled by older men.

Nellie decided she would seek refuge for those who were dismissed and perhaps get them some work among her many friends in County Meath. She set off with Máire Perolz to visit the shops where the employers' leaflets had been given out and took the names and addresses of the victims from sympathetic colleagues. In return, she gave them her own address at Temple Villas as a point of contact. Her enterprise proved, understandably, to be too intrusive for her parents, apart altogether from the ideological gaps existing between them, with sons in the armed forces and daughters who were proving to be rather in the nature of loose cannons. When Nellie lost the Temple Villas facility, Countess Markievicz stepped into the breach and offered a room at the top floor of 6 Harcourt Terrace where the work could be carried out.

The whole undertaking, however, was becoming more complex than finding shelter and work for dismissed young men. Shelter certainly was required in cases where fired apprentices had been housed over shops as part of their remuneration and also where those who had been made unemployed could not afford to rent. Some of the men who had come back from England and who were occasionally, and apparently unjustifiably, being questioned and even arrested by hostile DMP, were obviously Volunteer material.

Finally, Nellie's brother-in-law, Thomas MacDonagh, put it to a meeting of the Volunteers that she be given a room at its headquarters at 2 Dawson Street, an upstairs back room which had a comforting fire, table and chairs and a blackboard. She contributed a lawyer's tin box for documents, a ledger and an exercise book (the last two are still extant). She provided her own packed lunch, and, though the work was purely voluntary, she kept strict office hours. Because a detective from Dublin Castle constantly stood guard at the street door, watching those who crossed its threshold, she legitimised her business by calling it the Employment Bureau, which indeed it was. Dubliners make their own of any language. Their nonchalant rendering of the French language knows such gems as *bone chewer* (*bonjour*) and *a Jew* (*adieu*). So Nellie's *bureau* became the *burrow* and even the *burra*.

She had to be careful, and some of the names and addresses were written deliberately in erasable pencil. She had a code for names and job descriptions, but it is not very obvious, unless those recommended had their sponsor's name inserted. These were well-known republican names such as Pearse, Plunkett, Mellows and J. J. Walsh. What is quite clear, however, is that the skills going a-begging were manifold and included housepainter, watchmaker, porter, van driver, grocer, draughtsman, cabinet-maker, law clerk, bookkeeper, chemistry student, gardener and coremaker (a brass foundry craftsman). The addresses, mostly in Dublin, range from Kilmore Cottages in Artane to inner-city areas such as Emerald Street, Sherrard Street and Charlemont Street. Advertisements for clients and jobs were put in the papers, but most of the men came through Volunteer referral because those answering advertisements might be spies.

In her ledger, Nellie recorded her first impression of Michael Collins, who had come back from London and was seeking a job at her agency: 'A tall, loose-limbed young man, very much at home with himself. He gave me his reference and answered the routine questions.'[5] Joseph Plunkett, no longer with time enough to manage the family estate because of his involvement with the Volunteers, had turned to the good efforts of Nellie's 'Burra', and she recommended Collins to be his assistant:

Joseph came in his motor car – one of the first in Dublin. He had a lot of gaiety and a tremendous amount of vitality, so he breezed in, quite confident that out of the young men who sat around every day waiting, I would find someone to do the secretarial work he required.

Collins, on the other hand, was dour. Nellie's comment was that a stranger looking on might well think that Joseph was seeking the job and that Collins had the giving of it. She introduced the two men, watched them have a hurried chat, and they left together. The vacancy was filled.[6]

'The Burra' handled hundreds of cases, and acted as a meeting place for new arrivals, satisfied employers and employees. It also served as a recruiting mechanism for membership of the Irish Volunteers. It was both the brainchild and success of Nellie Gifford, a member of the Irish Citizen Army who lived in Anglo-Irish unionist Rathmines, a fact that is rarely, if ever, mentioned in accounts of the period.

13

HER EXILED
GIFFORD CHILDREN

In his proclamation of Ireland's independence, Pádraig Pearse was to speak not only on behalf of her 'dead' generations but also of 'her exiled children in America'. Like flocks of birds seeking better feeding grounds, they had taken flight to America from the seventeenth century on, each century's quota increasing with the advent of persecutions, famine and dire economic need. It was none of these factors, however, that motivated six of the Gifford family to sail there; being members of the Protestant ruling class, they were fairly sure of a decent livelihood at home. Whatever it was that moved them, there was a distinct dichotomy between the approach of the brothers Liebert, Edward Cecil and Gabriel and that of their sisters, Ada, 'John' and Nellie. The first two brothers were absorbed into army and navy careers, while Gabriel quickly blended into the heterogeneous American social and artistic milieux. Not so his sisters. They not only entered Irish-American society, but took part in it and initiated some of its most anti-British activities.

The Irish-American enclave had, for centuries, experienced from the WASPs (White Anglo-Saxon Protestants) the same bitter discrimination as at home. 'No Irish Need Apply' frequently accompanied advertisements for jobs, but the brute labour required for opening up the vast continent by canal, rail and road needed spade work, and the masters of these huge enterprises were forced to employ both Irish and Chinese workers, as well as the more acceptable Scots and Welsh.

Gradually, the Irish immigrants began to improve their lot, unconsciously forming ghetto-like supportive groups, often under their parish priests. From the very beginning, they saw education and politics as the twin saviours of their degraded status. The hedge schools and the Penal Laws had taught them lessons.

When you list the Irish insurrectionists who visited America you have a *Who's Who* of Irish history: Lord Edward Fitzgerald, the Young Irelanders, the Fenians (Devoy, O'Donovan Rossa and John Boyle O'Reilly), the New Departure disciples (Parnell, Davitt and Dillon), Labour personalities (Connolly and Larkin), the Irish Ireland insurrectionists (Casement, Pearse, Plunkett, Griffith, Collins and de Valera). They went in a steady stream, and they received warm welcomes and a great deal of money. Parnell and Dillon were invited to address Congress and were seen off by the Irish-American 69th Infantry Regiment. The American Land League was founded, and by June 1881, 12,000 branches had been formed and £100,000 sent to the Land League in Ireland.[1]

However, despite the help of Irish-American immigrants, Ada, 'John' and (later) Nellie Gifford had to contend with two impediments in their American endeavours. One was the fact that the very determined anti-Irish faction was trying, from 1914 on, to lure America into the First World War; the other was the dictatorial, anti-feminist leadership of Clan na Gael, particularly in the person of the old Fenian, John Devoy.

It was ironic that Isabella's three daughters experienced such hostility from the race to which their mother always claimed allegiance. The blessed, socially accepted ones in America embodied not only English emigrants but also their Welsh and Scottish neighbours. It was the natives of the neighbouring island, the fractious Irish, who were the undesirables, along with Blacks, Jews, Hispanics and other reviled peoples. Even more unacceptable to 'John' and Nellie was the disinterest, and even opposition, of Clan na Gael, which still embraced the old Fenian and IRB mores: armed insurrection to oust Britain forever from Ireland; social matters would then take care of themselves.

No more than Parnell, who treated his sister Anna's very successful solution to evictions with such overt disinterest and even contempt, so John Devoy saw women as wives, mothers and daughters, bakers of bread and laundresses of linen, *not* as shapers of politics nor its institutions. The old independent Gaelic queen from the west of Ireland, Gráinne Ó Mháille, would have given John Devoy nightmares. He had no idea of how, in Ireland, women were contributing to the movement. He had none of the pro-feminism of Griffith, Clarke or Connolly. Even Pearse and de Valera would not have patronised women emissaries as some of the old Clan na Gael leaders did.

The Gifford migration to America might be partly explained by the fact that their maternal ancestors, the Huguenot Bissets, had settled there. There was also the fact that they received family help in migrating: Ada had her passage paid out of Nellie's earnings as a domestic-science instructress, and when Gabriel had flown the maternal coop for America in 1915, his father had given him financial help.[2]

There is no suggestion anywhere that the Gifford men took any interest in Irish Ireland, either at home or abroad. Neither is there any indication that they had anything to do with the pro-British vigilantes. Gabriel became immersed in earning his artistic livelihood, in wooing and marrying his adored American wife, whom he met in the not unlikely Gifford ambience of amateur dramatics, and, later, in rearing lovingly their only child, Geraldine.

With Ada it was different, though she too settled well in America and kept in touch with her family intermittently. An early family story sets her in a neighbourhood in New York where dark-haired, olive-skinned children from southern Italy were fascinated by her golden-red hair. On one occasion they actually staked out her lodgings to see if the colour in this Irish lady's hair would wash out in the rinsing basin.[3] Apart from her artistic output – and family opinion placed her artistically very high – Ada had the distinction of being the first self-appointed woman spy engaged in working for the Irish-Ireland movement, a not-altogether-surprising activity for one whose independence of spirit had once expressed itself in the defiant drowning of two childhood hats. This most wayward of Isabella's daughters decided to spy for Irish Ireland and approached on her own initiative the vigilantes – anglophiles whose particular mission was to hinder any sympathy for the Irish-Ireland movement in America.

To appreciate her courage in taking on these men, it must be remembered that Dublin Castle was like a huge spider, spreading its webs not only over Ireland but over Europe and America as well. Claude Dansey, one of their master spies and arguably the most ruthless, saw killing as part of his job.[4] There is no doubt that Ada Gifford, in her own amateur spying for the Irish cause, was swimming in shark-infested waters. Her name, religion and accent were her protection. This Protestant lady was no Mass-going Bridget Murphy with an Irish brogue, so it was easy enough for her to pass herself off as pro-British and to ingratiate herself into the American Vigilantes, set up by an Englishman named Moffat and comprising English expatriates. When Ada presented herself for membership, she coined a name for a non-existent club to which she alleged she had belonged – the Betsy Ross Club – a very Daughters-of-America sort of name. On top of that, her own name, religion and accent were enough. She became an accepted member of the American Vigilantes.

A chief ploy of theirs was to insinuate that the Irish were German spies and to send gangs to break up Irish meetings. Ada was able to warn Clan na Gael when its meetings were to be attacked and was successful until her cover was blown when she was spotted in the company of known Mellows adherents and her career as a spy abruptly terminated. In a postcard photograph she sent to her mother at this time, bearing the words 'Greetings – hoping to hear from you soon', she looks like a young Mata Hari, dressed very stylishly in velvet coat, hat and fur stole and muff, trimmed with a bunch of violets. Was the picture saying, perhaps, 'Look Mother, your wild one has done well'? Isabella might have had a stroke had she known exactly what her wild one was up to.

When 'John' arrived in America in June 1914, her sister Ada was there to welcome her. She gave as her reason for going – against the advice of Thomas Clarke – that she wanted to acquire experience of American journalism, but travel was a natural eventuality for someone of her temperament. She did not return to Ireland for eight years, and during her time in America she married an émigré Hungarian lawyer, Arpad Czira, when they were both twenty-seven, and bore him a son in 1917 whom she called Finian, true to her Irish-Ireland sentiments.[5]

One of her first calls on her arrival in New York was to the offices of the *Gaelic American*, of which Devoy was editor, bearing a letter of introduction and recommendation from his close friend Thomas Clarke. 'John' was used to the men in the Volunteers accepting women as part of the movement: Inghínidhe na hÉireann, Cumann na mBan, its paper *The Bean*, Countess Markievicz's Fianna, her sister Nellie's part in Larkin's appearance in Sackville Street, Nellie's and Helena Molony's membership of the Citizen Army, Maud Gonne's enthusiasm, Arthur Griffith's acceptance of women's role in journalism, her sister Grace's contributions to *The Irish Review*, Alfie Byrne's willingness to support women's franchise: this was the pro-feminist atmosphere in which 'John' had matured politically. Instead of this accustomed good fellowship, however, Devoy treated her, in her own words, like 'a benevolent uncle who, to humour an impetuous child, pretends to ponder solemnly over her foolish chatter'.[6] 'John' referred to her articles which had been published at home, in both *Sinn Féin* and *Irish Freedom*. She offered her services to Devoy, on a purely voluntary basis, to promote Irish propaganda in the USA. He offered nothing, and she left his office, which she had entered enthusiastically and with high hopes, deeply disappointed.

However, *The New York Sun*, whose editor was a woman, printed 'John's' submitted articles, and she began to feel more confident that she would be able to earn her living and help Ireland in the ways she had promised her friends at home. After England had declared war on Germany, in August 1914, the arrival of two of those friends, Padraic Colum and his wife Mary, meant that things began to look up for 'John'. The Colums were popular and well known in American literary circles, and 'John' was soon meeting distinguished writers and artists, many of them with an interest in Ireland. Three chief topics of interest emerged: the vicious spread of anti-Irish slander from such groups as the American Vigilantes, the case against conscription for both Ireland and America in the First World War and, of course, the great surge towards Irish independence. Colum was parodying *Burke's Peerage* one evening, in an assumed upper-class English accent, when a deceived American, taking Colum for a member of the House of Lords, spoke rapturously of King Arthur and his Knights. Colum debunked his adulation so effectively that, to use 'John's' description: 'You could hear coronets rattling to the ground as he revealed how this commoner had got his title as a reward for political jobbery, that one for paying a royal prince's gambling debts, and others for their dark deeds in the British colonies.'[7]

But all this was merely a prelude to her drive to fulfil her promise to her friends at home: that she would collect funds for them and that she would start an American branch of Cumann na mBan. Clan na

Gael, not surprisingly, excluded women from membership, though the AOH at least had a ladies' auxiliary committee.

One evening, 'John' attended a lecture hosted by the Gaelic League and given by Teresa Brayton who had written the well-known song 'The Old Bog Road' during a visit to Ireland and who was giving her views on what she had seen and heard. Roused by something Teresa Brayton had said, 'John' Gifford rose and made a brief, impromptu speech on the Irish Volunteers, followed in the same vein by other members of the audience, including the brother of Terence MacSwiney, the Lord Mayor of Cork who would later die for Ireland on hunger strike. The chairman of the meeting called a halt, on the grounds that the Gaelic League was cultural and apolitical, the non-militant ideology approved of by Douglas Hyde. However, after the meeting, Gertrude Kelly, a member of the audience, invited 'John' to address a meeting in the McAlpine Hotel on the Irish Volunteers and Cumann na mBan. 'John' agreed but almost committed a gaffe on this, the first occasion on which she addressed a public meeting in the USA. Roundly castigating the AOH in Ireland for its support of Redmond during the Volunteer split, she became aware that the chairperson was frantically nudging her. Unaware that the bulk of her audience were members of the Ladies' Auxiliary Committee of the AOH, the day was saved when the Chair diplomatically pointed out that the *Irish* AOH, to which Miss Gifford had referred, was, of course, a very different body from its American counterpart. This distinction was greeted with loud applause and cheers.

The president of this Ladies' Auxiliary AOH, Mary MacWhorter, invited 'John' to address their convention on the Irish situation. She agreed and won over that body, heart and purse, when she spoke to them glowingly of a familiar subject, the Irish Volunteers. This body of Irish-American women worked very hard for Ireland and the impending War of Independence, and, following that address by 'John' Gifford, the first American branch of Cumann na mBan was founded, followed soon after by a second. Who wanted John Devoy when they could have Mary MacWhorter and 'John' Gifford?[8]

Then Devoy began to interfere in the affairs of the New York Cumann na mBan and even labelled as spies those who disagreed with him. He seemed to see himself as a sort of Irish leader *in absentia* and certainly as leader of all Irish Americans. In an effort to make money for a Volunteer arms fund, 'John' took it upon herself to write to the author Seumas McManus, asking him for a signed copy of one of his books for an 'arms' raffle. He obliged with six copies of his own books and those of his deceased wife, Eithne Carbery. For this most fruitful try, Devoy rebuked 'John', because she had not asked permission to write to McManus.

Francis Sheehy Skeffington, the pro-Gaelic pacifist, was also poorly received by the Clan. 'John' gave him a list of Irish Americans to avoid, which saved him a great deal of trouble. She also gave a great welcome to Nora, daughter of James Connolly, who arrived with a letter from Countess Markievicz asking 'John' to help. That help was readily given. Nora Connolly's mission to America was a peculiar one: her father wanted her to contact the German Ambassador to America, Count von Bernsdorff, to tell him that the British were building bogus ships in Belfast. These dummy ships were to lure the German fleet to the Kiev Canal where the British guns would strike. Von Skal, a German agent in New York, arranged a meeting for Nora Connolly with the German Ambassador in Washington, and 'John' Gifford went with her. Von Skal's wife had been deeply impressed by what she called clever Irish intelligence because the Irish girls knew her husband would be at home on the very day they called – after a year's absence. 'John' and Nora Connolly basked in this glory, unprepared to admit that their chance calling on that day was just the luck of the Irish.[9] Connolly had impressed on his daughter not to disclose to James Larkin the purpose of her visit and not to contact him until just before she was returning home. It was perhaps a justifiable precaution – the fewer people who knew the better – but it is interesting to note that 'John' Gifford was not precluded from the secret message.

After Redmond committed his Volunteers to Britain's war effort following the outbreak of the First World War, 'John' received a bundle of papers from Ireland which featured, among other items, news of the arrest of prominent Sinn Féiners for anti-recruiting activities. This name 'Sinn Féiners', borrowed from Griffith's newspaper and his followers, was applied indiscriminately in Britain to all those who were to take part in the Rising and the subsequent War of Independence. In Griffith's paper, *Sinn Féin*, she read a quotation from the *Liverpool Post* of 12 September 1914:

> Half a million recruits cannot be raised in this country without a derangement of industry. It is our sincere belief that if the Government of Ireland Bill received immediate signature of the King, then His Majesty could make a triumphal tour of Ireland ... there would be 300,000 Irishmen of all creeds volunteer for the front in less than a week.

It was an ingenious proposition: Irishmen would face German guns so that British tradesmen would be spared. Griffith's reply was, as usual, factual. His estimate, based statistically, was that there were 7,116,000 Englishmen between the ages of twenty and forty-five. In Ireland, he judged, there were only one-tenth of that number. In Britain, the standard height for enlistment was 5 feet and 6 inches; in Ireland it was 5 feet and 3 inches. Griffith claimed the extra three inches was to exclude some English tradesmen who could thus be kept at home. He concluded his propagandist article with one of his aphorisms: 'England expects every Irishman to do his duty.'

Delighted with her ex-editor's handling of the question, 'John' Gifford brought the particular issue of the newspaper to John Devoy, thinking he would be eager to publish it in support of the Clan's own anti-recruitment drive. True to form, because he would not associate with the non-militant Griffith, Devoy rejected the offer. 'John' brought it straight to another publisher, Patrick Ford, whose *Irish World* had up to then represented the more right-wing, conservative Irish-American readership. He printed both the *Liverpool Post* article and Griffith's rebuttal. Congratulatory letters flooded in, and the reaction was so palpable that the paper's policy changed from being pro-Redmonite to being supportive of the Irish Volunteers. If Irishmen were to fight, it was to be for their own country, not for their age-old oppressor. 'John' Gifford was responsible for this important change and became a frequent contributor to the 'new look' paper, writing about Irish organisations and profiling their leaders. She had become a conduit for the Irish-Ireland ethos to the Irish in the USA.[10]

It must be remembered also that 'John' was not *sent* as an agent to America. She went of her own free will. The British government, on the other hand, was determinedly sending specially trained agents to woo the various strata of American society into a military commitment against Germany. They proposed England as 'The Mother Country of America' which, to many, it was. But an Irishman, Hugh Harkins, retaliated with a street-wide banner from his house bearing the message: 'EUROPE: MOTHER OF AMERICA'.[11] Neither mentioned the native American Indians.

Newspapers took sides. The bulletin board of one paper which later became the *New York Herald Tribune* displayed daily news favourable to the Allies. A mêlée of people congregated at the board each day, infiltrated by British agents who spread their good news; sometimes they enforced their arguments with fisticuffs if any Irish contradicted them. Tom Tuite, an old Fenian and then secretary to Thomas Addis Emmet (Robert Emmet's grand-nephew), was badly beaten by British agents when he denounced them as warmongers at a pro-war demonstration in Madison Square. The police warned him – probably for his own good – to stay away from such demonstrations.[12]

During 'John' Gifford's work in Ireland as a propagandist journalist for Seán Mac Diarmada's *Irish Freedom*, Mac Diarmada had commissioned her to write a serial summary of the memoirs of the old patriot Myles Byrne, another Fenian. Thomas Addis Emmet had so enjoyed this series that he invited 'John' to work in his New York library translating some old pamphlets and texts into modern English. Among them was the original copy of Oliver Cromwell's order to the dispossessed Irish: To hell or to Connaught.

Addis Emmet, a wheelchair invalid with enormous influence in New York's intellectual circles, loved Ireland passionately. From behind the screen in the library where she worked, 'John' heard several requests from British agents that Addis Emmet lend his voice to their recruiting campaign. His answer was always 'no'.

Before the 1916 Rising, 'John' met two members of the Plunkett family in America: Mimi and her brother Joseph. Joseph Plunkett wrote to her from a New York address, asking that she meet him. She observed in her memoirs that he was not engaged to her sister Grace at the time but that he was 'friendly' with her. However, she was obviously piqued because neither of them told her the purpose of their visit. They went to lunch in a Turkish restaurant and spent the afternoon chatting. Perhaps the fact that he told her neither that he had been in Germany nor the reason for his presence in New York may have dictated her reaction to his visit. It seems wise that he should disclose his attempt to negotiate for German arms to as few people as possible, and this visit he obviously saw in the nature of a social call on his girlfriend's sister.[13] Though she considered he looked well, and he himself said he was a new man since he had joined the Irish Volunteers, 'John's' other observations are certainly not adulatory. Nellie had liked Plunkett, and she, and those who knew him well, always spoke of his pleasant laughter which often cloaked the pain of his illness. 'John's' summing up was, however, that she had always found him 'reserved and incapable of light conversation'. It does not match any other description of Joseph Plunkett's personality. She may have met him when he was quite ill in Ireland, and she was perhaps influenced on that afternoon in America by his diplomatic reticence. She never saw him again after that lunch.

14

ROMANCE AND REBELLION

Meanwhile, events in the Gifford family in Ireland were following their course. Claude left the legal practice shared with his father to become an officer in the British army. Ernest was pursuing his career as an electrical engineer in England. Kate returned from Germany, married a man named Walter Wilson in Wales in 1909 and settled in Dublin, involving herself in the movement. Muriel lived happily in Oakley Road, Ranelagh, with her two children, Donagh and Barbara, and her husband, Thomas, who was co-opted, in April 1916, to the military council of the Irish Volunteers. Nellie continued to run her 'Burra' in Dawson Street, a much more ongoing and demanding activity than her 1913 role as stand-in niece to James Larkin.

Grace had been quietly working away on *The Irish Review* and falling in love with its young editor, Joseph Plunkett. Closeness fostered their affection, and so did their interest in Catholicism, as stated by Grace.[1] There was a tentative suggestion made in the emotional aftermath of the troubled times, as the whole period from the Rising to the ending of the Civil War was described, to publish in their entirety the love letters Joseph Plunkett wrote to Grace. Happily, better judgement prevailed. Reading such letters may leave the reader with the presumption that nothing is sacred, even the most personal expressions of human affection. Nonetheless, the only record we have of the progress of this most tragic love affair lies in the young mystic poet's letters to Grace. Enough may be quoted to reveal the measure of his love while leaving the rest in the relative privacy of the archives.[2]

The first letter is dated 28 November 1915. The salutations, deepening in affection, are indicative of the writer's growing love for his lady, and it is significant that when Grace became ill in her declining years and when money troubles were pressing, and she negotiated the sale of some of her husband's military documentation, the love letters were never proffered.

All Plunkett's moods are there. He is passionate, prayerful, playful, tired, longing, whimsical, determined. He quotes from G. K. Chesterton and from Francis Thompson. He encloses a mystical poem he has written for Grace. Occasionally Volunteer material creeps in. His ill health is shrugged off. In that first November letter the salutation is a sober 'Dear Grace' and is signed 'Joseph', but it contains his ideas on mystical love and finishes, 'All things are in some way beautiful but of all things on earth the most beautiful are the human soul and body for these are the likest God [sic].'[3]

Two letters were sent on 2 December 1915. The salutations have become much warmer and the message very clear: 'Darling Grace, you will marry me and nobody else.' The question of their marriage is pursued: 'Dear, dear Grace, I hope to become more worthy of loving you … By the way I am actually a beggar. I have no income and am earning nothing. Moreover, there are other things desperate, practically speaking, to prevent anyone marrying me.' He is presumably referring to his ill health. But two days later he forgets such doubts and writes playfully, 'By the way don't forget I have it [your heart] and don't go looking for it – also don't give mine away … I haven't been but at Heartquarters and Headquarters.' Six days after that he tells her, banteringly, that Seán Mac Diarmada has been speaking to him about their engagement, so he suggests it would be a good idea for her to make the usual press announcement: 'Of course it should be done by your mother!' The exclamation mark is significant. Isabella did not approve of the engagement on account, it is believed, of Plunkett's health. The announcement eventually appeared on 11 February 1916.

On St Stephen's Day 1915, in a letter marked 'midnight', Joseph had addressed Grace as 'my darling child', though he is only a year her senior. In the same letter he called her the Arabic 'Babbaly' and told her, 'You have taken the harm out of all my troubles and made the whole world beautiful for me. You have made me happy – never forget that, whatever happens.'

Sometimes in this correspondence he makes appointments to see Grace at Sibley's restaurant, at a Percy French burlesque or to dine in his family home. Jocosely, on another occasion, he uses Dublin idiom: 'Of a Friday January 7th in this year of Grace, Sweetheart … Could you drop down to Oakley tonight (or anywhere else) and let me know by this messenger. If you are not … able to bunk out, well then how about tomorrow?'

He has started to sign his letters with the symbol that reflects the name of his book of poetry which Thomas MacDonagh had edited, *The Circle and the Sword*. He addresses Grace by her two Christian names: 'Grace Evelyn, I mean my darling dear.' There is playful flirtation. His Volunteer work is treated flippantly, cloaking its importance to him. He borrows the concluding phrase from Pepys:

I went to my sixteen-hundred sub-committees and then tea … in the DBC [Dublin Bread Company] and at eight a hellish old staff meeting (to decide the war) and congrats from Padraic Ó Riain and Shane Lester on my approaching marriage (their words) and … back here bloody awful late … and so to bed.

This letter ends with a veritable litany of endearments:

My heart's delight,

My thousand treasures,

My thousand loves,

My secret love,

My heart's music.

On 26 January 1916, Grace is again 'Dearest Babbaly', and he translates it this time for her as 'Gate of God'. He quotes a love poem he wrote in Algiers, disclaiming it as a poor thing in a mixture of self-mockery and playfulness: 'That's no good I'm afraid. It was wrote [*sic*] to nobody at all (cross my heart) in Algiers.'

The following day he explains that his left arm is stiff, due to too much beer drinking. His sister Geraldine asserted that Plunkett was often in pain during this time, but this is typical of how he made fun of it.

There is great poignancy in the concluding words of another letter: 'Nothing can ever separate us.' The very next day, the first day of spring, he is writing to say how he misses Grace and describes how he has spent the evening 'in fifty places and then a staff meeting and then more talk till all hours'. He was 'not very chirpy and should not have had to go out at all' and then banteringly asks, 'Some sleuth told me you were at the Red Bank today – is that so?'[4]

The following day he is confined at Kimmage with a heavy cold and a snow blizzard prevents her from visiting him. Two days later, the overworked postman delivers a letter in which Plunkett expresses his longing to see her. He is 'cultivating patience', but he details his worries about her, referring to her in the third person: 'Perhaps she is not well and not able to come – perhaps she is tired out – perhaps something is worrying her – perhaps she is unhappy and, worse, fears that I won't write – but never any doubt that she would love to come if she could.'

St Valentine's Day 1916 produces a brief letter: 'My darling Grace, will you come and see me?'

On 28 February his letter is headed 'Hic et Nunc' (here and now). He calls Grace 'Our Live Artist at the Front', a reference to her political propagandist cartoons. There are playful, repetitive expressions of love, an admission that he nearly came to blows when he was ordered to stay in bed 'on account of the weather disagreeing with me'. Then he becomes playful: 'Tomorrow I expect – sh! Tell it not in Rath – a leap year proposal.[5] Can you come early and avoid the rush?'

On her birthday, 3 March, Grace receives good wishes for the year:

> … and every year thereafter and the wish of your heart and a nice husband – that's me … you know I only snatch glimpses of you and we never have time to finish a talk … I'm an enchanted prince … I will love to do everything I can to make you happy … You must know how much and little that is … but it will be the whole of me.

Even his own address he infuses with poetry: 'At the Field of Larks near Kimmage. St Joseph his feast day, 1916' and uses, sometimes, old Gaelic endearments like 'A Rún', 'A chuid de'n tsaoighil' (My share of the world). He admits finding it difficult to 'love in black and white'. Poetry is the only vehicle for his love, but 'Poems are like love, they will not come for wishing.'

Joseph and Grace were to have been married in a double wedding ceremony, with his sister Geraldine and her fiancé Thomas Dillon, on Easter Sunday 1916. The Rising took over, however, and Joseph writes to Grace from Fitzwilliam Street on Holy Saturday 1916, when all is ready for taking over the General Post Office:

> My darling sweetheart, I got your dear letter by lunch as I was go-ing out at 9 this morning and have not had a minute to collect my thoughts since (now 2.45) … here is a little gun which should only

be used to protect yourself ... Here is some money for you too and all my love forever. Joe.

The gun and message were brought to Grace by Joseph's aide-de-camp, Michael Collins, and she gave this gun to Nellie, who was leaving Temple Villas on her way to her Citizen Army outpost at the Royal College of Surgeons.[6] The following day, which was to have been the day of their marriage, Grace received Joseph's final pre-Rising letter:

> Larkfield, Easter Sunday 1916, 9 p.m.
>
> My dearest heart, keep up your spirits and trust in Providence. Everything is bully. I have only a minute. I am going to the nursing home tonight to sleep. I am keeping well as anything but need a rest. Take care of your old cold, sweetheart. All my love for ever, darling, darling, Grace. Joe.

These were among the letters sent by Joseph Plunkett to Temple Villas during the six months leading up to the Rising on Easter Monday 1916. It is unlikely that you would find anywhere else in the world a bundle of such letters opening with a definition of mystical love and concluding with a penultimate letter accompanying a gun. But they reflect Joseph's life during these first months of 1916: a young man deeply in love and a young man determined to call England's bluff about the ever promised, never granted Home Rule for a country which her liberators declared to be a separate nation.

15

AN UNEASY CITY

For narrative purposes I must backtrack a little. While he wooed Grace, Plunkett was deeply involved in the politics of arming the Volunteers for a rebellion still not envisaged by either Roger Casement, an executive of MacNeill's Dublin Brigade of the Irish Volunteers, or its chief officer, MacNeill himself. Both men resented how easy it had been for the Ulster Volunteers to arm to oppose Home Rule, and neither man supported Redmond's solution to entice the granting of Home Rule by expending Irish lives in the trenches. Both did, however, see the need to improve their military strength against unionist aggression, and the Irish Volunteer Executive had sent Casement to Germany to seek help. The philologist and scholar Kuno Mayer disclosed that John Devoy actually cautioned the Germans about Casement, whom he mistrusted undeservedly. In fact, Joseph McGarrity, one of the most important men in Irish-American circles at this time, said it was a separate group – not Devoy's Clan na Gael – who arranged Casement's arms mission. Casement himself sought not only arms but also to create an Irish Brigade from the captured British army POWs who were Irish. The Devoy interference could not have helped his cause, and Casement met with a poor response from both the German diplomats and the POWs.

When it was decided to send Joseph Plunkett to Germany to join Casement, he started to talk of his health requiring another trip abroad. He grew a beard and destroyed various photographs of himself. On his arrival in Berlin, whereas Casement had dealt with politicians and prisoners, Plunkett went to the military authorities and to the German high command. His extraordinary thoroughness was only disclosed in 1991 when papers were acquired by Lieutenant Colonel J. P. Duggan, having lain in German archives since 1915.[1] They were described by the late Fr F. X. Martin as 'nothing short of sensational', and, according to Dr Donal McCartney, 'They show that it was not a question of a group of poets going out with a harebrained scheme.'[2]

The documents fall into three categories:

1. a briefing on the Irish Volunteers, 1915
2. a detailed disposition of British forces in Ireland
3. a survey of coastline and maritime counties of Ireland

Dr McCartney agrees with Fr Martin's assessment of their importance: 'Maybe I expected that there was a military plan all along but I feel that this is not the complete outline. Obviously Joe Plunkett, apparently carrying all the details in his head, could not have spelled them out fully.'[3]

To ensure the trustworthiness of any recruits from Germany for the Irish Brigade (a low figure of fifty is mentioned), their bona fides would be established by the password 'Aisling' and also by the use of the old circle and sword emblem used on Plunkett's letters to Grace.

However, the strategic sketch unearthed in 1991 by the German archivists is the most impressive component of the find. It is all there, relayed enthusiastically, supposedly from memory, to the Germans by Plunkett: the British camps, the garrison towns, the troops, the artillery depots, the batteries of guns, the store depots, the number of infantry, the field howitzers, the forts, the RIC placements, the drop in manpower as British troops were deployed to Europe.

Plunkett's argument, it is believed, was that the Irish Volunteers needed hands-on help to meet their age-old enemy. He gave, it is alleged, all the above from memory and, also from memory, the number and deployment of the Volunteers. To have memorised and relayed such detail would be impressive but almost essential. Had such documentation been found on his person by a British agent, it would almost certainly have been the end for both the messenger and the message. Nevertheless, a grandson of Geraldine Plunkett, Dr John O'Donnell, has in his possession a hollowed-out walking stick belonging to his great-uncle Joseph Plunkett and it is believed this may well have been the hiding place for the aforesaid details. The only way to determine which story is correct would be to ascertain whose handwriting appears on the papers. Either way, Plunkett had to know facts and figures to argue them.

Unfortunately for Irish hopes, the Germans, at this stage, were faced with heavy battles, including the notorious Somme. However, they did not totally reject the request for help. Plunkett went home to relay their promise of captured arms only, then went on to America, to give details there of a planned uprising. Back home again, his health deteriorated once more, but that did not prevent his working with Rory O'Connor on munitions and telegraphy, nor his pursuing of romance with Grace. He had also drawn up an operational plan for the Rising and showed it to an enthusiastic Connolly, who worked with him to improve it. Strategic, strong, Dublin buildings, forming a rough ring around the city centre, would be occupied, and the arms promised from Germany would be landed on the Kerry coast and distributed about the country. The stage was set, but the opening performance was to encounter several hitches. The wonder of it was that a military engagement took place at all.

It was, in fact, an order made in code by the Castle authorities, the Castle Document, that precipitated the Rising. This proposed not only making sweeping arrests of leading Volunteers and of those with non-militant cultural interests, such as Gaelic Leaguers, but also launching raids for arms, occupying the homes of Volunteer leaders and surrounding some buildings, including the archbishop's palace. A Volunteer undercover man named Smith in Dublin Castle had brought the document to the Volunteers, in stages, as secrecy allowed. Decoded by Plunkett, the translation was printed on a hand press at Larkfield by George Plunkett and Colm Ó Lochlainn.[4]

The British authorities were anxious to wash their hands of any immediate responsibility for the rebellion, but the Castle Document showed their intention to be the first to strike. When the decoded version was published, the Castle denied its authenticity, causing it to be termed a bogus ploy of the insurgents. Grace left an unequivocal testimony to its veracity: 'Although it was published in Holy Week, it had come from the Castle some time before that. It did come out from the Castle that is quite certain. I know who brought it … Mr Smith was in the Castle.'[5]

There was chaos at Liberty Hall and at St Enda's; indeed, there was chaos everywhere. The Dublin Castle authorities proposed to arrest about 100 Volunteers. Pearse's reaction was immediate: it was a case of who would strike the first blow, Castle or Volunteer? It must be the Volunteers. At Liberty Hall, the reasoning was 'now or never'.

The non-belligerent Chief of Staff of the Volunteers, Eoin MacNeill, whose house was amongst those to be isolated by the British, instructed his men to resist arrest, but only defensively. On hearing a rumour that an armed Volunteer confrontation was planned, however, he stated angrily that the *raison d'être* of his Volunteers was not aggression and agreed to approve mobilisation only on hearing of the awaited German guns which made armed confrontation seem inevitable. The German vessel *Aud*, however, with its cargo of rifles and machine guns, was cornered by the British HMS *Bluebell* on 22 April 1916. Its quick-thinking German captain sank the ship – cargo included.[6] Moreover, Roger Casement, who had arrived back in Ireland on a German submarine, had been taken into custody shortly after landing the day before. MacNeill immediately cancelled the mobilisation order.

The Rising was postponed for twenty-four hours, but on Monday, 24 April 1916, north of the Liffey, the GPO and Four Courts were occupied. South of the Liffey it was Bolands Mills, St Stephen's Green (including the Royal College of Surgeons), Jacob's factory and the South Dublin Union, with outposts. Dublin Castle and Trinity College were not occupied: this had been intended until the confusion of the counter-order and the loss of the *Aud*.

It was as jumbled an army as you could find. There were in fact two armies: the Citizen Army under Connolly and the Irish Volunteers under Pearse. This division became blurred, however, and eventually they became known as the Irish Republican Army. The Hibernian Rifles also took part, and the fact that Britain continued to call them all Sinn Féiners (who never had an army at all), or Shinners, added to the mixture. There was also a great discrepancy in their training and their gear: Howth rifles, guns, historic pikes (acquired from Professor Donal Ó Buachalla), DMP and RIC batons, automatics, a Russian rifle from the *Aud*, even a Carson rifle from the north of Ireland inscribed 'For God and Ulster'.

As to dress, some wore the stipulated full uniform; others wore a bandolier as the only available indication of their military status. In between these two extremes various compromises were made to achieve a military look. Mostly those involved had paid for their gear from their own very limited resources.

The participants and sympathisers were equally varied: two knights, Casement and Sir Thomas Myles (who assisted at the Howth gunrunning), a knight's daughter (Louise Gavan Duffy), a countess, two professors, a lecturer, poets, novelists, Éamonn Ceannt (who had played Irish music for Pope Pius X), teachers, an auctioneer, a judge of the circuit court, trade-union leaders, an engineer, an alderman, a surgeon, medical students, a scientist, the head of an old Gaelic clan, printers, actors and actresses from the Abbey, a Protestant woman called Nellie Gifford who used to teach domestic science in rural Ireland, two Swedish sailors on leave who joined in enthusiastically, as well as a mêlée of clerks, carpenters, bricklayers, shop assistants, railwaymen, plumbers, decorators and some unemployed. A veritable conglomeration, but they showed an enthusiasm that soared when they saw the flag symbolising the Irish nation waving above the garrisons they held about the city.

Thomas MacDonagh had bidden a tearful farewell to his wife Muriel. Plunkett sent the gun to Grace at Temple Villas. Emotions ran high as Pearse stood outside the GPO and declared the rebirth of a nation, reading from the statement headed, 'Poblacht na h-Éireann: The Provisional Government of the Irish Republic to the People of Ireland.' The seven names at the bottom of the statement were Thomas J. Clarke, Seán Mac Diarmada, Thomas MacDonagh, P. H. Pearse, Éamonn Ceannt, James Connolly and Joseph Plunkett.

16

IN THE GARRISONS

There have been many cameos recorded of what went on in Sackville Street (now O'Connell Street) during that historic week, some unforgettable: the dignified Pearse standing outside the GPO on Monday 24 April 1916 declaring the birth of their Republic to mostly disinterested passers-by; the building behind him being prepared for siege with sandbagged windows; those who had been on the premises already made prisoners; Pearse's steady voice calling out the emotive phrases:

> In the name of God and of the dead generations ... supported by her exiled children in America ... We declare the right of the people of Ireland to the ownership of Ireland ... In every generation the Irish people have asserted their right to national freedom ... six times during the past three hundred years they have asserted it in arms ... we hereby proclaim the Irish Republic ... The Republic guarantees religious and civil liberty ... We place the cause of the Irish Republic under the protection of the Most High God ... no one who serves that cause will dishonour it by cowardice, inhumanity, or rapine.

It has been said that this man's proper milieu is among the church's saints even though his detractors say otherwise. In a tribute, one of his pupils, Alfred Dennis, described Pearse's relationship with his students: 'They did not tell him lies, because he believed every word they said.'[1] General Blackadder, president of the court martial that tried the insurrectionists, observed regretfully, 'I have had to condemn to death one of the finest characters I have ever come across. I don't wonder that his pupils adored him.'

When biographers undertake a description of Joseph Plunkett's part in the GPO garrison, they seem committed to the inclusion of two matters and little else: his frailty and his jewellery, and that little else is not always accurate. Thomas Coffey mentions his filigree bangle and two antique rings, his emaciation, the surgical bandage around his throat (Plunkett had undergone surgery on his tubercular glands the previous week) and his uncertain step; yet he concedes that the young, post-surgery invalid showed an astonishing flow of nervous energy when the fighting got under way.[2] Charles Duff speaks of him tottering about but doing all he could, though he may have been 'ready to fall at any moment', but Duff admits his signing of the Proclamation and giving the Rising all his *moral* support.[3] Ruth Dudley Edwards records the particular contributions of Connolly, Pearse, Clarke and Mac Diarmada. She allots just one sentence to Plunkett: 'Plunkett was dying of consumption.'[4] In Kenneth Griffith and Timothy O'Grady's work, *Curious Journey*, the jewellery has proliferated into 'an assortment of rings, bracelets and bangles'.[5]

The illness and a ring and a bracelet were valid observations, but they were looking at a half-full vessel and seeing it half-empty. Quite different are the observations of those who were actually in the GPO. To start with, the Army Council of the Volunteers had replaced Eoin MacNeill with Plunkett as Chief of Staff of the Volunteers. He had already done a man's part in the movement by his theatre work, his journalism, his journeys to the USA and Germany, and his plan of the city's garrisons in his capacity as Director of Operations, as approved by Connolly. Now, despite post-operational fatigue, in that blazing, smoke-filled building, he played his part as leader, as those who were there have recorded. Desmond FitzGerald remembered his cheerfulness and that, despite his fatigue, he reassured, smilingly, those who were concerned for him as they set out initially from Liberty Hall for the GPO.[6]

In the GPO, when the shelling was at its worst, it is recorded that no one was more assiduous than Plunkett in keeping up morale, and, walking past the men at the windows, he called out when an enemy barricade was on fire. Within that barricaded building, as the fighting progressed, he is reported as redirecting Fergus O'Kelly and his men back to the premises of the Dublin Bread Company, a building strategically important because of its position between Abbey Street and Eden Quay. O'Kelly had received an order from Connolly to evacuate the tower of the building (vulnerable to snipers), and there had been a misunderstanding that the whole of the building was to be evacuated. O'Kelly explained this to Plunkett, who looked up from what he was doing and said, 'I know. Collect your men and go back.' O'Kelly did so. Then Plunkett sent his younger Volunteer brother, George, across Sackville Street to stop the looting in the shops.[7] George, revolver in hand, gave a 'stop looting or else' ultimatum to the looters. Finally, as the shelling intensified and the possibility of the sandbagged windows catching fire increased, Commandant Plunkett gave orders to douse the sandbags with water.

In between all this, he was writing a sort of war diary. Enough has been preserved to show he was very much au fait with what was going on – not 'laying down his maps and thinking of Grace'. He has recorded in the diary the taking over of the post office and the reading of the Proclamation, also the repulse of an attack by the Lancers. Obviously dispatches were coming in, and he records the attempt to take Dublin Castle. Entries for Easter Tuesday are on missing pages but, as Director of Operations, Plunkett was also interested in another dispatch relating to the extraordinary success of Commandant Ashe in Garristown in defeating the police, and also the movement of 200 IRA men from Navan to Dublin. Recorded also are the injuries to James Connolly's arm and leg, especially the fractured shinbone. The burning of Linenhall Barracks, in possession of the enemy, is noted, as are the boring through of buildings. There is a copy also of the 'unconditional surrender' notice sent by Brigadier General Lowe. Other entries refer to practicalities about food, signals and barricades.

Desmond Ryan, who was there, tells us of Plunkett, 'During the worst stages of the shelling no one was more assiduous in keeping up the spirits of the defenders. He walked past a long line of men at the front windows, smiling.'[8] He is there, up to the end, rallying his men as they make a dash from the GPO inferno through a hail of machine-gun fire and rifle bullets: 'Plunkett orders a van to be dragged across one of the lanes down which the machine-guns rattled, a feeble screen enough but it served its turn while Plunkett stood there shouting: "Don't be afraid … On! On! On!"'[9]

He was with the Pearse brothers, the wounded Connolly, Clarke and Mac Diarmada in the precarious security of 16 Moore Street when it was decided to hand in their guns. Nurse O'Farrell brought them Brigadier General Lowe's orders for surrender, and Ryan describes Willie Pearse, Plunkett and Seán MacLochlainn heading the surrendered garrison, 'waving white flags as if they were banners of victory'.[10]

It is difficult to conceive what inner physical and psychological reserves this young leader called on to carry him through those nightmare days and nights. Back from Germany, illness in Spain and a trip to America, he was supposed to be resting when he returned to Ireland. Instead, he had worked on munitions and on other preparations for the big day. He had meetings with the Military Council at midnight on Holy Saturday, lasting till 2.30 a.m. The next morning at 8 a.m., the Military Council met again. Later that day, Joseph wrote the letter to Grace commiserating with her on her 'old cold' and declaring that he was 'keeping as well as anything' but had to go into the nursing home to rest that night – in preparation for the next day. On Easter Monday morning, his aides-de-camp, Michael Collins and Commandant W. J. Brennan-Whitmore, called for him. Clarke and Mac Diarmada were advised to reach the GPO at their own pace, owing to Clarke's general health and Mac Diarmada's polio limp. But Plunkett, the man 'dying of consumption', marched from Liberty Hall with Pearse and Connolly at the head of the men, some of whom had trained at his family home at Larkfield.

Apart altogether from the recent vindication of Plunkett by the unearthing of the documents from the German archives, he developed the innovative idea of broadcasting the birth of the Republic to the world by wireless telegraphy. He ordered the closing of the official station at Ventry in County Kerry and the setting up of their own. The disaster of the *Aud*, a vessel which incidentally did not have a radio, put an end to that imaginative idea.

An article on Plunkett by Lieutenant P. B. Brennan features one soldier evaluating another: 'He followed orders, made his own and thought in broad sweeps ... he was prepared to die for his beliefs.'[11]

On the matter of his choice of garrisons, as director of military operations, the buildings chosen were well spaced out and strong, even the thick-walled stone buildings of the outpost distilleries and Jacob's, a biscuit factory, with towers commanding a panoramic view of the city.

Survivors of the GPO garrison have left several records of the special relationship between Connolly and Plunkett, men from two very different rungs of the social ladder. It has been recorded that some of the garrison, including Winnie Carney, Connolly's redoubtable secretary, at first looked askance at this young director of military operations who wore 'geegaws', a Dublin flippancy for accessories or jewellery. But Connolly assured her that in military matters none equalled Plunkett. She soon forgot her prejudice because he displayed such virtues of command in that extraordinary siege. He was pragmatic, commanding, decisive and encouraging, even if he did have to rest a little.

To set the antique-ring record straight, on the day Grace was received into the Catholic Church by Fr Sherwin, 7 April 1916, her fiancé presented her with a poem: 'For Grace on the Morning of her Christening.' One of her gifts to him was an antique emerald ring, a family heirloom, when they became engaged.

Muriel MacDonagh played her quiet part in the drama of Easter week. She had the two children to think of, but her home at Oakley Road, Ranelagh, became a rendezvous for the anxious wives of the rebel commandants. In the early part of the week she is said to have reached the GPO and to have spoken to Plunkett, who gave her a message for Grace. The route to Jacob's, where her husband served, was more inaccessible. Even Brigadier General Lowe had to meet MacDonagh quite a distance from that garrison. When the surrender came, MacDonagh wished that he might see his wife 'one last time', but when he was asked by Nurse O'Farrell if she would try to get Muriel to come to see him, he looked around dejectedly at the process of evacuation and surrender and said simply, 'Not like this.'[12]

Nellie Gifford worked hard at the Royal College of Surgeons garrison, under Commandant Michael Mallin and Countess Markievicz. Her later account of her stewardship there, published in *An Phoblacht*, misprinted her name as 'Mary Donnelly'.[13] Her description shows an innocence of things martial and a certain insouciance from this daughter of a comfortable unionist household who had once more publicly and gladly cast her lot not only with republicans but with the working-class members of the movement.

In an (unpublished) account, Nellie starts off by describing how she had breakfasted on the Easter Monday with Grace, the only sibling left in the Gifford household.[14] There were also, as well as her parents, a resident nurse required for Frederick, now bedridden following a stroke, and one resident maid. Fortunately, Isabella did not breakfast with her daughters that morning and so did not see the parting of the girls when Grace ran down the steps and insisted that a reluctant Nellie take, for protection, the small gun Joseph had sent to her through Michael Collins. Nellie was not at all sure, any more than many of the Volunteers, what 'reporting for manoeuvres' meant, especially in view of the apparent initial shilly-shallying. The Dublin Brigade mobilisation order, for instance, simply instructed that an overcoat, haversack, water bottle and canteen be brought, with rations for eight hours. Arms and ammunition should be carried, and everyone with a cycle or motorcycle should bring it. Those who were to serve under Commandant Éamonn Ceannt in the South Dublin Union got the strongest clue: they were asked to bring, in writing, the name of their next of kin. The first real hint of war that Nellie Gifford received was when she left her home – from a Rathmines neighbour who said there was shooting in the city.[15]

On reaching St Stephen's Green, Nellie met Margaret Skinnider, a Scot who had aligned herself with the movement and who was later badly wounded. 'You're late' was her greeting, though indeed punctuality was not an outstanding feature of this insurrection, with men drifting in to their various posts as they heard that the countermanding order of MacNeill had itself been countermanded.[16]

Nellie found St Stephen's Green occupied by the Citizen Army, with armed men behind the railings, trenches being dug and a tent erected by Countess Markievicz opposite the Royal College of Surgeons. The fine day became a kind of picnic, and Nellie's duties began to take shape: bringing required medicine, providing tea and scones, and carrying dispatches. She asked Andy Dunne to sing a rebel song that Countess Markievicz had written, but he baulked, in case it might seem like gloating and offend a prisoner who had been taken. A laden bread van trundled by, and its contents were commandeered, with a precise receipt for the bread handed to the astonished driver. Somewhere a rebel was ticked off for a breach of duty. 'Aw give us a chance,' he said, 'it's me first revolution.'[17]

Night fell, and things were not so cosy. It turned chilly, and the British had mounted a machine gun at the Shelbourne Hotel, overlooking the Green. Nellie and her mates slept on the hard benches of the summerhouse, normally used to shelter performing bands. It was decided to evacuate the Green on the Tuesday and to occupy the adjacent College of Surgeons, emptied of students for the Easter break. The lone watchman would not open the door to them, so he was warned to step aside while they blasted it in. In twos and threes, as instructed, they made their way from the Green under heavy fire. Once inside, they knelt down and said the Rosary. When they settled down for the night, they were glad to be under a roof. The women in the garrison were given pieces of carpet to keep them warm, less lucky than their sister rebels in the Four Courts garrison, who wrapped themselves in the ermine-trimmed robes of the judiciary.

Years later, Countess Markievicz was asked when she had decided to become a Catholic. She had no problem identifying the time: it was when she knelt down with the rebels saying the Rosary in the College of Surgeons in 1916.[18]

Tuesday brought with it several tasks. Between the College and Grafton Street was a row of shops, the overhead apartments of which were rented. Their occupants had fled, and Commandant Mallin's men broke through the walls of these adjoining buildings, stationing men on guard in each. One of Nellie's jobs was to reach them with food – not an easy task because, as she explained, the floor levels differed and often there was quite a drop into the next house, especially difficult when carrying food. In the heat of attack, one young rebel was found, white-faced and red-eyed from lack of sleep and very hungry from a twenty-four-hour lack of food. When they fed him, he collapsed into sleep on the spot. Two country boys had subsisted on nothing but plum jam for two days until Nellie reached them. There were mouthwatering accounts of a French pastry shop nearby which was never reached, and there are glimpses, here and there, in various accounts of the siege, of Nellie Gifford not only supplying tea, scones and porridge, but also furnishing with spirits the First Aid post run by Nora O'Daly of Cumann na mBan. Acquiring food was a problem. The wives of two Citizen Army men called to see if their husbands were there or at the GPO. The Countess gave them money to buy food and they returned later, laden with a very welcome variety.

Carrying dispatches, sometimes verbal, sometimes written, was a common job. One such mission involved Nellie and Chris Caffrey being sent to the Jacob's garrison to get needed ammunition. Their main fear was not the British army but the 'Allowance women' who got one shilling per day if their men were at the front and who wanted no noble-minded patriotism to rob them of what was, in some cases, their drink money. On reaching Jacob's, through heckling groups of these women, they saw Major MacBride, husband of Maud Gonne, at an upper window. This man, who had fought with the Boers in their war with England, had wandered into their Rising but was delighted to stay to oppose a familiar enemy. He pointed humorously to his slouch hat and asked for their approval. The men had just been issued with them. All the doors of the factory were closed so Nellie and Chris were hauled up through a window. Thomas MacDonagh went to get ready the required ammunition, and Nellie also asked for a tin of biscuits as a bribe to ensure their safe return.

> Inside [Jacob's] we rested while awaiting the reply to dispatch [ammunition]. We unloaded our news re our stronghold and heard their story. Máire Ní Shúilaigh [Abbey Theatre actress] was there. It was agony to Commandant MacDonagh, who was the soul of chivalry, to let two girls go out there alone to face those Separation Women [they had attacked a dispatch carrier earlier that night]. Someone engaged his attention and we gave him the slip and stole out of the factory.

The Separation Women were waiting for us like a pack of wolves and started to scream 'Sinn Féiners' at us and surged up to us in a threatening way. Chris' coolness made them doubt their judgement for a moment. She saw their hesitation and calmly handed them the biscuits which Commandant MacDonagh had given us, insinuating that that was the object of our midnight visit to Jacob's. Nevertheless they followed us like some awful tidal wave. We took to the road and I dared not go on the path lest they suspect our destination. My knees wobbled and it was only when we were level with the side door of the College of Surgeons that we dived over and panted through the keyhole the password for the day – 'Success'.[19]

Incredibly, once inside, Chris Caffrey's comment on the episode was, 'Where in the name of fortune did Commandant MacDonagh rustle all those red-haired Cumann na mBan from?'[20]

Most of Nellie's descriptions of her service in the St Stephen's Green garrison were light-hearted, the only exception being on the occasion one night when, candle in hand, she found herself in a room that contained embalmed parts of the human body. It was, of course, not so surprising in a building calling itself the Royal College of Surgeons.[21]

17

SURRENDER

The trim, military uniforms of today's Irish army bear no resemblance to the scorched, soot-stained, assorted garments of Pearse's GPO garrison in 1916. For all that, some of the weary, embattled ones making their way out of the doomed GPO in their conglomerate clothing, would be among the first members of the Irish National Army, and the standard cap badge of that army today, embodying a sunburst and a reminder of the legendary Fianna, was the same one introduced by Professor Eoin MacNeill for his Irish Volunteers in 1914, based on his Celtic studies.

Pearse's exhausted men, who had sniped all week from windows and high roofs or burrowed their way from building to building, were now ordered to make a dash for it, in small groups and at sporadic intervals, to the comparative safety of Henry Place, parallel to Sackville Street and leading circuitously to Moore Street, where the military council eventually holed up in Nos 15 and 16. The last act of Pearse, Clarke and The O'Rahilly had been to free their prisoners from the basement, where they had been housed for safety from the battered roof and its falling timbers. There is a street now called after The O'Rahilly, close to where that wealthy head of his clan was killed as he led a small group to Parnell Street.

It was being confronted by the devastation of the streets around them and reluctance to lose more lives that persuaded Pearse to surrender. The badly wounded Connolly was not enthusiastic about giving up. They had discussed the possibility of retreating through Jervis Street, but he agreed eventually to allow the intrepid Nurse Elizabeth O'Farrell, under a white flag, to initiate the surrender. That lady's extraordinary bravery, her coolness as she walked towards the enemy ranks, reflected the dedication of the women involved. Shamefully, the figure of Nurse O'Farrell was airbrushed out in the familiar photograph of Pearse surrendering.

The Four Courts garrison surrendered immediately after the GPO evacuation. The Jacob's garrison, as well as those at Bolands Mills, under Éamon de Valera, and the South Dublin Union, under Ceannt, were still well entrenched in their positions when the surrender order arrived. MacDonagh, now in overall charge with the arrest of the headquarters' staff, was reluctant to surrender. Brigadier General Lowe went out of his way to encourage him to do so, perhaps influenced not only by his regard for Pearse but also by the presence of a remarkable Anglo-Irish officer, Captain Henry de Courcy Wheeler, whose neighbours in Robertstown, County Kildare, including the Volunteers, had given him an affectionate farewell on his way to the trenches in 1914. Lowe offered his car to two Capuchin friars, Fathers Aloysius and Augustine, who reached Jacob's and persuaded MacDonagh how essential it was to obey Pearse and Connolly's surrender order. He agreed to meet Brigadier General Lowe at St Patrick's Park, which was as near as Lowe's car could safely reach, and at that meeting MacDonagh explained that it would be advisable for him to contact Éamonn Ceannt personally at the South Dublin Union. Lowe agreed, and MacDonagh honoured his promise by returning to St Patrick's Park at 3 p.m. and formally handing over his belt and revolver in the age-old ceremony of surrender. He had persuaded a reluctant Ceannt to do likewise.

Éamon de Valera had awaited MacDonagh's decision. He had shown himself a very able commandant, hoisting his flag on a building close to his garrison so that the firing from the British gunboat, *Helga*, was deflected there, but now he, too, surrendered.

The personnel at the Royal College of Surgeons were also still well entrenched in their positions when the surrender order came. But it was obeyed, again reluctantly. Nellie Gifford found fresh towels, and the dishevelled men cleaned themselves up before the doors opened and they followed their two commandants to Captain Wheeler, waiting outside to receive their surrender. Countess Markievicz refused the captain's offer of a lift to prison, saying she preferred to walk at the head of her men. She kissed her Mauser before handing it over to him. Then, looking defeat in the eye and turning it on its head, she remarked: 'We have done better than Emmet anyhow.'[1]

The women were sent first to Ship Street Station, from there to Richmond Barracks, and finally to Kilmainham Gaol, where they were lodged four to a cell. The Countess was placed in a cell on her own from where she was sent to England. Nellie wound up in a cell with three others. For the first time in her life – but not the last – Isabella Gifford, niece of Sir Frederick Burton, had a jailbird daughter.

Not all the military dealt with their prisoners as honourably as Brigadier General Lowe, both at the headquarters surrender by Pearse and in his later negotiations with MacDonagh. Nevertheless, sympathetic discretion was shown by other British officers, some of whom quietly sent the youngest, teenage Volunteers home to their parents with nothing more than a dismissive cuff on the cheek. Others were vicious in their behaviour. On 26 April 1916, the day on which Seán Heuston's surrendered garrison was treated with contempt, a far more heinous act was committed on three unarmed civilians at Portobello Barracks. Captain Bowen Colthurst ordered the killing, without trial, of three civilians, Francis Sheehy Skeffington, Thomas Dickson and Patrick J. McIntyre. Sheehy Skeffington was a pacifist and had been trying to stop looting.

Another military crime was committed at 177 North King Street, a licensed premises owned by a Mrs O'Rourke. Two bodies were discovered, fully dressed and buried twelve inches below the cellar floor. One was the mutilated remains of Patrick Bealon, foreman at the premises, and the other that of James Healy, a clerk at Jameson's Distillery. At the subsequent inquest on Patrick Bealon, Lieutenant Colonel H. Taylor, commanding the 2nd/6th South Staffords, denied that his troops were culpable. The jury found otherwise:

> We find that the said Patrick Bealon died from shock and haemorrhage, resulting from bullet wounds inflicted by a soldier, or soldiers, in whose custody he was, an unarmed and unoffending prisoner. We consider that the explanation given by the military authorities is very unsatisfactory, and we believe that if the military authorities had any inclination they could produce the officer in charge.[2]

A similar verdict was passed in the case of James Healy. The two victims were neither armed nor in the Volunteers – and neither were the other eleven men and two teenagers who were killed by Taylor's men, who went on a murderous rampage in the area.[3]

In the limited ground space outside the Rotunda, where the Volunteers had been founded so auspiciously three years before, upward of 400 prisoners from the GPO and the Four Courts, including some women, were packed together. It was a chilly night, and they did not receive as much as a drink of water for thirty hours. Even before he became really drunk, the officer in charge, Captain Lee Wilson, behaved atrociously towards them. He called his prisoners animals and would not allow them to get up to relieve themselves. He is said to have contemptuously snatched Joseph Plunkett's will, leaving everything to Grace, from his pocket, sneering that it was proof that the rebels knew they would be defeated. He knocked the walking stick away from Seán Mac Diarmada, and he had Thomas Clarke, the senior leader, stripped to the buff so that he could be searched, during which search he passed derogatory remarks. The veteran Clarke, survivor of the notorious imprisonment meted out to the Fenians, was stoical.[4]

You cannot indict a whole army for the vicious behaviour of some of its members, and the surrenders effected 'by the book' must balance the others. It should be remembered also that the women involved were not subjected to any indignities, beyond a few ribald remarks. Most of the GPO ladies found their extremely hazardous way home, but Winnie Carney had refused to leave the wounded Connolly. In fact, Winnie recorded that on reaching Richmond Barracks, chilled to the bone from their ordeal at the Rotunda, the women were shown great kindness by Captain Robert Barton. She asked him if they could have tea, and when he had it brought to them with it were also very welcome 'sticky buns'.[5] It was to be their last food and drink until the next day. In fact, this Captain Barton was so taken with the spirit and thinking of the rebels that he later embraced their freedom ethos and became a Sinn Féin delegate at the Treaty talks in 1921. Nor was he the only convert from the British side.

Sometimes a junior officer's kind intent was overruled, as when Lieutenant Lindsay assured Ned Daly at the Four Courts that Dr Brigid Lyons and the other young women would be taken home. His superiors decided otherwise, and the women were jailed.

18

SIXTEEN FUNERALS AND A WEDDING

James Connolly had prophesied, before the insurgents had manned their posts, 'We are all going out to be slaughtered.'[1] Certainly, whatever the kindness shown to the rebels by some of the British forces, the official reaction was otherwise. Retribution was swift. The man appointed to effect it was General Sir John Grenfell Maxwell, General Officer Commanding-in-Chief of the forces in Ireland.

Maxwell approved Lowe's handling of the military situation and confined his ire to the Castle politicians who had allowed the Irish to arm and carry out their manoeuvres all over the country. He first made public his intention of burning to the ground all buildings harbouring rebels and then decided that the execution of 100 rebels would put manners on the unruly Irish: 'I am going to ensure that there will be no treason whispered for 100 years.' That he was to ensure the very opposite was not due to carelessness on his part; the arrangements for the executions and burials were meticulous:

> After each prisoner has been shot, a medical officer will certify that he is dead and his body will immediately be removed to an ambulance, with a label pinned on his breast giving his name. When the ambulance is full, it will be sent to Arbour Hill Detention Barracks, entering by the gate at the garrison chapel. A party there will put the bodies close alongside one another in the grave (now being dug),

cover them thickly with quicklime (ordered) and commence filling in the grave. One of the officers with this party is to keep a note of the position of each body in the grave, taking the name from the label.[2]

Both the size of the grave, more of a pit in that it measured twenty-nine by nine feet, and the disintegrating nature of the quicklime, suggest reasons for affixing labels, though that directive was not carried out.[3]

No time was lost. The executions started five days after the surrender, on 3 May 1916, in the execution yard attached to Kilmainham Gaol. Within hours of the 'trials' (with no defence), the shootings began. The first of the 'funerals' – though the unceremonious disposal of the bodies could hardly be so-called – were those of Pádraig Pearse, Thomas MacDonagh and Thomas Clarke. No one was in the yard excepting the firing party and the attendant priest who stayed with them to the end. A lorry awaited at the side gate of the yard, and the remains of the three men were driven to the pit at Arbour Hill.

Thomas MacDonagh had kept photographs of his two children with him in prison. He sent them to Muriel, whose attempt to visit him in Kilmainham had been frustrated and to whom he sent also his last, loving tributes. His son, Donagh MacDonagh, has left this recollection of news of his father's death being brought to Oakley Road, when he was a very small boy:

One of my earliest and most vivid memories is of Fr Aloysius coming to our house in Oakley Road with the news of the executions. I was playing in a rockery and fled in terror from the bogeyman who came riding on a bread van with news which terrified; and later I remember the British soldiers lying on the ground with their guns sighted on our house as we walked away.

In 1908, Thomas MacDonagh had written a play, produced by the Abbey, called *When the Dawn Is Come*. It had foreseen a future Ireland in which, oddly prophetically, seven captains would lay down their lives for their country. He was the third of the seven signatories of the Proclamation to be executed. A British officer said of him: 'They all died well but MacDonagh died like a prince.'[4]

Fr Augustine, OFM, Cap., saw Joseph Plunkett at Richmond Barracks, resting with a group of other tired Volunteers on a stretch of grass, his body thrown back slightly, and his position supported by his two hands pressed against the grass. Plunkett had been in a fainting condition after the march from the Rotunda, and Seán Mac Diarmada, who had also found it a huge strain, suggested that Plunkett be given an old quilt from the Royal College of Surgeons, which was rolled up to form a pillow. Easter Week in the GPO, a night in the chill air outside the Rotunda with nothing to eat or drink and a forced march on an empty stomach: these were hardly the doctor's orders for a tubercular surgery convalescent. Fr Augustine may not have known all this, but he was told the young commandant was awaiting court martial, and he recorded that his heart went out to him, resting there on the grass.

The banns for the marriage of Joseph Mary Plunkett and Grace Evelyn Vandeleur Gifford had been read out, in Rathmines church, weeks before the proposed wedding to be held there on Easter Sunday. The wedding, in fact, took place in Kilmainham Gaol. No bride can have had more distressing eve-of-wedding preparations, all to be accomplished in a few short hours.

Ironically, while Joseph Plunkett's letter dated 29 April (the sixth day of the Republic as he so dated it) was not received until Winnie Carney's release, his last letter to Grace, dated 2 May, was delivered to her without delay by the British soldier to whom it was entrusted. More ironically still, this final letter was written on the back of Plunkett's Last Will and Testament which had lain in his pocket for nine days and which had been the subject of Captain Wilson's ribald comment. It reads as follows:

> The Will of Joseph Mary Plunkett, 23rd April, 1916.
>
> I give and bequeath everything of which I am possessed or may become possessed to Grace Evelyn (Mary Vandeleur) Gifford.
>
> Signed: Joseph Mary Plunkett
>
> Witnessed: George Oliver Plunkett.[5]

The letter on the back of the document appears to have been written after Plunkett's court martial but before sentencing.

> Richmond Barracks,
>
> Tuesday May 2nd, 1916.
>
> My darling child,
>
> This is my first chance of sending you a line since we were taken. I have no notion what they intend to do with me but I have heard a rumour that I am to be sent to England.
>
> The only thing I care about is that I am not with you – everything else is cheerful. I am told that Thomas was brought in yesterday. George and Jack (Plun) [sic] are both here and well. We have not had one word of news from outside since Monday 24th April except wild rumours. Listen – if I live it might be possible to get the Church to marry us by proxy – there is such a thing but it is very difficult I am told. Father Sherwin might be able to do it. You know how I love you. That is all I have time to say. I know you love me and so I am very happy.
>
> Your own,
>
> Joe

The Fr Sherwin mentioned was the priest who had received Grace into the Catholic Church in the University Church on St Stephen's Green. Whether she consulted him or her parish priest at Rathmines

– perhaps both – she was obviously advised that the clergy at James' Street looked after the Kilmainham area and if permission for the wedding was granted by the prison authorities a priest from that parish would attend. Permission was granted, but although the couple had discussed various possibilities when the Rising cancelled their Easter Sunday wedding, Grace was now faced with implementing them. She knew that her mother, occupied in caring for her sick father, disapproved of the marriage. Nellie was in jail, and the family was also trying to cope with Muriel, who was stunned at the sentencing to death of her beloved husband. It was no wonder that the jeweller from whom Grace bought the plain gold band, Dermot Stoker of Grafton Street, was taken aback when a young woman emerged from a taxi which stopped outside at closing time, entered his shop and asked to buy a wedding ring. She cried a little as the purchase was completed, and he, now upset himself, asked the reason for her tears. She told him simply that she was to marry Joseph Plunkett that evening, a little while before his execution.

On her wedding day, Grace Gifford wore a gingham dress with white collar and cuffs and a brimmed straw hat with a veil. This is the ensemble shown in her passport picture of 1928. It was questioned if a twelve-year-old picture would have been acceptable for passport purposes. The *Catholic Bulletin* of February 1917 comes to the rescue and shows the identical picture of Grace, with the great sad eyes of a woman, still in her twenties, who has lost a young brother, a brother-in-law and her husband.[6] It is one of the most sorrowful faces in the pages of Irish photography. There is another picture, taken at Larkfield, where she went after the Rising, wearing a pretty, flounced dress and cuddling a kitten. Such a dress might have been out of place at the wretched ceremony in Kilmainham.

It is best to allow Grace herself to tell the details of that sombre wedding:

> I entered Kilmainham Jail on Wednesday, May 2nd, at 6 p.m., when
> I saw him for the first time in the prison chapel, where the marriage
> was gone through and no speech allowed. He was taken back to his
> cell, and I left the prison with Fr Eugene MacCarthy [*sic*], of James'
> Street. We tried to get shelter for the night, and I was finally lodged
> at the house of Mr Byrne – bell founder – in James' Street. I went
> to bed at 1.30, and was wakened at 2 o'clock by a policeman, with
> a letter from the prison commandant – Major Lennon – asking me
> to visit Joseph Plunkett. I was brought there in a motor, and saw my
> husband in his cell, the interview occupying ten minutes. During the
> interview the cell was packed with officers, and a sergeant, who kept
> a watch in his hand and closed the interview by saying: 'Your time
> is now up.'[7]

Other facts emerged: that her groom had come to her handcuffed;
that the 'cuffs' were removed for the ceremony and the signing of the
register and were then replaced immediately before he was marched
away; that because of a gas failure the prison was in darkness, light
provided by a soldier holding a candle, with another soldier acting as
witness to the wedding. Grace said, even years afterwards, that she
could still see that soldier's face.

Before being brought to her husband's cell, when she was recalled
to the prison at 2 a.m., she had an astonishing conversation in the
damp, dark building with one of the officials, which she recorded, as
well as further details of the time allowed with her husband:

> I was gratuitously informed in May, 1916, by the officer in charge of
> prisoner's effects, that my husband, being in bad health when taken
> prisoner (he had entered the fight only a few days subsequent to an
> operation) was specially given hospital treatment, and lodged in the
> infirmary. The hospital treatment consisted of an extremely small cell
> with an extremely small window, a table on which (I presume) lay

his 'hospital diet' – i.e. a tin bowl of some unspeakable, semi-liquid concoction, with no implement with which to eat it, and a stool so small that he had to kneel beside me during our ten minutes conversation (regulated to exactitude by a soldier with an open watch).

His bed consisted of a plank, with one blanket, although the coldness of the disused prison had made it necessary for a roaring fire in the commandant's room and in the guard room. He was also left without a light. Also, his last moments with his wife were not rendered more bearable by the presence of as many soldiers and inane officers as could be crammed into his cell – we who had never had enough time to say what we wanted to each other found that in the last ten minutes we couldn't talk at all.[8]

This was the 'hospital treatment' accorded to a man used to dining with cut glass and fine linen. The conditions for the other prisoners would have been much the same, but they were squeezed three and four to a cell. How constrained and awkward the newly-weds must have felt in that cell of alert ears. Perhaps it was for their benefit that Joseph Plunkett spoke glowingly, as he did, of Pearse, MacDonagh and Clarke, executed only that morning, and of The O'Rahilly, who had deprived Maxwell of another execution when he was shot by a sniper in the retreat from the GPO.

On the certificate of marriage, the address of Grace's husband was given as Kilmainham Prison. She gave, as her own, Muriel's address, 29 Oakley Road, though she appears to have been brought temporarily to Kate's home in Marino before going to the Plunkett residence, Larkfield House in Kimmage, where Nellie also went.

There was certainly no going back to Temple Villas. At that stage Isabella must have had her fill of republicanism. Already coping with the strain of a husband still invalided after his stroke, she now had a daughter, Nellie, in jail (a circumstance Isabella attributed to association with Countess Markievicz); her well-liked son-in-law,

Thomas, was dead, leaving her daughter, Muriel, a widow and her two grandchildren fatherless; and now Grace had contracted a marriage with a man about to die. In fact, Isabella, probably tired and a bit distraught, told a journalist that Grace 'was always a very headstrong and self-willed girl': if she was, one may wonder from whom these characteristics might have been inherited.

Fr Augustine described 4 May 1916 as 'a hurried morning'. Before 3 a.m. soldiers arrived at the Church Street Capuchin monastery and said that he and his fellow priests should come urgently to Kilmainham Gaol. Four were to be shot that morning, and the Governor had got a slight postponement to enable the priests to attend. *Hurry* was the word. Fr Augustine roused three of his fellow monks, Albert, Columbas and Sebastian, so that each of them could attend spiritually to the condemned men. There was no delay when their ministrations were completed, and the order of dying was Edward Daly, Willie Pearse, Michael O'Hanrahan and Joseph Plunkett.

Plunkett's niece, the late Eilís Dillon, made an extraordinary revelation regarding her uncle's execution. She was writing of Kilternan Abbey, where the Plunketts lived during their childhood, and of the nearest big house on the Dublin side, which was the home of the Protestant rector. His children and the Plunkett children played and grew up together in what Eilís Dillon called 'a warm friendship'. She went on to say:

As time went on the Plunkett family became involved in the IRB and the plans for The Rising of 1916. The Rector's sons, their old friends, naturally joined the British army at the outbreak of the 1914 war. In the fullness of time my oldest uncle was court-martialled and condemned to death and of all people his old boyhood friend was instructed to command the firing party which would execute him. He refused, was himself court-martialled and cashiered from the army and died not long afterwards, or so I have been told. But I have not checked the end of this painful story. There may have been many such incidents in those mad times.[9]

A substitute officer was appointed to the firing party, and the four Volunteers fell to their fire.

One of the most merciless acts of the authorities was to deprive Mrs Pearse of both her sons. The gentle, artistic Willie had actually pleaded 'guilty' at the trial. It is said in some analyses that he wished to stand by his brother. Be that as it may, the mortal remains of the four men were put on the waiting lorry and brought to join those of their three comrades who had died the day before. In Plunkett's case, gone with the rebel was also gone the small boy who had booed his Firhouse neighbour for lashing her horses, the youth who was offered the job of skating instructor in Cairo, the mystic poet who wrote one of the best-loved poems in Irish Christian literature, the international envoy of the Military Council of the IRB, the husband whose lady was his 'share of the world', and the commandant who had ignored his illness to encourage his men in the stifling, smoky atmosphere of the shelled GPO.

There was already a flood of commentary about the executions and the tragic bride, but years later Brendan Kennelly embraced both tragedies:

Surely Joseph Plunkett was right
to take Grace Gifford for a bride
in the untold desolation
of the morning that he died.
She – lover, wife and widow,
almost in a single breath –
understood. He, tautly poised
upon the threshold of his death,

179

knew simply that in little time

he'd stretch to frenzied lead,

prone, alone on the barrack square,

his unshared bridal bed.[10]

The executions proceeded with military efficiency, the firing parties consisting of six kneeling soldiers and six standing behind them. The prisoners were placed, blindfolded and with a white card marking the heart, some fifty feet from their executioners.

Major John MacBride had the doubtful privilege of being the only prisoner executed on 5 May. He famously asked not to be blindfolded because he said he had often looked down the barrels of English rifles (referring to his Boer War activities). Protocol overruled his request, and he was blindfolded like the others.

On 8 May, the executed were Seán Heuston, Michael Mallin, Éamonn Ceannt and Con Colbert. A pre-execution visitor to Colbert, Mrs Séamus Ó Mhurchada, noted that he had not even a plank bed or a mattress and that, on that bitterly cold night, he had only one blanket.[11] Fr Augustine, who was with Colbert to the last, felt obliged to correct a description of his end which had appeared in the *Evening Herald* on 31 May 1916. The Capuchin described how Colbert, reverent and calm, had suggested that the soldier preparing him for execution should perhaps pin the required white square a little higher to cover his heart. The kindly soldier, touched by the young Volunteer's bravery, asked if Colbert would shake his hand. Confused, Colbert extended his hand, which was shaken warmly by the soldier, who then proceeded to bind his prisoner's hands behind his back and gently blindfolded him.[12]

The loving thoughts of Nellie Gifford's commander at the Royal College of Surgeons, Michael Mallin, were with his wife ('pulse of my heart') and with their children: 'Our manly James, happy-go-lucky John, shy, warm Una, Daddy's girl and oh so little Joseph, my little man … he will rest in my arms no more.'[13] Una became a Loreto nun, and James and Joseph entered the Jesuit Order.

Éamonn Ceannt was the bridegroom who used French gold coins at his wedding ceremony to avoid using English sovereigns. He wrote in Irish to *Áine, a mhíle grádh* (Anne, my thousand loves). In Irish also he addresses a letter *Dom' mhaicín bhocht Rónán* (To my poor little son Ronan), asking him to look after his mother.[14]

On the eve of his execution, in a letter to his sister Mary, a Dominican nun, Seán Heuston urged her to teach Irish history 'as it should be taught'.[15] He was visited in his cell by his family and Fr Michael Browne (later Cardinal). A young British soldier who was present was so deeply affected he was crying. Theresa, Heuston's sister, heard one officer say, 'These men must be got away by three.'[16] It was, in fact, 3.45 p.m. when her brother was led to the execution yard, prayerful and serene, as described by Fr Albert. His last act on this earth, blindfolded, was to kiss the crucifix held by the priest.

It was generally felt that the twenty-five-year-old Heuston, not a signatory of the Proclamation and with a very small garrison, was executed because he had inflicted such a humiliating hold-up and such losses on the British troops trying to make their way down the Liffey quay, with numbers approximately 400 to his tiny ill-armed garrison of twenty plus. For whatever reason, Heuston was now dead, and by 4 p.m. the four bodies were on the lorry to Arbour Hill.

On 9 May, Thomas Kent was executed in Cork Detention Barracks. It is one of the vagaries of history that two of the sixteen executed, though not related, should bear the very un-Irish name of Kent. Even the Christian names of the Kents of Bawnard House, Castlelyons, County Cork, had no Gaelic resonance about them. Thomas, David, Richard and William were determinedly holed up in their home in the early hours of 2 May 1916, when news of the unwelcome Dublin surrender came through. A pitched battle ensued with a party of RIC men under Head Constable Rowe. The Kents' mother, eighty-four years old, loaded the guns for her sons. Head Constable Rowe and Richard Kent died in the battle, and Thomas, court-martialled on 4 May, was executed five days later. His last recorded words were, 'I have done my duty as a soldier of Ireland and in a few moments I hope to see the face of my God.'[17]

There are two versions of the death of James Connolly, the fourteenth and last of the rebel leaders to die in Kilmainham Gaol. At his court martial on 9 May 1916, Connolly stated his philosophy:

> We went out to break the connection between this country and the British Empire, and to establish an Irish Republic ... We succeeded in proving that Irishmen are prepared to die endeavouring to win for Ireland those national rights which the British government has been asking them to die to win for Belgium.

Three days later his gangrenous leg, operated on and 'mummified' with thick bandages, made his condition appreciably worse. Fr Aloysius found him tired and feverish during his visit to Dublin Castle, in whose military hospital Connolly had been placed following the surrender on 29 April. The priest told him to rest himself and that he would bring him Holy Communion the following morning. Anxious about his condition, the Franciscan contacted Captain Stanley, the officer in charge. The captain reminded him that the question of Connolly's execution was being debated at Westminster that evening and that there would be no more executions pending the outcome of that debate. Reassured, Fr Aloysius returned to the monastery at Church Street, but at 9 p.m. that night he received a call indicating that his services would be required at the Castle the next morning at 2 a.m. Despite international questioning of the executions, especially that of a very sick man, not only Connolly but also Mac Diarmada were to die the following day.

The most memorable characteristics of Mac Diarmada were his ease of manner and his sense of fun. Kathleen Clarke gave an account of the difference between a visit to her husband's tobacconist's shop by Pearse and one by Mac Diarmada. Pearse was all courtesy, raised his hat and enquired formally if Mr Clarke were available. Mac Diarmada, on the other hand, breezed in, gave her a hug and asked after Tom. He ignored, as far as he could, the lameness left by polio and happily flirted and laughed his way through social gatherings. But this extrovert held two things very dear: his faith and his love for Ireland. Just before his death he wrote of his abhorrence of Ireland's slavery. He declared he died 'bearing no malice to any man, and in perfect peace with Almighty God ... I meet death for Ireland's cause as I have worked for the same cause all my life.'[18] He so died at 3.45 p.m. on 12 May 1916.

About Connolly's execution, Fr Aloysius recorded that, having given Holy Communion to him at Dublin Castle, he accompanied the stretcher-bound patient in the ambulance, along with Fr Sebastian, to the execution yard at Kilmainham Gaol. Owing to his weakened condition, Connolly was to be shot just inside the gate instead of at the far end of the yard like the other prisoners. Fr Aloysius says very little of the actual execution, merely that he 'was present at the execution' and that he 'stood behind the firing party at the execution. Fr Eugene McCarthy chaplain to Kilmainham Gaol, anointed Connolly immediately after the shooting.' The usual version of Connolly's execution is that the prisoner was tied to a chair to prevent him from becoming an unstable target for the firing party. A much more distressing scenario, however, was recorded by the Sacristan to the Parish of St James during the Rising and its aftermath:

In giving a description of James Connolly's execution Fr McCarthy told me that the prisoner, who was in a bad condition, elected to stand like the rest but failed. He was then tied to a chair but slumped so much that he overbalanced. Finally, he was strapped to a stretcher and placed in a reclining position against the wall ... The sight left an indelible impression on Fr McCarthy.[19]

Westminster, subjected already to worldwide criticism about the executions, and Connolly's in particular, would be reluctant to have such a scene depicted abroad.

As against its inhumanity, Fr Aloysius recorded his appreciation, and that of James Connolly, for the kindness and consideration shown to them all by the British officer in charge at Dublin Castle. The priest also recorded observations made in his presence by Lord Powerscourt and a group of British officers, one of whom summed up their general feeling for the republicans: 'They were the cleanest and bravest lot of boys I have ever met.'[20]

One last execution: Roger Casement, shorn of his knighthood, was hanged in Pentonville Prison, after his trial for high treason in the High Court of Justice in London. Unlike the other fifteen executed, Casement had counsel to argue his case. But he argued his own with great skill, the nub of it being that Ireland meant much more to him than Empire and that loyalty to his country, which was Ireland, was held in Britain to be a crime. He was received into the Catholic Church by an Irish priest and was hanged on 3 August 1916. His was the sixteenth funeral of the executed.

Sixteen funerals and a wedding were to cause the first crack in a powerful empire's grip on Ireland, and in other of her colonies about the world.

19

FRONGOCH

World reaction to the executions was such that General Maxwell could not fulfil his intention of executing the rest of the 100 condemned men. Immediate arrangements were put in place, therefore, to imprison them in Britain, and they were among the approximately 2,000 prisoners who were marched via the Dublin docks to cattle ships waiting to take them away. They were the 'lucky' ones. As for the journey itself, it was hardly a case of 'dining at the captain's table'. Joseph Sweeney, one of the prisoners, described how they were put into the hold of the ship and recorded, 'we all got lousy as a result of the trip over to Holyhead'.[1]

Most of them eventually wound up in the Welsh village of Frongoch, in a disused, converted distillery. One of the prisoners there was to become a leader in the War of Independence: Michael Collins, the same man for whom Nellie Gifford had found a job, through her 'Burra' in Dawson Street, with the Plunkett family at Larkfield; the same Collins who had, with Commandant Brennan-Whitmore, helped their commander, Joseph Plunkett, from the nursing home at Mountjoy Square to take part in the Rising and who had brought Grace the gun from her fiancé.

It was Frongoch, more than any other place, that epitomised the unusual nature of the 1916 internments. In effect, the British government was unwittingly providing a kind of residential military university whose activities were orientated towards the creation of a new, free Ireland. Frongoch was simply buzzing with such activity, so, faced with all the problems attendant on acute overcrowding, the authorities arranged route marches and drills, both grist to the prisoners' mill in keeping them fit for the future fight for freedom. There was sport too: Gaelic football, skittles and handball. Sports days were organised, with track events. Hurling, where each player would have a weapon of sorts, was naturally excluded. At night, though it was lights out at 9.45 p.m., cards, draughts and chess were allowed. When gambling crept into the card-playing, their elected camp adjutant, W. J. Brennan-Whitmore, admonished them with a concluding phrase: 'In God's name do not let us smirch our beautiful ideals.'[2]

From 2 to 8 p.m., there being no shortage of imprisoned teachers, journalists and poets, classes were provided in five European languages, including Irish and Latin. There were also classes in maths, shorthand, bookkeeping, telegraphy and Irish history. On the cultural side, instruction was provided in choral singing, step-dancing, drama and debates in English and Irish. Creativity found expression in sketching, writing poetry and fashioning small works of art from the most unpromising material: bones from the kitchen were carved into perfectly contrived Celtic crosses, spoons were fashioned into bracelets, coins into rings and twine into quite beautiful macramé belts and bags.[3] Many homes in Ireland today have such relics, apart from those in museums.

Concerts were held regularly, including one to honour Wolfe Tone and another to honour the Manchester Martyrs. There were fiddle players, pipers, dancers, reciters of poetry, singers. The songs included the increasingly popular 'The Soldier's Song' as well as 'We Will Have Our Own Again', 'The West's Awake' and 'Gallant Men of '98'. A resounding finale was the singing of 'A Nation Once Again' by hundreds of lusty, untrained, emotional male voices. At times there were improvised 'plays', one of which included a mock fair, with the voices of various 'bids' for cattle as well as the sound of pigs grunting, donkeys braying and cows lowing.[4]

'The Last Post' was sounded, and the Catholics (the vast majority of the prisoners) knelt down to say the Rosary. No one has ever called the twentieth-century struggle for Irish freedom the Rosary Revolution, but this communal prayer forms part of contemporary descriptions time and again.

There were downsides to this prison life, especially as the cold winter approached. The food was largely appalling and inadequate, though parcels sent lovingly from home helped out. Lack of proper heating and ventilation were problems, the latter being so abusive of their health that a name was coined for their suffering: *Tired Frongoch Feeling*.

One of the most interesting of all the prisoners' activities was the cult of the autograph book. These books, from all the jails, bear similar characteristics. Some of the recorded names were to become significant in the Irish nation, then still only a dream, names such as Seán Mac an tSaoi, Earnáin de Blaghd and Éamon de Valera. There were bantering, and often very comic, stabs at poetic expression as well as nostalgic images of the Irish landscape and expressions of the sort of good fellowship that emerges from hardship shared. More than any of these, however, one positive, dominant note was struck: a commitment to renew the struggle on the men's release. Typical of this determination is that from Michael Brennan's autograph album:

Is mór dúinn na daoiní móra mar atáimíd féin ar ár glunaibh. Éirímís.
(Those we deem great seem only so because we are on our knees. Let us rise.)
The sword we hold may be broken, but we have not dropped the hilt.[5]

Reflecting this positivism, just as the Progressive League in New York was displacing Clan na Gael, so in Frongoch the first prisoners' council, which called itself the General Council or Civil Government of the Irish Republic, was replaced by a council comprising officers of the Irish Volunteers and the Citizen Army. The old council concerned itself with social matters, but it had become obvious that the real council was a military one, and so the military organisations took over. Their emphasis was on drill, smuggling in and studying military manuals, and studying firearms and tactics. Frongoch lacked Sandhurst's comfort and equipment but wanted for nothing in determination. Men such as Collins and Richard Mulcahy became the natural leaders for the struggle that lay ahead. Collins made it his business to learn what he could of the widespread locales from which the prisoners came – as far west as the Aran Islands (part of Mellows' Rebellion), as far north as Tyrone and as far south as his own Cork. Friendships were formed and characters quickly assessed. Collins met the nucleus of his squad and flying columns at Frongoch. All in all, one could say that the inmates graduated as Irish revolutionaries and that men such as Collins, Mulcahy and Tomás MacCurtain took their doctorates in leadership.

The Giffords' friend, Constance Markievicz, was jailed in Aylesbury, with none of the camaraderie of Frongoch and the other prisons. She wore prison garb, and her cellmate was a gangster's moll, 'Chicago May', who developed a surprising affection for the rebel aristocrat. Constance endured the rough prison garb, poor food, filthy bathtubs, appalling kitchen hygiene and forced labour. She was losing weight and one day stole and ate a raw turnip through sheer hunger. This woman, whom Isabella Gifford saw as a corrupting influence in her daughters' political involvement, was the last of the 1916 leaders to be released, in June 1917. She had left Ireland known by few and resented by many. She came back to a tumultuous reception in the streets of Dublin.

General Maxwell's conviction that the Easter executions would put paid to Ireland's dream of freedom proved utterly wrong, and this was nowhere more evident than in Donegal, where Pearse, MacDonagh and Plunkett had studied Irish. They had impressed the Gaelic speakers during their stay there, and one of them, young Niall Ó Baoighill, had such admiration for Joseph Plunkett that his friends called him Niall Pluincéad. This is how Pádraig Ó Dónaill describes it in *Scéala Éireann:* 'A special place should be reserved for the name of Niall Plunkett O'Boyle. He was called Plunkett because he thought so highly of Joseph Plunkett.'[6] Young Niall Pluincéad Ó Baoighill of the Rosses, who was to fight heroically the Black and Tans and to give his life for his ideals, was only one of innumerable instances of the effect that Maxwell's actions had on Irish minds. The War of Independence, conceived in Frongoch, was the fruit of the executions, and that war was to be served by the Gifford daughters, both at home and abroad, but not by the Gifford sons.

20

IMMEDIATE AFTERMATH

Nellie Gifford, being a member of the Royal College of Surgeons outpost, was marched with her fellow prisoners to Richmond Barracks and on to Kilmainham Gaol. She has left a description of her time there: three to a cell, she knew neither of her two cellmates but remembered taking charge, especially in the matter of frequent exercise. It was a bitterly cold spring, and she could see snow on the mountains when her cellmates lifted her up to the window to get a view. However, they were all fortunate in their icy lodgings in that the matron had suffragette leanings and was chuffed at having under her authority two countesses (Markievicz, before her transfer to Aylesbury, and Plunkett) and one lady doctor (a rarity in those days), Kathleen Lynn. She allowed her prisoners the much-needed luxury of hot baths and new blankets, there being no bedding in this deteriorating old prison when the sudden influx of women prisoners arrived. With as many other little alleviations as possible, she made their stay as comfortable as anyone could in the cold, damp fortress. Dr Lynn, before being deported with Countess Markievicz, thanked the matron on behalf of them all.

In other parts of the jail, not so cossetted, had been Nellie's brother-in-law Thomas MacDonagh and Joseph Plunkett. The Plunkett parents and their two younger sons, George and Jack, were also held in the jail. Nellie shared something else with the Plunkett family: both she and the Count had lost their official jobs as a result of their actions – he as director of the National Museum of Ireland and she as 'the cookin' woman'. Countess Plunkett met Nellie in the jail's exercise yard when she faced deportation to England with her husband and offered her the opportunity to stay at Larkfield House in Kimmage on her release, no doubt aware of Isabella's antipathy to the Rising. When news of a general release filtered through, the Countess approached Nellie again, kissed her affectionately and repeated that she would be welcome at Larkfield House and that the servants had been instructed to treat her as one of the family.

Josephine Plunkett was aware not only of Isabella's hostility but also of Frederick's illness. Her offer of hospitality to Nellie and also to Grace and many other members of the movement provides a warm, pleasant image of Joseph Plunkett's mother, despite less happy matters yet to come.[1] This daughter of the Gifford family was very glad of the proffered hospitality. On her release she returned to her home in Temple Villas, from which she had gone to St Stephen's Green as a member of the Citizen Army: Nellie's ring on the door was answered not by a maid but by Isabella herself. Her words were curt: 'You can't come in here.'[2]

Nellie wanted, above all, to say goodbye to her sick father, because already she had thoughts of leaving for America. She had been, after all, his favourite, the little girl whom he had brought with him on his trips as land agent to various rural areas, the youthful hostess who had attended him and his friends, the Yeats men, with her toddy and hot scones. Nellie was allowed to say her goodbyes to him, and she left her childhood home which she was not to see again. Her father she would also never see again. Without funds, she thought of Countess Plunkett's offer of hospitality and made her way to 'The House of Larks', so called, poetically, by her late brother-in-law, Joseph.

The Plunkett residence was an old-style mansion with a large entrance hall, stairs on either side and a balcony facing the entrance door. Nellie was not the only 'refugee'. Two other republican activists, the Skinnider sisters, were there along with other waifs and strays of Easter Week. It gave them a respite to consider how to pick up the threads of their unravelled lives. Grace Gifford – now Plunkett – was also at Larkfield. Grace became friendly with Joseph's younger sister, Fiona, and it was there that the aforementioned picture of Grace, cradling a kitten in her arms, was taken.

Nellie did not go straight to America from Larkfield House but went first to Liverpool where she stayed in the friendly home of a republican, Peter Murphy. Liam Mellows was also there, and his life was to become very much a part of the Giffords' lives in America. Mellows was a wanted man, and so Nellie dyed his hair blond, though he had not thought, as Nellie observed wryly, of his dark eyebrows and eyelashes.[3] The same Peter Murphy later wrote to *The Irish Press* in reply to some items which had appeared from Hanna Sheehy Skeffington, Frank Robbins and a Mr H. Harvey on the subject of Mellows' escape to the USA:

The facts were as follows: When Liam Mellows came to my house and made himself known to me, I undertook the work of getting him into America. He stayed at my house for a fortnight and I was with him night and day. The only ones who engineered his safe passage were myself and my *aide-de-camp* in the Shipping Federation. Many pleasant evenings we had, too, during that time; and Miss Nellie Gifford (now Mrs Donnelly) may remember them; for instance, the night she dyed Liam's hair and made him jump as she worked on his brows and lashes. She was also 'on the run' at the time, waiting to sail to America on a false passport, and they sailed within a few days of each other.

The Federation official and I arranged the details for Liam to sail as a coal-trimmer named John Atheridge with a doctored book on a tramp steamer. I left him at Lime Street station as a member of a scab crew, going to Devonport to join the 'tramp' which sailed to Barbados; and Mellows did not reach New York until six weeks later.[4]

One of the most remarkable – and most forgotten – men of the Rising, at the age of twenty Mellows had been given orders by Pearse before Easter Week to 'mobilise the west', which he unquestioningly proceeded to do – on his bicycle. The northern Volunteers had been instructed to join Mellows. On the fateful Easter Monday he had rallied 15,000 men for whom his supply of arms consisted of thirty rifles and seventy guns – one weapon to every 150 men, unless they were able to equip themselves with improvised weaponry. For all that, there did take place a confrontation in arms against Britain in the west of Ireland, and it has gone down in history as Mellows' Rising. Despite his troops' restricted numbers and paucity of arms, the youthful leader brought them success in capturing several RIC barracks, ambushing RIC and British army forces, cutting off communications, holding Moyode Castle in County Galway and generally creating mayhem in the west. When news of the surrender came, Mellows' Rising was in full swing, but he obeyed orders, disbanded his men and made good his escape, avoiding imprisonment. He was still a wanted man, however; hence the disguise.

When Nellie secretly reached New York in late October 1916, the 'terrible three' of Bridget Hamill's nursery were reunited. Gabriel and Ada, her partners in childhood adventures, received her with open arms, and, of course, 'John', the baby of Temple Villas, gave her just as hearty a welcome. It is easy to imagine the talk that went on into the small hours, that first night, the cups of tea, the tears, the memories. News of the Rising was a source of mixed emotions. How were Grace and Muriel bearing up? How were father and mother reacting? That the tricolour had flown over the GPO and other places seemed to be particularly welcome news: the symbol of a free Ireland. Gabriel, as the only unionist among them, must have felt the odd man out.

Ada, however, fired with enthusiasm, went about the business of celebrating the flag's symbolism in her own inimitable manner: after the Easter Rising she had bought three pieces of cloth – green, white and orange – and made what may have been the first Irish-American tricolour. In Carnegie Hall her home-made flag was flown conspicuously from the balcony and was greeted by a standing ovation, with delighted cheering and clapping of hands.[5] Happy with this outcome, the intrepid Ada mounted a trolley car the next morning, the flag concealed beneath her coat, and went onto the top deck. The driver could not understand the extraordinary respect his car was receiving as he passed the New York cops on the beat. They were giving him, or rather the improvised tricolour (of which he was unaware), a full military salute as the trolley car passed. Ada was delighted with her ploy and waved her flag with gusto.[6]

All the siblings' enthusiasm, however, was tempered by their losses: the tragic wedding, the execution of their brothers-in-law, Thomas and Joseph, who had been, for years, such a favourite with them all, even Isabella; the grief of their widowed sisters, Grace and Muriel. They grieved also at the thought of their small niece and nephew, Barbara and Donagh, left fatherless. Gabriel was part of this family grief, for all his unionist sympathies, nostalgically remembering the sketch he had done of Thomas. A particular shock had been the news of Grace's midnight wedding and her short-lived marriage to Joseph. A description of Nellie's imprisonment in Kilmainham Gaol brought more distress, and for 'John' there was the added grief of Countess Markievicz's jailing and deportation and the details of the deaths of the other leaders, especially the three men who had so encouraged her in her journalism; James Connolly, Seán Mac Diarmada (with his *Irish Freedom*) and especially Thomas Clarke, whose letter to John Devoy had been intended to cushion her entrance to American republican journalism. These were all personal sorrows in the midst of general Irish-American grieving.

Nevertheless, despite the initial reaction felt even by those outside the movement and the personal loss of those intimately involved, positive thinking began to subsume the sorrowing. Pádraig Pearse became the Irish standard bearer of the theory that martyred blood is an essential to gain freedom from a determined conqueror, but, in fact, the other executed men had, in either prose or poetry, in one way or another, subscribed to the same political theory – for it *was* politics, of the most dramatic kind. Why else would they have engaged in an armed confrontation whose optimum goal had been to hold out for six days? The 'red rose of patriotism' had been nourished by the execution squads as predicted and was putting out fresh blooms, even on another continent. It is obvious from Plunkett's mentioned reservations to Grace in the Moore Street letter and from Pearse's reason for surrender that these men had no bloodlust. Perhaps the defining factor was that there is a moral difference between a war of conquest and one of liberation.

Nellie was to find, as had 'John', that the relationships between the émigré Irish and their descendants, on the one hand, and the Irish emissaries of the movement who had come over from Ireland to seek help were not always perfect. Even the matter of Devoy's anti-feminism was not singular because American life was strangely out of tune with the freedoms women were gradually achieving in Ireland and in Europe generally. Even such a non-political matter as smoking, which in Ireland had become generally acceptable for women, was frowned upon in America, and there was even a law forbidding women to smoke in public.

Ada was never a prolific writer – she told her stories with her paintbrush – but both Nellie and 'John' have left interesting records of their time in America. 'John's' style (in *The Years Flew By*) is professional, but Nellie's unpublished notes have a compensatory warmth. She had not been six months in New York when she received an invitation from a professor and his wife to spend a week's vacation in their home. The journey took eight hours by train and then about one hour by horse transport. She spent a pleasant week, and the professor left her back to the station to catch her New York-bound return train. A train drew in while they were chatting, but he dismissed it as the wrong one. It was he who was wrong, however, as Nellie discovered to her grief, and she spent several cold, miserable hours on the bleak station platform waiting for the second New York train of the day. Not only did it not arrive at its destination until after midnight but it had no dining car, and she had had neither bite nor sup since an early breakfast. So she waited, huddled miserably, collar up against the extreme cold. The ticket collector saw her plight and shared his coffee and sandwiches with her. He said that if she had any difficulty on her arrival she was to return to the depot and they would fix her up somehow for the night. He also warned her that she was to speak to no one except a policeman. It is a very human story with its absent-minded professor and kind ticket collector, solicitous for a young woman's hunger and safety.[7]

Three of Isabella's daughters, Ada, Nellie and 'John', were now working hard in America for recognition of Ireland's nationhood. To this was added a plea for economic help for the bereaved families of the Volunteers who had been killed in the Rising. Hanna Sheehy Skeffington toured America with the objective of raising funds. The Gifford involvement in this push for help was not hugely significant, it is true, but it was consistent and determined, and there is no doubt that they made an impact in spreading the gospel of republicanism and in collecting funds for the almost destitute families of some of those executed or interned. In fact, in some areas of Irish-American republicanism the Gifford influence was to become quite dramatic.

At home, their three sisters, Kate, Muriel and Grace, were trying to come to terms with the deaths of the two executed men who had been husbands and brothers-in-law. Kate was the quiet stalwart in the background, her home in Philipsburgh Avenue on Dublin's northside a haven for Grace when she left Larkfield. Muriel, like many widows before and since, had to put aside her sorrow with two children to rear and a capital sum of £300, which constituted the assets her husband had left.

Grace found herself in a rather different position. She became a sort of icon as the story of her Kilmainham Gaol marriage filtered into the public consciousness. Some years ago, a senior citizen in Coolock, who wished to remain anonymous, recalled a poem she had learned at school in Castleplunkett, Castlerea, County Roscommon, in the 1920s:

Grace Gifford, I warn you.
The lion's revenge knows not justice nor law:
he will preach the world over of justice and freedom
while Ireland lies mangled and crushed 'neath his paw.

In a more romantic view, Father Leonard Feeney wrote emotionally:

Two dresses laid she by at night
and loosed her flowing hair.
She rose at dawn and stood in fright
and wondered which to wear?
Should it be white for her delight
or black for her despair.[8]

Grace's presence was enough to heighten the emotions at any function. In fact, of course, far more tragic was the plight of those widows, like Muriel, who had children to support, such as the widows of Thomas Clarke and Michael Mallin. However, Grace's slim, black-clad figure represented a particular tragedy, which was 'milked' by the organisers of the republican electioneering campaigns of 1916 and 1917. Her presence on a platform was a dynamic: at one recruitment drive in James' Street, after Pádraic Ó Conaire had spoken in Irish against recruitment, the crowd hoisted Grace onto the platform to voice a similar rejection in English. That was the end of any further recruitment that day. Ó Conaire's use of their ancient language reminded them of their nationhood; Grace was a reminder of what had occurred at Easter, and why.

She helped also with by-election posters for three Sinn Féin candidates, all successfully elected, including a North Roscommon seat won by her father-in-law Count Plunkett, and she was photographed with the Count and Countess, apparently electioneering. One of her election posters (below) featured many aspects of British misrule in Ireland. To show their contempt for British government, the three successful Sinn Féin elected victors refused to take their seats in Westminster.

In 1917, Crissie Doyle of Cumann na mBan wrote a book called *Women in Ancient and Modern Ireland.* Áine Ceannt wrote the preface, and Grace Plunkett designed the cover. Another instance of Grace using her art as a political weapon was her own recollection, in later years, of lying on the floor to paint a twenty-foot slogan streamer which was to stretch from one side of North Frederick Street to the other.

Though no one ever thought of Grace Gifford as a political animal, least of all herself, nevertheless she was elected to the Sinn Féin executive at its convention in the Mansion House on 19 April 1917. The three other women elected with her were Countess Markievicz, Mrs Kathleen Clarke and Dr Kathleen Lynn: a historic foursome.

The tragic deaths of the 1916 leaders left deep emotional wounds and also financial problems. While Thomas Clarke shared the poetic dreams of the poet philosophers, he had been too long associated with hardship not to ask economic questions as well. The leaders of the Rising all felt death was almost certain, but it was Clarke who had the foresight to deposit with his wife, Kathleen, the residue of the IRB funds, so arduously collected in America, Ireland and Britain, so that relief would be available for the inevitable financial distress. It amounted to £3,100, and on the Tuesday after her husband's execution his widow set up the Irish Volunteers Dependants' Fund, with offices at 1 College Green, Dublin. The committee comprised Kathleen herself and her sister Madge Daly, Áine Ceannt, Muriel Gifford-MacDonagh, Sheila Humphries (The O'Rahilly's niece), Con Colbert's sister Lila, Michael O'Hanrahan's sister Eily, and the Pearse brothers' mother, Margaret. Their twin aims were financial relief and keeping alive the national cause while the bulk of the remaining leaders were still imprisoned.

Another body, the Irish National Aid Association, represented those whose sympathies had been stirred by the executions but who had not taken part in the Rising. Amalgamation was an obvious step, but Kathleen Clarke agreed to their joining only when she was assured that no parliamentarians were involved.

The united bodies became known as the Irish National Aid and Volunteer Dependants' Fund, eventually administered by Michael Collins.[9] It had been decided to give a holiday by the sea to those women whose husbands had been executed. It was a good thought, bringing them together for mutual support and getting a healthy break from the problems of their daily living. The Association rented a beach house called 'Miramar' in Skerries, County Dublin. Other activities included distribution of food and clothes from America, delivering comfort parcels to camps and prisons, first-aid training and fundraising by flag days, fairs, *céilí móra* and concerts.

A brief account in the *Catholic Bulletin* of the widows' holiday at Miramar and of Muriel's conversion to Catholicism reads as follows: 'Mrs MacDonagh made her First Holy Communion on May 3rd 1917, the anniversary of her husband's execution, and since then has been a devout and weekly communicant ... During her stay in Skerries she and all her friends said the Rosary in Irish in common every night.'[10]

Unfortunately, the holiday which was to help heal the wounds of 1916 was the scene of another tragedy. On 9 July 1917, Muriel went swimming, got out of her depth, and drowned. She was not being foolhardy because she was a strong swimmer from her lessons with 'the swimmin' woman' in her youth at Greystones. There was a fanciful theory at the time about a plan she had to fly the tricolour from Shenick Island, just off the coast of Skerries. The story was that she had bound a tricolour flag around her body and meant to swim to Shenick to flaunt it from the Martello tower there, in defiance of the wireless station in the field at Holmpatrick behind the Old Mills Bakery, from which the very first intimation of the Rising was said to have been wired to Britain. It was manned by a 'naval' unit of four. In Easter Week 1916, the highly trained 5th

Battalion, Fingal Brigade, of the IRA, led by Tom Ashe, and with Richard Mulcahy as second-in-command, had been a most effective unit, with a capture tally of five barracks and nearly 100 RIC men. The wireless station was an obvious target, but Ashe obeyed Pearse's order to surrender, however reluctantly. Anyhow Jack McGowan, sent by Ashe to destroy the station, was too late and had to inform his officer-in-command that the South Staffordshire Regiment had arrived in Skerries Harbour.

One can see the emotional stimulation in all this for Muriel's alleged gesture – but no such flag was found on her person.

Far more plausible was the explanation of Paddy Halpin, long-time resident of Skerries.[11] He remembered boating near Shenick waters when he was in his twenties, and, seeing that the waters were getting treacherous, he got frightened, felt out of control and thought he might not make it home. That was the reality for Muriel and the tragedy for her children. They were collecting shells on the beach with their Aunt Grace when she noticed that her sister was in difficulty. She frantically alerted a boat's crew to the danger, and Jimmy O'Dea, the Dublin comedian, was among those who rushed, unsuccessfully, to help, but, too late, they succeeded only in retrieving Muriel's lifeless body. The first of the Gifford girls to marry, she was now the first to die.

Muriel's removal from Miramar to the railway station was given full military honours, accompanied by the Irish Volunteers of Skerries, Rush and Lusk, preceded by four priests, the last of whom, Fr Albert, represented the Capuchins, who a year before had been so close to the executed leaders during their last hours. Huge crowds formed to meet the Skerries train at Amiens Street, and there were enormous numbers the next evening at the Pro-Cathedral and the following morning at Glasnevin Cemetery. The funeral was filmed for the Irish Events Newsreel – the first indigenous newsreel produced in Ireland, the first issue of which appeared in cinemas from 17 July 1917. It showed the funeral procession, which took place on 12 July from the Pro-Cathedral to Glasnevin, accompanied by a wide representation that included Irish Volunteers in uniform, Cumann na mBan and Na Fianna.

Kate and Grace took the two orphaned children home to Kate's house in Fairview. The MacDonagh family, perhaps not aware of Muriel's recent conversion to Catholicism, were uneasy that the children might not get a sound Catholic education, as they saw it. One evening, as Kate and Grace were preparing to go out with Donagh and Barbara, their attention was diverted for a moment, and when they turned to the children they saw, to their astonishment, Donagh and Barbara being whisked away in a MacDonagh-driven car.[12] It was obvious that the little niece and nephew were going to a kind and loving home and the Giffords, especially Kate and Grace, never lost touch with them. The MacDonagh action seems shocking but may, perhaps, be excused by virtue of worry and prejudice. Kate was an exceptionally wise lady, and she elected to let matters rest.

If the south of Ireland was badly hit by imprisonments and deportation, the north of Ireland's innumerable Catholics lost both homes and jobs. Police turned a blind eye as the feared UVF revived. Catholics were stoned or even shot at in the street, and homes were raided.[13] Ireland was by no means at peace – north or south.

That year of 1917 brought another loss for the Gifford family. Just two months after his daughter Muriel's funeral, Frederick Gifford died on 19 September, in the old family home at Temple Villas after a protracted illness. Frederick had named Isabella and Kate as executors of his estate. Money was allocated meticulously among his children and his grandchildren, Eric (Claude's son), Donagh and Barbara. No one was deprived because of association with republicanism, and Frederick went to some pains in his will to explain that Gabriel was omitted because he had already received his share – presumably on his departure for America. The most curious thing about this will is the appendix by the Chief Registrar:

> This grant is made upon the condition that no portion of the assets shall be distributed or paid during the War to any beneficiary or creditor who is a German, Austro-Hungarian, Turkish or Bulgarian subject wherever resident, or to any one on his behalf, or to or on behalf of any person resident in Germany, Austria, Hungary, Turkey or Bulgaria or whatever nationality, without the express sanction of the Crown ...

Sidney Gifford-Czira ('John') was not excluded by virtue of her marriage to a Hungarian.

Isabella did her husband proud with the purchase of a double grave and a dignified headstone in Deansgrange Cemetery. She herself, however, elected to be buried in the modest single grave of her son, Gerald, in the cemetery of Mount Jerome in Harold's Cross – not with the man for whom she had borne thirteen children. She gave as her reason that she wanted to be buried 'near her neighbours', Rathmines being much nearer the Harold's Cross cemetery of Mount Jerome than the Deansgrange location.[14] Following a lonely childhood with neither parents nor siblings, Frederick Gifford, a kind, good man, now lies buried in isolation, the headstone lying broken across his grave.

After her father's death, Grace seemed to withdraw gradually a little into herself and became a less sociable person. Considering this young woman's personal bereavements within the relatively short span of sixteen years makes this understandable. In that time she had lost her younger brother Gerald, her husband Joseph, her brother-in-law Thomas, her sister Muriel and now her father Frederick. In two of the bereavements, those of Joseph and Muriel, she had been the last family member to speak to them. There is another alleged loss:

that of a miscarriage she is rumoured to have had during her stay at Larkfield. Her sister-in-law, Geraldine Plunkett Dillon, has recorded this supposed miscarriage, but several factors oppose its acceptance. First, Geraldine disliked Grace – a sort of sister-in-law animosity, exacerbated perhaps by the fact that she and Joseph had been so close when they lived together after one of his bouts of illness; second, in an interview given to me, Geraldine's daughter Blánaid Ó Brolcháin said that both her mother and her grandmother the Countess were inclined to divide the Gifford girls into two categories: the sweet ones (Kate and Muriel) and those with a 'rather sharp wit': Nellie, Grace and 'John'. Neither Geraldine nor the Countess had ever met Ada, but one may definitely presume she would not be grouped with Kate and Muriel.

The dislike also came out in the Plunkett annoyance at Grace, during her stay at Larkfield, because she converted a Paisley shawl she had found there into a cushion cover. They were also annoyed because she was 'always asking about an emerald ring'.[15] This was almost certainly the antique family heirloom that Grace had given to Joseph on their engagement. Another fact that makes the miscarriage allegation questionable is the suggestion Geraldine makes that Joseph might not have been the father of the child. The term 'bias' hovers about that suggestion, but there is perhaps some excuse in that a nonagenarian's memory, such as that of Geraldine, might have been inaccurate as well as prejudicial. Geraldine's brother Joseph would not have thanked his sister for that unacceptable suggestion of promiscuity against his beloved Grace. There is also the fact that Geraldine had left the family home on her marriage and before Grace arrived there, but Fiona, who was at Larkfield, denied that there was a pregnancy. Lastly, Nellie's daughter Maeve, who was very close to her Aunt Grace, never heard of the baby, and Joseph's nephew, Eoghan, totally rejected the idea.[16]

In any event, when all is said and done, it would not be regarded today as extraordinary for a couple so much in love, who were to have been married on Easter Sunday, to have anticipated their honeymoon. Eve-of-battle conceptions may not have been rare, with heightened emotions and the shadow of death threatening a final parting. Nevertheless, the allegation is unproven. Not at all uncertain, however, is the fact that a small Joseph or Josephine would have been a joy in Grace's lonely years and a grandchild for the Count and Countess to have perpetuated the goodness that made Joseph Plunkett the kind of man he was.

21

THE GIFFORDS CONFRONT THE VIGILANTES ... AND CLAN NA GAEL

Nellie had been less than three months in New York when she met a handsome young Irish-American named Joseph Donnelly, who was a master printer, publisher and a friend of James Connolly. He came from a comfortable, Catholic family in Omagh, County Tyrone, who owned a large drapery shop in the town. Joseph's older brother, Alec, practised law in Omagh, and his other brother, Nicholas, was a doctor in London. Nellie and Joseph had much in common: a family connection to the law, mutual grief at Connolly's execution, and, of course, their politics. It was a whirlwind romance, but it was also a mixed marriage, so they married in a registry-office ceremony. Countess Markievicz sent a beautiful Tara brooch to mark the occasion, and Liam Mellows wrote a delightful congratulatory letter to Nellie, his erstwhile hair colourist. A year later a daughter, Maeve, was born.

The young publisher had printed a magazine Connolly edited and did his friend proud in his edition of the labour leader's classic, *Labour in Irish History*. The book was tastefully presented in hardcover, in a soft reseda green, with details on cover and spine in gold lettering and with a narrow ribbon of green satin as a bookmark. A twin volume produced by the Donnelly Press was Connolly's *The Re-Conquest of Ireland*. Other publications included Hanna Sheehy Skeffington's

Democracy in Ireland and James Fintan Lalor's *The Rights of Ireland* and *Faith of a Felon*. A particular success from the Donnelly Press was *Ireland,* by a Canadian, Katherine Hughes. She went first to England as assistant to the agent general of Alberta in London. A visit to Ireland shocked her so deeply that she began careful economic research, leaning heavily on English documentation. Reviews of her book from such publications as the *Evening Post, America, The Gaelic American* and *The Monitor* were euphoric. Her dramatic conclusion was that England had been 'disembowelling' Ireland for over seven centuries. Her cure was Griffith's Sinn Féin policy, which, she claimed, would rescue Ireland from its subjection. In Irish-American circles there was universal praise for Hughes' *Ireland,* and *The Gaelic American* concludes its particularly complimentary review by praising the 'able' author and her 'directness, completeness and conciseness' with the following recommendation:

Ireland is a book which should be in the hands of every person interested in the cause of Irish liberty, every seeker after the truth about Ireland, whether he or she be Irish or American, and every citizen who believes that nations should not be governed against the will of their inhabitants by brute force.

This praise had added value when it is recalled that *The Gaelic American* was John Devoy's paper and that a woman's contribution was, for once, considered meritorious.

Not only did Nellie's husband specialise in Irish-Ireland material, but he also made his printing works at 164 East 37th Street available for meetings of a new Irish society called the Progressive League, a name embodying perhaps a veiled innuendo that older Irish societies were less than progressive in their leanings towards erecting monuments to the past rather than planning for the future. The League nurtured those rejected by Devoy and Clan na Gael. For instance, when Hanna

Sheehy Skeffington arrived in America with her seven-year-old son, Owen, she expected no encouragement from Devoy. He had treated her husband, Francis, as he had treated Casement – with suspicion. It seems unfair to pile such recriminations on this old man who had, with little help from anyone, achieved economic success. Nonetheless, he did seem to have his mind set against anyone with Protestant Ascendancy links, had deep reservations about 'political' women and seemed to see himself as head of an Irish government *in absentia*. The redoubtable Hanna, however, managed to address over 250 meetings on her American tour, including colleges and politicians, actively helped by the Gifford sisters. Naturally her dynamism was fired by the killing of her gentle, idealistic husband, but while she spoke everywhere of his murder by Bowen Colthurst, she spoke also of the proposed Peace Conference in Europe, at which she – and all Irish republicans – felt that Ireland's rights should be recognised. There was an idea that the leaders of the Rising, Pearse in particular, had been determined to hold out for at least five days, because that was the time that would be required for recognising a nascent nation, but it had proved only a theory as far as Europe was concerned.[1]

It is worth noting that in August 1916, Hanna had been offered an apology for her husband's murder, following a Royal Commission of Enquiry. Herbert Asquith had offered her £10,000 either as compensation or as a bribe to forego a public enquiry. Whatever the motive, she rejected the money. Even this did not endear her to Clan na Gael but Joseph Donnelly, the Giffords and the Progressive League gave her all the support she needed.

Apart from pushing for recognition at the peace conference of the Republic declared by Pearse, Hanna had a brief also to raise badly needed money for those who had been widowed and orphaned in the conflict and for those whose breadwinners had been jailed as a result of the Rising. Although President Wilson proclaimed that the rights of small nations must be upheld, his roots were in the unionist north of Ireland, so he did not see Ireland as a nation with sovereign rights. The Progressive League was well aware of this and, at a meeting in the printing works, it was decided that Joseph Donnelly should go to Washington to organise a monster meeting at which Hanna Sheehy Skeffington and Margaret Skinnider would speak, as well as John Devoy, Judge Daniel Colohan and other influential Irish Americans. Donnelly dismissed the suggestion, however, because he was so busy, and said that his wife should go, showing that he had faith in Nellie's organising abilities.

The committee decided to engage a theatre opposite the White House for the big event and a room for Nellie in the Ebbitt Hotel in which Hanna Sheehy Skeffington was staying. She was given a list of 'true Irishmen' but quickly became disillusioned when she discovered that many names on the list were unwilling to rock the boat of Wilson's war effort. Many Irish Americans were evasive or unwilling to speak at the meeting, and Nellie's correspondence with one Irish-American loyal luminary illustrates this perfectly. She had written to Judge Colohan to invite him to speak, but his secretary informed her by letter that the judge regretted he would be out of town at the time of the proposed meeting. An observation written by Nellie in Dublin, in 1953, notes caustically, 'At time he was invited to speak *no date* for meeting was set, even approximately.'[2]

The high point of Irish-American commitment to Ireland may well have been characterised by the amazing trilingual outdoor concert which had been held in New York on 30 April 1916, when news of the surrender had reached them. Even though this was before the executions, emotions ran high. Devoy and the widow of Jeremiah O'Donovan Rossa led the huge 'choir', comprising Irish Americans, German Americans and general anti-British sympathisers. Their very unusual repertoire included the American national anthem, 'Deutschland Über Alles', 'A Nation Once Again', 'Watch on the Rhine' and 'The Wearing of the Green'.

Nevertheless, a year was to elapse between that open-air concert and America's entry as Britain's First World War ally in April 1917. Even Irish Americans who had used Ada Gifford's spying activities, the work of her sister Nellie and the writings of her sister 'John' to help their campaign to promote Irish nationhood and keep America out of the war so that they would not become an ally of Britain, now reconsidered the situation. They had frustrated Anglo-American attempts to engage America in Europe up to 1917, but now the position was different. The American part of them resented the loss of their sailors to German U-boat attacks, after Germany started unrestricted attacks on all shipping in early 1917, just as much as the Irish part of them resented the post-Rising executions. Min Ryan, Nellie Gifford-Donnelly, her sisters 'John' and Ada, and others, became aware of growing reservations and of subtle barriers being erected to curb their activities. Such was the case when Hanna Sheehy Skeffington proposed to address a meeting in Carnegie Hall and it was obvious that details of her husband's murder were bound to rouse anti-British feeling. In an attempt to prevent her speaking she was advised that, allegedly, her voice would not carry at a meeting in this vast hall, but she ignored the advice and was given good coverage in the press for her address.

At times, however, the relationship between these two new-found bedfellows – Irish-American and English allies – was strained. Angry Irish and Irish-American demonstrators forced the withdrawal of the British film *Whom the Gods Would Destroy*, which depicted Irish Volunteers as apelike creatures, similar to the demeaning, racist cartoons of Irish people in *Punch*. When a Jewish cinema owner, unaware of the movie's implications, rented it, he needed only an explanation of its purpose – to demean the Irish race – to have no further truck with it.[3]

The lengths to which the anti-Irish element in America was prepared to go is perhaps best illustrated by Nellie's experience in rousing support for the Progressive League's monster meeting at the theatre opposite the White House. Leaflets giving the time and venue were printed, and it was part of Nellie's job to distribute them as widely as possible. Fortunately, a friend had warned her about the 'dirty tricks' brigade: Washington had never had such a big Irish meeting before, and it was possible that the booked venue might become mysteriously unavailable after the advertising leaflets had been printed. Nellie was advised to quietly book an alternative venue for the night, just in case. When she called ten days before the meeting to check if anything needed attention, the manager told her that he had told her committee in New York that the theatre would not now be available. However, Nellie continued to distribute her leaflets (called 'dodgers') and, on the big night, stood on the steps of the offending theatre with an Irish-American friend, displaying a notice in large lettering which read: BIG IRISH MEETING – TWO BLOCKS WEST, ONE BLOCK SOUTH. She and her friend chanted the message for good measure, directing the audience towards the 'shadow' venue she had booked. The Irish-American cops on duty were appreciative of her ingenuity and clapped her heartily (and somewhat boisterously) on the back. The meeting was an unqualified success.[4]

Another incident, this time in the behaviour of Clan na Gael towards Liam Mellows and Dr Patrick McCartan, riled the Giffords, who, along with those of the Irish-American community of more recent immigration, revered Mellows and called him their commandant. He was among the young group who sported a kilt and, when he had first come to America, was employed by Clan na Gael on *The Gaelic American*. A problem emerged from a New York meeting to celebrate the first anniversary of the Rising, just after America had entered the war. Before that, the Clan had been pro-German (and, *ipso facto*, anti-British), but platform speakers at the anniversary meeting urged the young men present – Irish and Irish

American – to join the American forces. Those who had fought in the Rising, including Mellows, dissented, and there was a stormy confrontation. The young rebels refused to take down their tricolour when the stewards ordered them to do so.

Meetings at which Mellows was chief speaker were organised to put forward the Irish republican viewpoint, but the American Vigilantes tried repeatedly to break up these meetings and incited mobs to attack the Irish by labelling them German spies. On one occasion they even tried to get American sailors to attack a Mellows meeting, but the Irish got to the Americans first to put their view, and it was the Vigilantes the sailors routed. The Vigilantes themselves were composed largely of Englishmen, led by the notorious Moffat.

Mellows lost his job on *The Gaelic American* on account of this, and, forced to take labouring work, he collapsed one day from starvation. Fr Magennis, a sympathiser of the Irish republican cause, gave him a job, and they became great friends. However, when Mellows and McCartan wanted to return to Ireland, Devoy and Colohan, anxious perhaps after the centenary confrontations, told them that there were no ships sailing for Europe and that they could not leave America. 'John' Gifford's friend, Lucie Haslau, knew otherwise, and 'John' made plans for the two men to leave. She warned Mellows to tell neither Colohan nor Devoy of the plan, but McCartan said, thinking of Devoy's past, that it 'would not be fair to the old man'. Because of this well-meaning kindness, both men were imprisoned in what was known as the 'Tombs' prison in Manhattan, as a result of the disclosure. The deceit of the Clan na Gael diehards was exacerbated by the fact that they had told both Nora Connolly and the Gifford sisters that neither Mellows nor McCartan wanted to be bailed out because, allegedly, they felt 'safe' in the Tombs.

Ada Gifford scotched that fabrication. She visited the prison, and Mellows assured her that they were most anxious to get out but that no one in the Clan had been willing to pay the bail. When 'John' heard this, she decided to approach Barney Murphy, a wealthy saloon owner who had Irish republican sympathies. He was responsive, but Colohan told him, 'You don't want to get mixed up in this German plot.' However, Murphy paid the bail and left the Clan. Mellows and McCartan were released.

Mellows' ingenuity had shown itself when, on his arrest, he had quietly managed to toss a bundle of incriminating papers through the window of the police car taking him away. He had also feigned non-recognition of the ship's captain of the vessel on which he was to have sailed for Europe. The captain later wrote and thanked him for the presence of mind which had saved him from a long imprisonment. The ability of Mellows and McCartan eventually to make that journey was, in no small measure, owing to Isabella Gifford's daughters: Ada, whose visit to the jail disclosed the Clan's duplicity, and 'John' who elicited the necessary bail from Barney Murphy for their release.

Sibling rivalry is not an uncommon human characteristic, and, in describing the fortunes of the Progressive League, we find great dissimilarity between the descriptions of involvement and responsibility in the League's affairs given by 'John' in *The Years Flew By* and by Nellie in her Washington notes. 'John's' summing up is given to absolutes and contains no reference to the part Nellie or her husband played:

A new organisation came into existence called the Progressive League. We set up a shop, the front part of which was devoted to Irish books, pamphlets, periodicals, postcards, badges and the usual propaganda material. This must have been 1918 because we had in the window a map which we used in the way that war maps were used at that time, by sticking pins with little flags to indicate the constituencies in which Sinn Féin were victorious in the election ... I was in charge of the premises and was chief saleswoman. The back part was used for committee meetings and lectures. We had many visitors and recruited new people into the movement.[5]

The ubiquitous 'we' of this extract supposedly covers Joseph Donnelly and his wife, who were not only involved in the setting up of the League but whose shop it was and who are not even mentioned in the extract.

Nellie's record is fuller and, on balance, seems more accurate. Though it is a minor point, the Progressive League seems to have been started in 1916. Nevertheless, Nellie, too, excludes from her record the fact that 'John' must have played an appreciable role in the League, given her longer stay in America and her journalistic and other contacts. Joseph Donnelly's premises were first used for the meetings; only when the membership swelled did they consider seeking bigger venues. They were not only attracting blue-collar workers (who, as Nellie recorded, gave generously from their limited means) but also the more well-heeled members of the Irish-American community, among them a society doctor, some of whose patients were among New York's wealthiest.

The meetings soon became an intrusion on the printing works, and Nellie had the job of finding a new venue, helped, she readily admitted, by a Mrs Hickey, a seasoned New Yorker. The premises they finally chose had a counter which served as a reception desk. Fired with 1916 anniversary zeal, Nellie lit small candles in the window before the patriots' portraits but the lights were quickly extinguished by order of a representative of the New York Police Department who told Nellie she was breaking the law by having naked lights in the window. She said he admonished her with a twinkle in his eye. Also, it was Nellie who the League sent to book the theatre for the monster meeting – very successfully, as has been seen.[6]

'John' could surely have spared Nellie a word of recognition in her summing up of the League in *The Years Flew By*. Perhaps this was due to the old nursery groupings, with Gabriel, Nellie and Ada being the 'middle three', as Nellie sometimes called them, excluding the 'babies', the youngest of whom was 'John'? The chronological groupings may have been accentuated by the fact that Nellie and Ada, of the six sisters, remained Protestant, like their brothers, while 'John', Grace, Muriel and Kate became Catholics. The split is there, even in the later correspondence of their middle age. However, leaving aside this different approach in recording the affairs of the Progressive League, it still remains obvious that all Isabella's 'Yankee' daughters were fighting Ireland's cause, in one way or another, while their fellow republicans at home were mending gaps and erecting new patriotic fences for the struggle yet to come.

While Nellie, Ada and 'John' Gifford had found their American work for Ireland greatly impeded since the USA had become Britain's ally in the Great War, at home Grace was increasingly finding herself a platform heroine against conscription. In fact, such proposed conscription, as Britain became desperate to fill the depleted trenches, became a boom time for Sinn Féin. Better to take your chance in an Irish ditch fighting for Ireland than in a French trench, gassed to death for England. Both Woodrow Wilson and Lloyd George later admitted that economics rather than German expansion per se was the motivation for their part in this war. In Ireland, their reasons did not matter: the executions of Easter Week and incidents such as the hunger-strike deaths of Tom Ashe and Terence MacSwiney had killed any residual desire to fight on England's side, in any war, for any reason, among an increasing number of the population.

22

THE WAR OF INDEPENDENCE

From the time of the Volunteer split of 1913, two sides, political and militant, ploughed individual furrows towards freeing Ireland. Paradoxically, it was the non-violent side, represented by Redmond's National Volunteers, who were responsible for the greater bloodshed – a substantial part of the 50,000 Irish who fought England's war in the deadly trenches for 'the freedom of a small nation' – not Ireland, but, allegedly, Belgium.

During the years immediately following the Rising, while an uneasy sort of peace prevailed, Dublin Castle kept close watch and detailed documentation on even the merely cultural aspects of the Gaelic revival.[1] The tumultuous welcome that greeted the returned prisoners who had been imprisoned after the Rising, underlined for Britain the damage the executions and internments had done to its power.

After Easter 1916, republicans continued to take part in the democratic elections. Time and again, Sinn Féin nominees, even those in British prisons, defeated Redmondite candidates at by-elections. Furious reaction from the authorities included police raids, confiscation of arms and criminalisation of seditious matter. Moreover, no blind eye was turned any more to manoeuvres or marches about the streets of Dublin.

Following the Sinn Féin Ard Fheis on 25 October 1917 where Éamon de Valera was elected president of the party, on 27 October delegates also met in Dublin to formally reorganise the Irish Volunteers, electing de Valera as President, Cathal Brugha as Chief of Staff and Michael Collins as Director of Organisation. The first two offices sounded more imposing, but, in the coming war, it was Collins who effectively ran the Volunteers.

A 'German Plot' was allegedly 'discovered' by Dublin Castle in May 1918, which accused some of the republican leaders of holding secret talks with the Germans: de Valera, Count Plunkett, Griffith and, in fact, the entire leadership of Sinn Féin, were jailed as a result. Collins was busy all over the country, using his Frongoch contacts to weave together a loyal, clever web of espionage agents. He could play the British at their own game with his men in state and semi-state posts – his biggest coup was placing some of them as detectives into the DMP. Collins' planned guerrilla tactics – not open warfare – would be swift, sly and utterly necessary, given the IRA's (as the Volunteers had become known) dearth of arms. He was born for the job, but this powerful, charismatic man – like all others – had his flaws: he seemed to disparage Plunkett when he faulted the strategy of Easter Week conceived by his commander (and civilian employer), despite Connolly's approval of its garrisoned, ring-around-the-city plan, the plan that has since been defended, never more admirably than by the professional soldier Colonel P. J. Hally.[2]

It was not as if guerrilla warfare, however brilliant a tool in Collins' hands, was something new in Ireland. Over the centuries, young rebels such as Rory O'More, Art MacMurrough Kavanagh, Fiaich McHugh O'Byrne and even Collins' contemporary, Liam Mellows, had seen its appropriateness. Plunkett certainly had been as well aware of this as Collins, but it took the dramatic GPO stand and the subsequent executions to rouse the spirit of nationalism. There would have been no Frongoch without Easter Week, and there would have been no safe houses without Frongoch and the executions.

The end of the First World War in November 1918 precipitated a

general election, and both Kate and Grace worked hard for the Sinn
Féin candidates. Then the fateful decision was made: that elected Sinn
Féin candidates would not take their seats at Westminster. They swept
the electoral board, winning more than twice the seats of the combined
other parties, and the first meeting of Dáil Éireann was held in the
Round Room of the Mansion House on 21 January 1919. They elected
de Valera as president of the First Dáil, ratified the Republic declared
at the GPO, voted in a constitution and declared a Bill of Rights. Some
of the elected members were in His Majesty's custody, some on the
run. For example, Éamon de Valera was still incarcerated in Lincoln
Jail in England. Collins decided to set up an escape in February 1919.
A key was duplicated, put in a cake and sent in to the prisoner. De
Valera escaped and presided at the second session of the First Dáil
in Dublin. The British found the whole idea of an Irish parliament
absurdly pretentious and were comfortable in the belief that the IRA
was dormant and that this ridiculous Dáil Éireann would not last.

Yet the scene outside the Mansion House on that historic day
should have given them food for thought. Dawson Street was chaotic,
with crowds milling about the Dáil's first meeting place, almost
opposite the IRA's headquarters, which had housed Nellie's 'Burra'.
There were two policing bodies keeping order: the *de jure* force, the
DMP, was using all its efforts to keep the trams going, and a de facto
policing body, the Irish Volunteers, was trying to keep the crowds
orderly.[3]

From then until the end of the War of Independence there was
a duplication of offices of state, one appointed by Westminster and
one by Dáil Éireann, which from then on met secretly, either in the
Mansion House (with escape routes carefully planned) or in a private
house in Mountjoy Square.

The Giffords had many friends and acquaintances in the First
Dáil: Grace's father-in-law, Count Plunkett, became Minister for
Foreign Affairs; Arthur Griffith, who had ferried them around

Dublin Bay and sponsored 'John' in her early republican writings, was Minister for Home Affairs; Countess Markievicz, their friend and Nellie's commandant at the Royal College of Surgeons, was Secretary for Labour; Michael Collins, who had brought the protective gun from Joseph Plunkett to Grace, was Secretary for Finance; Larry Ginnell, the cattle-rustling MP so admired by Nellie and 'John', was Minister for Propaganda and was also, appropriately, on a committee to consider land policy; Thomas MacDonagh's brother Joe was on a select committee to determine financing the Dáil.

During the August 1920 (private) session of the First Dáil, the oath of allegiance was administered to two other friends of the Giffords from America: Dr Patrick McCartan and Liam Mellows. The Giffords had not only got them out of jail but had also helped to facilitate their passage from America. Dr McCartan was appointed Envoy to the USA.

The financing of Dáil Éireann started with the initial loan of £2,000 made by Anna, sister of The O'Rahilly, in January 1919. In April of that year, Collins was given carte blanche '[w]ith further reference to Dáil to receive all monies which he can obtain from the proceeds of Anti-Conscription refunds, the issue of Republican Bonds, and all other sources for the purposes of Dáil, and to apply these monies to such specific subjects as the Ministry (when not reduced below five in number) shall unanimously approve'.

The funding from then on was a conglomerate affair, amalgamating the great generosity both from the Irish abroad, especially in America, and from those at home, even on the lower rungs of the economic ladder. Some of the better-off Irish citizens (such as the O'Dalys of Limerick) paid income tax directly to Dáil Éireann. The money flowed in, despite British suppression of newspapers carrying advertisements for the first Dáil national loan. Total trust was involved, as instanced by the occasion when Daithí Ó Donnachadha, Secretary to the Trustees of Dáil Éireann, ran from a raid by British forces in Limerick, carrying in his suitcase the considerable Dáil loan money that had just been checked by George Clancy, newly elected mayor of the city. Ó Donnachadha deliberately took a first-class carriage to Dublin the next morning and read his newspaper with apparent calm during a search which did not include first-class passengers. He stoically smoked a cigar while the headlines before his startled eyes told him that Mayor Clancy and others had been murdered by Auxiliaries during the raid from which he had barely escaped, complete with the precious suitcase resting snugly on the rack above, which might well have been the object of the raid. The amateur handling of this money obviously relied on people of honour. Kate Gifford-Wilson was such a person and was appointed a registrar of the Dáil loan. (Her husband, Walter Wilson, had fallen victim to the Spanish flu epidemic.)

The Sinn Féin courts illustrate one of the most successful and intriguing duplications of offices of state from that time. The English system of justice, administered with bias and selectivity over the centuries, with rigged juries and hanging judges such as Peter the Packer, held all the paraphernalia of law.[4] Theirs was the magnificent Four Courts overlooking the Liffey, as well as various, dignified-looking halls of justice about the country; they had also their retinue of bewigged and begowned barristers and judges. Sinn Féin had none of these and held its courts in schoolhouses and kitchens in townlands and villages. What that party did have, however, was the allegiance of the people, who recognised these makeshift courts and shunned the others which were, from then on, used generally only by those known as 'West Britons'. So, around a kitchen table, with an oil lamp for light, land disputes were settled in a country where land was much more than just wealth and where many a lifelong vendetta had ensued over as trivial a matter as the right to cross a ditch. The litigants almost always accepted the courts' decisions, even if they favoured the landlords. The soul of the nation was lodged firmly in the parliament that called itself Dáil Éireann.

The directive issued by Dublin Castle to all Irish newspapers, that the proceedings of Dáil Éireann were not to be reported, was ignored. The various streams of labour, politics, militancy and culture were in confluence, making for the harbour of freedom. Anything Britain could do at that stage was to prove merely a stopgap to this great, historic flood.

The IRA had been dormant since the Rising, it was true, with just three of its supporters killed and several RIC wounded in minor skirmishes about the country. However, on the day the First Dáil sat, the sound of rifle and revolver shots broke the still air at a quarry in Soloheadbeg, not far from Tipperary town. These were the first (unauthorised) volleys fired in the often brutal, though ultimately successful, War of Independence. The shots came from the rifle of Seán Treacy and the revolvers of Dan Breen and Seamus Robinson, all members of the 3rd Tipperary Brigade of the IRA. They had hoped to capture what proved to be 160 pounds of gelignite destined for the quarry. The IRA men knew that, apart from two civilian 'loaders', there were only two armed RIC men to guard the consignment en route from Tipperary town. The plan was to ambush the small party near the quarry. In his autobiography, *My Fight for Irish Freedom*, Dan Breen stated that the plan was to ambush *only*, with no intent to kill, but that the RIC men reached for their weapons, and, in reaction to this unexpected resistance, fatal shots were fired and the two servants of the Crown lay dead on the roadway.[5] However, Breen later left a personal statement in the Bureau of Military History to the effect that Treacy and he had deliberately set out to kill the police escort, members of the most important force of their enemies.[6] Their deaths would start the war for freedom. One reaction to this statement has been the suggestion that Breen might have regarded it as an honour to have kick-started the war which ultimately brought and end to British rule in Ireland. Whatever the reasons, the shooting of the RIC men was a very quick, physical reaction, and a blueprint for many of the incidents of the ensuing war.

Owing to comments from Breen about the shooting a price of £10,000 was put on his head. It was never collected, but Tipperary town was earmarked for special attention: fairs and markets were forbidden, the roads and lanes of Tipperary were alive with manned lorries and the hated vehicles nicknamed black marias, and even an aeroplane was used to try to spot the three marked men.

But this episode was like a rallying cry to the IRA all over Ireland. By the end of December 1919, eighteen RIC men had been killed and the more remote RIC barracks were being closed. Retirement from the force was rife and recruitment negligible. British reaction, allegedly 'unofficial', was crude and violent. When a jury refused to find the death of an ambushed soldier 'murder', 200 British soldiers inflicted damage on the jury members' houses to the extent of £3,000. No one was brought to account. The IRA continued raids for arms; the British raided for insurgents.

Atrocities multiplied. Tomás MacCurtain, Lord Mayor of Cork and Officer Commanding Cork No. 1 Brigade of the IRA, was shot in front of his family; the unionists in the north of Ireland conducted pogroms against the nationalists, who were unprotected by either the British army or the police. Volunteers for the depleted RIC had to be found in England and came to Ireland with no training and a makeshift uniform, the mixed colouring of which gave them the feared name of the Black and Tans. In July 1920, an elite corps under General Crozier arrived, armed with bayonets and revolvers. On 14 October, Seán Treacy (of the Soloheadbeg raid) was shot in Dublin's Abbey Street; eleven days later, Terence MacSwiney, who had succeeded Tomás MacCurtain as Lord Mayor of Cork, died on hunger strike following a seventy-three-day fast; on 1 November, Kevin Barry, an eighteen-year-old medical student, was hanged in Mountjoy Jail followed by the hanging of eight more IRA men. There was dismayed world reaction to the deaths of MacSwiney and Barry. British prestige abroad was low, yet Lloyd George was foolish enough to boast, on 9 November, 'we have murder by the throat'.

Twelve days later, Collins organised the assassination of fourteen British agents who had been sent over to wipe out Collins' own men. The response was predictable: three men, Dick McKee, Peadar Clancy and Conor Clune, were shot 'while attempting to escape' according to the official report. One of the men, Clune, was entirely innocent. Their bodies showed bruises and marks consistent with bayoneting. They were formally buried, with Collins acting as a pall-bearer. A still more dramatic reaction came from the Castle, however; the Black and Tans went to Croke Park where a Gaelic football match was being played. They mounted a machine gun and indiscriminately shot into the crowd. Twelve people died and sixty were injured. The retaliation earned the name of 'Bloody Sunday'.

Then, at Kilmichael, County Cork, on 28 November 1920, Tom Barry and members of his Cork No. 3 Brigade ambushed two army lorries manned by Auxiliaries. A false 'surrender' by the Auxiliaries ended up with two of Barry's men dead. After this hoax, Barry ordered all eighteen Auxiliaries to be shot, burned the two lorries and confiscated the British arms and ammunition. A most instructive comment was made by Barry in the aftermath of this fateful incident: he said his men were so disturbed by the outcome that he had to march them up and down the road to regain their equilibrium.[7] It is a reminder that these were not hardened, professional soldiers; they were small farmers, tradesmen, labourers – amateurs – pitted against well-armed, paid troops from Britain.

The demands on Collins were enormous, trying to keep up the pressure with an extremely small army holding very limited arms. When de Valera returned from a fund-raising trip to America there were still raids and street murders. Drunken Black and Tans walked the streets. In England the hard-line diehards were losing ground, and their compatriots felt a peaceful solution should be sought to the Irish problem.

In a general election in May 1921, Sinn Féin was victorious in the south, except for Trinity College's four seats. The status quo became less defendable, but Britain held on, and Dáil Éireann declared its elected authority. Then, later that month, the Dublin Brigade of the IRA burned down the Custom House, destroying the documentation which had recorded the ruling of Ireland for centuries. The following month, Lloyd George proposed a peace conference. On 11 July 1921, a truce was declared. The IRA, strained to the limit for both active servicemen and munitions, was quietly relieved. So were those who hated warfare, with all its loss of lives.

Twenty thousand British troops had confronted the sparsely numbered flying columns and active service units of the IRA. Michael Collins, 'the Big Fella', had finally won. In hunting terms, the mighty British lion of heraldry had been trapped in what might well be termed a military mousetrap.

In most wars, women are less prone than men to take an active part in armed conflict; in Ireland, women played a hands-on part in the struggle and even when their men were executed or interned, there were none more anxious than the women of Cumann na mBan, the Irish Citizen Army and even those outside these organisations, to carry on the fight. Among them, to the end of the War of Independence and even beyond, were the names of Lynn, Despard, Pearse, Clarke, Ceannt, Plunkett, Sheehy Skeffington, Carney, Mac Diarmada, Daly, MacBride, Connolly, Markievicz, fFrench-Mullen, Molony, (Ada) Gifford, Gifford-Plunkett, Gifford-Donnelly, Gifford-Wilson, Gifford-Czira and Comerford, all working for a free Ireland. Grace continued to publish her political cartoons, while Ada and 'John' kept up their work in America to raise support for Ireland's freedom. At this point, however, Nellie was back in Ireland with a small daughter to rear, so she was unable to play an active role for the time being.

23

THE TREATY AND
ITS BITTER FRUIT

The word 'treaty' has a peaceful connotation, but the Treaty ending the Irish War of Independence brought in its train a bitter civil war and the jailing and killing of those on either side who had been, for three years, comrades-in-arms, friends, neighbours, even brothers, united against their common foe.

When the Irish delegates signed the Treaty, the families of the executed leaders of Easter Week would have none of it, and its narrow victory in Dáil Éireann – sixty-four votes to fifty-seven – reflected the scope of the division and was a warning of the horror that was to come. Cumann na mBan returned an overwhelming 419 votes to 63 against the Treaty. None of the Gifford daughters favoured it.

Both sides, for and against, tried at first to compromise, but they also began to build up their armies. The new pro-Treaty Free State, as it was called, was eventually recruiting its soldiers at the rate of 300 per day under the Minister for Defence, Richard Mulcahy, and the Chief of Staff, Eoin O'Duffy. Both men were determined to defeat the anti-Treaty republican army. Many of their Free State recruits were desperate for a paid job.

The opposing, republican army was under the leadership of men such as Liam Lynch, Liam Mellows, Cathal Brugha, Oscar Traynor, Tom Barry and Rory O'Connor. De Valera joined them later. Revolted at what was happening to fellow nationalists in the north of Ireland they aimed to form a military dictatorship and to continue the War of Independence. The Westminster government was seen by them as duping the Treatyites with their promise of a boundary commission, which was supposed to safeguard northern nationalists.

In the south, sporadic killings were inflicted on and suffered by both the Free State and republican armies, but just as the shots at Soloheadbeg historically marked the opening of the War of Independence, so the occupation of the Four Courts by a detachment of the republican army marked the first significant confrontation of the Civil War.

R. M. Fox's metaphorical reference to Grace Gifford-Plunkett on the roof of the Four Courts in June 1922, blowing a bugle to summon support for the republicans has, on occasion, been taken literally: 'Sometimes she seems a gay, graceful figure … with a reed to her lips, dancing on; then I see her as the young bugler – whom I saw perched on the dome of the Four Courts in 1922.'[1]

But Grace climbed no roofs nor did she use either bugle or reed. She did speak, however, with her artist's brush and, apart from her letters to the press disavowing the Treaty, produced one of her devastating political cartoons: Griffith had called Erskine Childers, who opposed the Treaty, a 'damned Englishman'. Her cartoon depicts Griffith and Collins, dressed in Union Jack swimsuits, entering a sea marked 'British Citizenship'. Childers is turning back to the shore marked 'Irish republicanism'. Neither Griffith nor Collins can have been amused.

During those Civil War years, women republicans remained active and supportive of the men, just as they had during Easter Week and during the War of Independence. The statistics bear this out: hundreds of women were jailed by the Free State. In fact, what might be called the Easter Week names, such as Pearse, Plunkett, Clarke, Connolly, Mac Diarmada, MacDonagh, Heuston, MacBride, Mallin, de Valera, Daly and Ceannt never featured on pro-Treaty documents.

The women of these families remained opposed to the Treaty, an embarrassing thorn in the Free State body politic's side. The anti-Treatyites included all five of the surviving Gifford daughters, in both Ireland and America.

Nellie came back to Ireland in 1920 with her little daughter, Maeve. Her marriage was in trouble, and her mother, Isabella, who had accepted, only with some misgivings, the marriage of her other daughter, Muriel, in a Catholic church, asked of Nellie's wedding, 'What can you expect of a registry-office ceremony?'

Sadly, Maeve, child of the union, retained only one vague, visual image of the handsome father she so resembled – a man coming towards her with a balloon in his hand, so pathetically reminiscent of the memory of her cousin, Donagh MacDonagh, of his father Thomas: 'A uniformed figure on a motorbike, who gave me a red wagon.'[2] Joseph Donnelly gave support for Maeve until she was about twelve years of age. His mother had also disapproved of the American registry-office marriage, and the Gifford family believed that on his visits home she deliberately introduced him to marriageable Catholic girls.[3] Joseph did remarry, though Nellie never did, and had another daughter with his second wife. She and her daughter contacted Maeve years later. Maeve, however, though she availed of an invitation to their home, and though her father and mother were long dead at this stage, did not pursue the proffered friendship. She felt it would be disloyal to her mother.[4]

Things were tight for Nellie financially, but she acquired a small red-brick house near the Royal Canal in Drumcondra and let a side flat to supplement her income. Her heart and soul were anti-Treaty, but she felt, trying to cope with straitened circumstances and with her young daughter to rear, that she could not devote time to politics as she had in her single days.

'John' had a different approach. When she returned to Ireland in 1922, the Civil War was under way. Her American marriage was over, the result of both partners wanting to settle in their native place: Arpad Czira went back to Hungary, leaving her with four-year-old Finian to rear. Despite that, she immediately identified herself with the 'Mothers', anti-Treatyites one and all, who were given this patronising title by the 'Free Staters', though their relationship with the jailed or executed anti-Treaty leaders might have been mother, daughter, cousin, girlfriend or sister. 'John's' relationship was sister-in-law – twice over – to Plunkett and MacDonagh, and that made her a 'Mother'.

Before leaving for America, apart from her budding career as a republican journalist, 'John' had always identified herself enthusiastically with many facets of the nationalist movement, from her submission of republican articles to Arthur Griffith in her teens, to her membership of Inghínidhe na hÉireann with a view to helping to launch the women's paper which became *Bean na hÉireann*, seeking the betterment of women's health and lives. There was later a general enlargement and embodiment of aims so that the Inghínidhe could amalgamate with Cumann na nGaelhael and later with the Dungannon Clubs (IRB). That organisation's paper, *Irish Freedom*, replaced *Bean na hÉireann*, but 'John' was as happy writing for one as the other. She had never contributed to such publications as *The Irish Homestead*, whose images were those of the 'Irish Coleen' in red petticoat and shawl, and she had alienated the Irish Women's Franchise League (IWFL) – the Irish suffragettes – by her suggestion that a significant move for Irish women would be another all-Irish school. As far as the IWFL was concerned, the Gaelicisation of Irish women took second place to their enfranchisement. An interesting letter to the *Irish Independent* from Grace repudiates the necessity for a women's franchise league because the 1916 Proclamation clearly granted women equal status.

Despite this and other differences, 'John' had become a distinctive voice in republican women's circles, and, before her American sojourn, she had reached executive status in Sinn Féin, along with Jenny Wyse Power and Countess Markievicz. Her fellow republicans welcomed her back from America with open arms, and she reciprocated with unbounded enthusiasm and commitment. She was a women before her time in that she managed to blend motherhood with her socio-political involvements, much as many women have learned to do with business and home today. Both she, Kate and Grace were frequent participants in the Sackville Street meetings of the 'Mothers', held symbolically on the debris of the ruined buildings. They were members of the Women's Prisoners' Defence League (WPDL) and frequently held public protests, including vigils outside jails against executions by the Irish Free State. They also smuggled guns, offered safe houses to republicans and sent food parcels to jailed prisoners. Grace lent her artistic talent by producing political cartoons, as usual, and Kate her general ability, especially on the matter of money management. It was like a continuation of the War of Independence, only the foe had changed: no longer Britain but now the Irish Free State.

The government of that state, however, was slowly but determinedly closing in on them. The WPDL was prorogued in January 1923, so the ladies changed the name and held a march in Sackville Street. Helena Molony mounted a lorry marked 'The People's Rights Association' and quoted Shakespeare to remind the Free State authorities – and her audience – 'a rose by any other name would smell as sweet'. So they continued shifting name and venue. These intrepid women seemed immune to being hosed with water and shot at and having their houses raided. Nor did they confine their activities to Dublin: 'John' Gifford-Czira addressed a protest meeting outside Portlaoise Jail.

In March 1922, before the taking of the Four Courts by the republican side, Grace wrote a letter to the press rebutting the expressed opinion of a journalist who urged acceptance of the Treaty as comparable to Plunkett marching with his white flag of surrender: both, he argued, were an acceptance of reality. Grace replied: 'Joseph Plunkett, marching with white flag, surrendered – but only his body. He gave his life rather than take a shameful oath of allegiance to the Empire.'[5] She argued that the Republic, including the whole of Ireland, was a living reality, the Treaty its abandonment. In another letter, however, she defends the contributions of both Griffith and de Valera to win that republic and asks that this not be forgotten in rejecting the Treaty, though nevertheless urging its rejection. This magnanimity changed, however, with the outbreak of the Civil War.

The lives lost in the Civil War were Ireland's loss. The execution of men such as Liam Mellows, Erskine Childers, Rory O'Connor, Joe McKelvey and Richard Barrett made a sad litany. In July 1922, Grace was among those who distributed leaflets at the funeral of Cathal Brugha, asking anyone who repudiated his anti-Treaty republicanism to leave the funeral obsequies. It was harsh, but many Free Staters obeyed and left.

Utterly strained with it all, Arthur Griffith died in August 1922. Ten days later, the bitterness reached its nadir with the ambush and killing of Griffith's fellow negotiator, Michael Collins, on 22 August. The country mourned Collins, on both sides of the divide. His commitment to the north of Ireland had never wavered, and he stated publicly in Armagh, before the London negotiations, 'No matter what the future may bring, we shall not desert you.'[6] Commandant General Tom Barry of the republican army gave an extraordinary description of the reaction of 1,000 republican prisoners in Kilmainham Gaol when they heard that their political opponent, Collins, had been killed by fellow republicans: 'There was a stunned silence before the prisoners spontaneously knelt down and recited the Rosary for their "enemy", and their one-time colleague and friend.'[7]

Griffith's successor, W. T. Cosgrave, handed over the quelling of the Civil War to the military authorities. They responded ruthlessly, some argue necessarily so, to avoid the possibility of anarchy. Violence of self-termed idealists was met by ruthlessness of self-termed realists. Deputy Seán Hales was assassinated by republicans. In retaliation, and without trial, Joseph McKelvey, Rory O'Connor, Liam Mellows and Richard Barrett fell to the executioner's bullets in Mountjoy Jail, and, at that, even Free Staters felt uneasy. But the authorities were inexorable. Apart from the executions, about 12,000 republicans were jailed, of whom 400 were women, amongst them two of the Giffords, Kate and Grace.

On 6 February 1923, a party of Free State soldiers arrived at Kate's residence at Philipsburgh Avenue and proceeded to ransack the house, looking for guns and incriminating documents. According to Maeve Donnelly, she, her mother (Nellie), her aunts Kate, Grace and 'John', with 'John's' five-year-old son Finian, were present when the raid occurred. Grace was the more distressed of the two resident sisters, and Maeve remembered this distress, and the reason for it.[8] Grace was a tidy person, and in the pre-nylon days ladies wore lisle stockings, which, when laddered, were carefully darned. Grace had two drawers for her stockings: one for her best (unladdered) and another for her second-best (darned). The sight of a young Free State soldier rooting through these drawers to seek a gun or papers was the cause of her chagrin. Had she known what lay in store for both her and Kate at Kilmainham Gaol, she might have been less concerned at the rummaging through her hosiery.

It was, of course, Grace's second visit to the awful jail. She knew well the discomforts of the dark old place – its dripping walls, lack of heating and small cells, without even basic furnishing. Yet there was another side to its discomforts: a sort of Frongochian comradeship got the women through their ordeal as it had done the men of Easter Week who were detained in Wales. Their friends were there, including Maud Gonne and also Dr Kathleen Lynn, for whom it was a second incarceration. They could have food parcels sent in, and their friends and family gathered outside on the banks of the River Camac to communicate with them, long distance, as shown in the picture of the hatted women visitors by John B. Yeats, shouting up their news to the prisoners who had gone to the top landing to 'communicate'. Yeats painted this while Grace and Kate were prisoners at Kilmainham.

Grace herself, in contrast, produced a typically humorous sketch of the visits – a 'glass half full' approach to the visiting restriction in contrast to Yeats' 'glass half empty' representation. Mary Kelly lived with her six children at 155 North Circular Road. Hers was a 'safe house' and had been visited by Connolly, Pearse, MacDonagh and, later, by Kate Gifford. When Grace was arrested during the Civil War, she left with Mary the gun which Joseph Plunkett had sent her on Easter Saturday 1916, which had been leant to Nellie for the Rising. Throughout Grace's imprisonment in Kilmainham Gaol during the Civil War, the Kelly family – Mary, her six children and the family dog Rex – visited her every Sunday, bringing her baked delicacies to supplement the prison diet. Eddie, the eldest boy, a teenager, brought her paints and brushes with which she painted the 'Kilmainham Madonna'. In a not untypical impish mood, Grace imagined and painted one visit where Rex became a lion or a panther, vaulting effortlessly over the closed jail gate. On his back was the eldest daughter, May, nonchalantly doing a dance, and with her are her five siblings – Eddie, Jack, Frances, Gus and Ciarán.[9] The guard, a Free State soldier, his rifle abandoned, is holding up his hands in surrender. Ciarán, the baby, is guiding their transporter with the reins and issuing an order: 'Put us down at Kilmainham please.' The sketch reflects Grace's buoyancy of spirit and also her appreciation of how those visits must have brightened the jail's drabness. Grace showed her appreciation materially when her circumstances improved, and she brought Mary with her on a holiday to Rothesay in Scotland, and later on, to Paris.

The sketch's light-heartedness was remembered over the years by three of the Kelly family. A phone call to an Australian Kelly, Aoife Duffy (née Kelly), was successful: the long-lost picture had been found, and its copy, reproduced below, adds a very interesting example of Grace's sense of humour.

With the paints and brushes which young Eddie Kelly had brought to the jail, Grace painted on her cell wall a very beautiful image of the Madonna and Child. Unfortunately, the deterioration of the prison before its restoration did not spare this historic picture. I have a very vague memory of seeing it as a child when I played in the crumbling jail with the caretaker's daughter. There is a misted, distant sense of its being more 'comfortable' than the usual images of the Virgin depicted in statues and 'holy pictures' – those blue-eyed ladies with doll-like babies in their arms.

In a Kerry newspaper a picture appeared with the caption *Copy of the Original Kilmainham Madonna*. Miss Hannah O'Connor of Ballymullen had admired the Madonna on her fellow prisoner's wall in 1923. Grace thanked her and promised to do an exact copy in Hannah's autograph book. She drew a very beautiful and very Jewish Madonna for Hannah, signing it with her name and address. It is not an *exact* copy: the infant – and cloak – are different, but there is still a palpable warmth about it, a little reminiscent of certain Renaissance Madonnas and Russian icons.[10]

In the 1960s, Thomas Ryan, later President of the Royal Hibernian Academy of Arts, was asked to 'retouch' the picture. At that stage, replastering, dampness and neglect had done their worst, and it is hardly fair to question, as has been done, Ryan's renovative work. He decided to change the Virgin's cloak from blue to red, and though she herself lacks the free-flowing gracefulness that characterised the original, the artist still avoided the relative lifelessness of the twentieth-century Italian madonnas.

As the men had done in Frongoch, the women imprisoned in Kilmainham also had classes – in language, history and dancing. Autograph books, a legacy of Frongoch, featured also in Kilmainham. Both Grace and Kate contributed. In some, Kate expressed determination for the cause; others she merely signed – bilingually, giving her prison number and her two prisons:

Cáit Bean Mich Liaim
(Catherine Gifford Wilson – 3102)
Kilmainham and NDU 29.viii.1923

In another of the autograph books, the NDU (North Dublin Union), an institution to which they were transferred in 1923, is described as Tig na mBocht (the House of the Poor), which, of course, it had been before it was taken over by the British military in 1918, and there is later a brief reference to an incident in prison: Grace is described as trying to escape through barbed wire by throwing a blanket over it. It would not have been out of character.[11]

In May 1923, the women organised a special commemorative ceremony of Easter Week: they marched into the execution yard, Grace unfurled the tricolour, laid a wreath and spoke about her husband; Éamonn Ceannt's sister-in-law spoke of his part in the Rising; and, to conclude the sad little ceremony, the Rosary was led by The O'Rahilly's sister-in-law. That emotional day concluded with a concert and included a recital of compositions by Plunkett and Pearse. It ended with the singing of 'Amhrán na bhFiann', an enthusiastic translation of 'The Soldier's Song' which became the Irish national anthem.

The pleasantries of Kilmainham Gaol helped, but the women were all to taste the darker side of imprisonment. The historian Dorothy Macardle was a prisoner there at the time and has left a vivid and disturbing picture of their efforts to stay in the prison to comfort two of the prisoners on hunger strike: Kate O'Callaghan (widow of Michael, Lord Mayor of Limerick) and Mary MacSwiney (sister of Terence, Lord Mayor of Cork) who had argued that the Treaty was 'the one unforgivable crime that has ever been committed by representatives of the people of Ireland'.[12] The women feared that the two hunger strikers would be force-fed if they were left as the only prisoners in the jail. Both women were quite ill, especially Kate O'Callaghan, and the other prisoners used to sing outside their cells every evening to cheer them up. The bulk of the women had already won some privileges by going on hunger strike, but this time the authorities seemed adamant: they wanted to isolate O'Callaghan and MacSwiney. At 3 p.m. one afternoon, the nineteenth day of the hunger strike, the Governor notified the objectors that the prisoners were to be removed to the NDU, the former poorhouse, that evening, leaving the two hunger strikers behind. The reaction was unanimous: the hunger strikers must first be released. At 9 p.m., Governor Begley sent word that eighty-one prisoners would be removed, if necessary by force. When asked if woman-beating was a soldier's work, he replied, unbelievably, 'I have beaten my wife.'[13] Then word came to the women of Kate O'Callaghan's release but not of Mary MacSwiney's. They decided on a sit-in on the top gallery of the compound, with instructions to resist but not attack and to avoid helping each other: passive but determined resistance was the idea, and no one was to cry out, to avoid upsetting the remaining hunger striker. They knelt and said the Rosary.

After that they stood three deep and sang Mary MacSwiney's favourite songs, fastening the doors of the cells as they waited in darkness, only one lit window illuminating the huge place. At 10 p.m. their leaders were called to Mr O'Neill, Governor of the NDU. Much softer in his approach than the wife-beating Begley, he promised that if eighty-one would go quietly to the NDU, no others would be sent away before Miss MacSwiney and that if they failed to cooperate, their privileges would be withdrawn. They had ten minutes to decide. Their answer was 'No'!

Next, a worried matron, carrying a lighted taper, came to tell them that it was not soldiers but the Criminal Investigation Division and military police who would eject them, both of whose members she described as 'horrible men'. She was wasting her well-intentioned intervention, but she was right about the men, whose violent rush up the stairs brought down the first two girls, crushed and bruised. Dorothy Macardle's words describe what followed:

Our Commandant, Mrs Gordon, was the next to be attacked. It was hard not to go to her rescue. She clung to the iron bars, the men beat her hands with their clenched fists again and again; that failed to make her loose her hold, and they struck her twice in the chest; then one took her head and beat it against the iron bars. I think she was unconscious after that; I saw her dragged by the soldiers down the stairs, all across the compound and out at the gate.

The men seemed skilled; they had many methods. Some twisted the girls' arms, some bent back their thumbs; one who seized Iseult Stuart kicked her on the stairs with his knee. Brigid O'Mullane, Sheila Hartnett, Roisín Ryan and Melina Phelan were kicked by a Criminal Investigation Department man who used his feet. Florence MacDermott was disabled by a blow on the ankle with a revolver; Annie McKeown, one of the smallest and youngest, was pulled downstairs and kicked, perhaps accidentally, on the head. One girl had her finger bitten. Sheila Bowen fell with a heart attack. Lily Dunn and May O'Toole, who have been very ill, fainted; they do not know where they were struck. There was one man with a blackened face. When my own turn came, after I had been dragged from the railings, a great hand closed on my face, blinding and stifling me, and thrust me back down to the ground among trampling feet. I heard someone who saw it scream and wondered how Miss MacSwiney would bear the noise. After that I remember being carried by two or three men and flung down in the surgery to be searched. Mrs Wilson and Mrs Gordon were there, their faces bleeding. One of the women searchers was screaming at them like a drunkard in Camden Street on a Saturday night; she struck Mrs Gordon in the face. In spite of a few violent efforts to pinion us they did not persist in searching us. They had had their lesson in Mountjoy. They contented themselves with removing watches, fountain pens and brooches, kicking Peg Flanagan and beating Kathleen O'Carroll on the head with her shoe.

I stood in the passage then, waiting for the girls to be flung out, one by one. None were frightened or overcome, but many were half-fainting. Lena O'Doherty had been struck on the mouth; one man had thrust a finger down Moira Broderick's throat. Many of the men were smoking all the time. Some soldiers who were on guard there looked wretched; the wardresses were bringing us cups of water; they were crying. The prison doctor seemed amused at the spectacle until the women were finally thrown into the waiting lorry, the whole procedure having taken five hours.[14]

The Mrs Wilson whose face was bleeding was, of course, Kate, the eldest Gifford daughter.

It was an ugly business, but just as ugly, in a different sense, was the observation of Kevin O'Higgins. He was Minister for Home Affairs at the time and referred contemptuously to the Kilmainham Gaol disturbances as being caused by 'hysterical young women who ought to be playing five-fingered exercises or helping their mothers with the brasses'. He conveniently forgot the huge input of the Easter Week women, from Countess Markievicz's command at the Royal College of Surgeons to the lone figure of Nurse O'Farrell carrying her improvised white flag of surrender through streets where she could have met her end at any moment. O'Higgins is said to have been the last minister to sign the execution order for the four republicans shot in Mountjoy in 1922, perhaps reluctantly because one of them, Rory O'Connor, had been best man at his wedding.

O'Higgins himself did not die immediately when shot by republicans after the Civil War had ended, and Roger Gannon, son of Bill Gannon, one of the three assassins of O'Higgins in 1927, approached his daughter Una O'Higgins O'Malley with an account of the shooting given to him by his father during his last illness.[15] The story was that O'Higgins had told his attackers that he understood why they had shot him, that he forgave them, but that this had to be the last killing.

Doubts have been expressed about the authenticity of this account, but Roger Gannon's disclosure emerged as a result of a commemorative Mass, publicly announced for 'Kevin O'Higgins, Tim Coughlan, Archie Doyle and Bill Gannon'. Its bonding of the assassinated and the assassins touched a chord and prompted Roger Gannon to pass on his story, and the account indicates magnanimity in O'Higgins, despite the four executions and despite his contemptuous dismissal of the role of republican women in the War of Independence.

The jailed women at Kilmainham, including Isabella's imprisoned daughters, Kate and Grace, were all duly bundled into the NDU from the lorries that had taken them from Kilmainham Gaol. Documents held there indicate a difference made between the sisters. The records are as follows:

Philipsburgh Ave. Fairview – PLUNKETT, MRS GRACE; date of
arrival 6/2/23. Also brought to NDU. Release date 13/8/23.
Prisoner number 3101.

Philipsburgh Ave. Fairview – WILSON, MRS CATHERINE; date
of arrival 6/2/23. Also brought to NDU. Release date 28/9/23.
Released from NDU, number 3102.[16]

These dates show that Grace was imprisoned for almost seven months. There is no indication why Kate was detained in prison for almost seven weeks longer than Grace, who, in fact, on being told of her forthcoming release, informed the authorities that she refused to go without her sister. They told her that she could either go quietly or be removed by force. No doubt Kate counselled her to go. Perhaps Grace's presence was an embarrassment to the Free State, her being the widow of a signatory of the Proclamation. Whatever the reason, her sister's detention order makes strange reading:

SAORSTAT EIREANN

Public Safety (Emergency Powers) Act, 1923
Public Safety (Emergency Powers) No. 2 Act, 1923

ORDER BY THE MINISTER FOR DEFENCE

WHEREAS Catherine Wilson, 49 Philipsburg Av, Fairview (hereinafter referred to as the prisoner) was at the date of the passing of the PUBLIC SAFETY (EMERGENCY POWERS) ACT, 1923, detained in Military Custody.

AND WHEREAS the prisoner was not before the passing of the said Act sentenced to any term of imprisonment of penal servitude by any tribunal established by the Military Authorities.

AND WHEREAS I am of opinion that the public safety would be endangered by the prisoner being set at liberty.

NOW I RISTEARD UA MAOLCHATHA an Executive Minister within the meaning of the said Act do hereby order and direct that the prisoner be detained in custody under the said Act until further order but not after the expiration of the said Act.

Dated this 8th day of August 1923.
Signed: Ristéard Ua Maolchata
Minister for Defence
Member of the Executive Council
of Saorstát Éireann.

This most gracious lady a danger to public safety? One wonders from where did *this* Kate emerge. The faces of all who knew her lit up at the mention of her name: soft-voiced gentleness, kindness and academic ability were the images conveyed – the paragon of the Gifford family, one of the Giffords whom Countess Plunkett and her daughter Geraldine found charming, the chosen executrix for both her parents' wills, the respected language teacher, the mother figure for her junior siblings, the lady who was to leave behind her a legacy of loving memories – *this* Kate Gifford-Wilson was considered by the Free State to be a danger to public safety. What on earth did her mother think of her solid Kate being described as a danger to the state? Of the six unlikely rebels whom Isabella had bred and nurtured, this lady was surely the most unlikely to be such a danger.

When Kate was released from the NDU on 28 September 1923, the Civil War was already over. Liam Lynch was dead, and Frank Aiken, the new Chief of Staff of the IRA, declared a ceasefire for republicans. The Irish Free State was tottering along awkwardly but determinedly, a nation taking its first steps of partial freedom since the twelfth century.

24

PICKING UP THE PIECES

After the Easter Week Rising, thousands of people had been affected deeply in their daily lives, both materially and psychologically. After the Civil War, however, the situation was immeasurably worse. The heroism and dedication of the executed in 1916 had been moral weapons against the foe, but many of the events of the Civil War were causes of shame.

It was a long time since Isabella's dolman-wearing callers had visited Temple Villas to exchange gossipy titbits about their sons fighting in far-flung corners of the globe for their empire. What would Isabella have had to offer after the Civil War, apart from tea and cakes? – two sons-in-law executed by His Majesty's government; two daughters married in Catholic churches; two in registry offices in America; one even married in Kilmainham Gaol; another daughter jailed after fighting with the working classes in the Royal College of Surgeons; two daughters jailed during the Civil War, the elder, Kate, held for being a menace to public safety. Fortunately, perhaps, Isabella's hospitality had been curtailed because of Frederick's illness, and, after his death, the house being obviously too big for her, she had arranged for its sale, with Kate's help, for £900 and purchased a house at Lower Beechwood Avenue costing less than half that amount. She later moved to Cambridge Road, Rathmines.

Grace did not stay with her mother again but elected, instead, to live in Mary Kelly's house on the North Circular Road until Kate's release. The sisters then resumed living together until Grace felt able to rent a place of her own. Likewise, when 'John' and Finian had returned from America in 1922, it was to Kate's home they had gone. In fact, though Grace and Nellie lived in straitened circumstances, 'John' seemed to be in the worst financial plight. There was some correspondence with her husband, Arpad, but there is no suggestion that he ever helped her financially after they separated. 'John' plunged straight away into her republican journalism and in the 1920s wrote for *An Phoblacht* with the *mostly* controlled passion of good journalism. In 1927, in an article entitled 'The Dark Days', she examined how the events of 1916 had moulded Irish public opinion (including her own), and she eulogised the leaders, especially Clarke, Pearse and MacDonagh.[1] In a continuing series of articles, one in the 24 September issue of *An Phoblacht* of that same year, 'John' gloried in the fact that Ireland had shown India the way to oppose England's enlisting campaigns. In yet another 1927 issue she told the story of Liam Mellows in America. In the 1930s, ardour undimmed, she covered such topics as the United Irishmen, Irish revolutionaries who served in the British army and Wolfe Tone's rejection of sectarianism. In 1932, she wrote a gleeful article on how the WPDL had managed to get around all the proclamations against it and how they had still held their meetings in the ruins of Sackville Street, or wherever they could. In 1934, she published an article on 'Tone and the Ascendancy' which had been rejected by *The Irish Press*. A later article in *An Phoblacht* considered the origin of the phrase 'the wearing of the green', and elsewhere she wrote of Frongoch. For all her work with the WPDL, 'John', unlike her sisters, never spent a day in jail.

Although old animosities die hard, and although none of Isabella's daughters went to live with her, the advent of grandchildren in such a situation brings a healing grace. Finian, Maeve, Donagh and Barbara were brought to meet their grandmother, and Claude's son, Eric,

243

stayed with her for a while in Cambridge Road. Maeve never heard a cross word from her gran, but nevertheless got an impression of She Who Must Be Obeyed.[2]

For all that, Isabella's will, set down after Frederick's death, makes poignant reading. She died on 15 January 1932.[3] Kate and Claude were executors, and Kate and Ada beneficiaries, as well as her sons, Claude, Liebert and Edward Cecil, the last two of whom had lost contact with the family. Gabriel is excluded because, Isabella specifically states, he had got his inheritance on going to America. Although her maid is remembered, as well as a couple of charities, there is the notable exclusion of 'John', Grace and Nellie. Even more revealing, perhaps, is the residual legatee, Liebert. Perhaps because he seems to have been less academic than his brothers, he had quickly dropped his solicitor's apprenticeship for a hoped-for enrolment in the Merchant Navy. A mother often especially reaches out to the less talented of her children, and, apart from her financial stipulations, Isabella concluded her will by a clause that might be called wishful thinking: 'If my son, Liebert, should return before I die I should wish him to mind my little dog as long as she lives. If my said son Liebert should not return before I die, I should wish my said dog to be put out of life by chloroform.'[4]

When he was President of Ireland, Seán T. Ó Ceallaigh wrote to Máire Comerford explaining how he had become involved in arrangements for the convening of the First Dáil.[5] It had been decided to invite all elected representatives of whatever party to attend, and he was appointed chairman of the subcommittee put in charge of arrangements. That subcommittee included J. J. Walsh, TD, a lively GAA Corkman, who shared the dream of both Michael Davitt and Éamon de Valera of reviving the old Tailteann Games of ancient Ireland, which had first taken place in 632 BC and which, they all felt, would be an effective badge of nationhood. Davitt's dream included not only sports events but also literary, artistic and industrial contributions. De Valera materialised the dream by voting an astonishing £10,000 in the First Dáil towards its realisation. Twice during the Civil War the games were postponed, but Walsh persevered and in 1924 they attracted, as they were meant to, people of Irish birth and descent from all over the world, as well as other Celtic peoples. He appointed Kate Gifford-Wilson as General Secretary because he had known her as Registrar of the First Dáil Loan, and her degree in languages and experience abroad in teaching made her an ideal appointee. *The Handbook and Syllabus of the Games*, published by Kenny's Advertising Agency, is proof of her excellence. Competitors came from Australia, New Zealand, America, Canada, South Africa and Europe. Between 2 and 18 August, twenty-one sporting events, ranging from archery to yachting, had to be accommodated and experts appointed to adjudicate. There were also five cultural categories: arts and crafts, dancing, literature, music and national costume. Under these sections some of the prizewinners were John S. Keating, RHA; Letitia M. Hamilton, RHA; Harry Clarke (the stained-glass maestro) and Evelyn Gleeson, tapestry weaver.[6]

Aonach Tailteann, as it was to be officially called, became an acclaimed success in every possible way – except financially. The efficiency of its organisation, relying to a great extent on the calibre of its general secretary, Kate Gifford-Wilson, was universally acknowledged. The games were held again in 1928 and 1932 but, despite much goodwill and genuine efforts to keep them going, they were discontinued.

During those three resurrected years it was obvious that, with the four-year gaps between, the staff would not be fully occupied. However, Walsh had another job for Kate. His portfolios of Postmaster General and Minister for Posts and Telegraphs put him in charge of initiating the proposed broadcasting service for the Irish Free State, and, though he was distinctly Gaelic-minded in his approach to what the cultural mode of the proposed station should be, he was not above conferring with Britain on its experiences of this new communications medium. During the preliminary preparations Kate was invaluable because she was capable of coping with both the work of assistant director and woman's organiser, although she was paid only as a temporary clerk.

The appointed director was Seamus Clandillon, a civil servant who hired Kate (no doubt on Walsh's recommendation) and also his own daughter, both without authorisation from the Department of Finance. He was told that the appointments would not be ratified. The power of both Walsh, 'Minister for Broadcasting', and its first director, Clandillon, were thus negated, and Clandillon's daughter and Kate were discharged at the behest of Ernest Blythe, Minister for Finance. Kate applied formally for the post of woman's organiser but was unsuccessful.[7]

There is often, in these post Civil War years, a hint of old animosities in the granting or withholding of privilege. The two ladies appointed as replacements for Kate and Clandillon's daughter were both married, and in those years that was supposed to bar them. In one of Nellie's old news cuttings P. S. O'Hegarty observes: 'Maighred [sic] Ní Ghráda succeeded Mrs Wilson.' Ní Ghráda used her maiden name for her work, which cloaked the ineligibility of her married status.[8]

'John' took the new medium in her stride. In an article entitled 'The Broadcast in Ireland's Eye', her use of irony is cleverly sustained.[9] While reassuring the Irish people of their country's prosperity, she argues, President Cosgrave should rustle the cheque showing the ministerial pay into the mike, and election promises should be woven into a programme of *Farmers' Bedtime Stories*. She feels a fog signal would usefully introduce an explanatory programme on the Boundary Question and a West British choir could sing 'The Exisle of Erin' while a Catholic choir from the north might choose 'Questions to a Free State'.

On 4 July 1926, in a programme commemorating American Independence Day, Frank Fay quoted Pitt's speech on England's war with America, F. R. Higgins recited the poetry of Walt Whitman, 'Marching through Georgia' was rousingly played, and 'John Brennan' spoke on American history. She was also responsible for an Irish ballads programme with Gerald Crofts in 1927: the series was called *The Ballad History of Ireland* and was typical of the station's determination to sustain a distinctively Irish approach.

There was often heated debate about such matters as the insufficiency of Irish music and language in the station's programmes, and 'John' became what was called 'the victim of political discrimination'. In 1927, a letter of hers was published in *The Irish Times*, in which she questioned the action of a senator who had mentioned the Volunteers in relation to the assassination of Kevin O'Higgins. Some members of that organisation were to be tried for O'Higgins' death. Her words were, 'If it were to become customary to attack prisoners in the Press or in the parliament while their cases are still *sub judice*, trial by jury would become a mere mockery.' The day after the letter appeared, 'John' was told that her services were no longer required in 2RN (the station). Her case was remembered in 1946 when Noel Harnett found himself in a somewhat similar position. Passions ran understandably high after O'Higgins' assassination, and 'John' did not regain a much-needed source of income for six years. Seán T. Ó Ceallaigh raised her case in the Dáil and said that, though their political opinions differed, he felt her treatment was harsh. His plea was fruitless, and she was not reinstated until Fianna Fáil came to power in 1932.

But if two of the Gifford rebels had been dismissed from the broadcasting station, there was a third member of the family waiting in the wings to play her part. Nellie was beset by financially harassing times, and she put pen to paper and launched herself as a freelance journalist. An early offering by 'EGD' (Eileen Gifford-Donnelly) entitled 'The Child and the Cinema' appeared in an advertising broadsheet in Omagh on 26 December 1926.[10] In January 1927, Máiréad Ní Ghráda (*bean stúirthóir* [woman's organiser]) – the lady who replaced Kate as woman's organiser in 2RN – wrote to Nellie accepting her play for children called *Mr Tipps*.

On 22 March 1927, the broadcasting programmes advertised in the daily papers included this item: '6.30 Uair I dtir na n-Óg: Songs Síle Ní Ceallaigh; stories Mrs Donnelly and F. J. McCormack.' On 30 March of that year, Nellie received another letter from Máiréad Ní Ghráda offering a May booking for her story *Wow*, an engaging tale about a dog. In July 1933, the Director of the Talks Branch of the station had his office in the GPO in O'Connell Street, opposite the hotel Nellie had entered with James Larkin twenty years before. He wrote offering an engagement to broadcast her submitted talk called *Suggestions*. It was to last fifteen minutes and carried a fee of two guineas. Her ideas included tourist attractions, waste usage and disposal and lowered kerbs for invalids – all matters later realised and some derived from what she had seen in America.

In June 1935, the same director engaged her for a series of four talks but advised that since she would be speaking for the station rather than as an outsider, it would be better to delete any suggestions about the government. He was even prepared to ask for funds for any suggestions sought from listeners. The talks started in August. In October, C. Ní Rodaigh, who also described her office as *bean stúirthóir* and who was the other replacement when Kate and Clandillon's daughter were dismissed, wrote accepting three of Nellie's children's stories for broadcasting: *Wow* (a repeat from 1927), *Mr Tipps* (also a repeat) and *Whistling Michael*.[11]

Apart from her success in broadcasting, Nellie also wrote short stories for adults. Her style and subject matter were in complete contrast to 'John's' academic and finely researched work. They included *The Turf Fire* and a moving story about a little girl called

Sheila, the eldest of eight though not yet ten herself: her widowed mother, desperate to make ends meet, has to break the news to the little girl that she must be 'farmed out' to work in another house to put some pennies in the family 'till'. Nellie had seen such poverty in Meath and succeeds movingly in conveying the anguish involved in what amounted to child labour in Ireland in the very early twentieth century. Occasionally she wrote profiles, such as that on Lady Gregory, and dabbled in poetry, though verse was not her forte. All this helped the precarious family budget, and, along with many others all over Ireland, these Gifford sisters were finding their feet in the matter of economic survival in a new state which had major problems, financial and otherwise, to resolve.

25

THE NEW STATE REMEMBERS
... AND FORGETS

After the Civil War, the Gifford daughters, diehard republicans though they were, tried to settle down with the new Irish Free State. One of the state's first hurdles to be vaulted was the Army Mutiny of 1924, dealt with decisively by W. T. Cosgrave. Unfortunately, in 1925, he accepted the iniquitous Boundary Commission Report, which spawned eighty years of strife in Northern Ireland. The following year, de Valera formed a new political party, Fianna Fáil, which was republican and firmly anti-boundary. When he entered the Dáil in 1927, de Valera took the Oath of Allegiance to Britain as 'an empty formula', only so as to have the presence and power to abolish it. Significantly, in 1929, the first Prime Minister of Northern Ireland, Lord Craigavon, dropped proportional representation in Northern Ireland – an electoral system that would have helped the nationalists there. In 1930, Ireland became a member of the League of Nations Council, and in 1931 it was given equal status with the other countries in the Commonwealth under the Statute of Westminster. A year later, de Valera was appointed prime minister, when Fianna Fáil swept to power in the General Election. Immediately he commenced dismantling the Treaty of 1921. In retaliation, Britain imposed sanctions against trade; de Valera responded, and so began the Economic War. The Governor General's powers were significantly curtailed by Dáil Éireann and in 1937 the powers of this office were completely abolished. In 1932 de Valera was elected President of the League of Nations and at his inaugural meeting made a historic appeal for peace. Also that year the 31st International Eucharistic Congress was held in Dublin. Not often was so much accomplished in such a short time. The infant state would have more teething troubles and growing pains, but it was definitely on its way.

Some of its begetters did not live to see those times – not only those who had died in the insurrection and the Civil War but also those whose span of life had ended naturally. Many mourned the death of Countess Markievicz, including the Giffords. Her funeral, in 1927, was very large, and most of the mourners were not dignitaries but the poor of Dublin, whose poverty and wretchedness she had highlighted. They had always had a problem pronouncing her name, but got round that obstacle by calling her 'Madam' or, more often, 'Madam Dear'. They followed her hearse in their shabby clothes; she was one of themselves in so far as she had died in a public ward in Sir Patrick Dun's hospital. Nellie's daughter Maeve recalled how, after Dr Kathleen Lynn had founded St Ultan's Children's Hospital, at Christmas the Countess would bring Maeve and the Coughlan children, in whose home she was staying, to visit Woolworths.[1] Their task was to choose presents that would be suitable for the boys and girls at the hospital. Armed with the choices of her marketing advisers, 'Madam', at this stage by no means flush with money, made her purchases for the children at St Ultan's.

It was not until the advent of the Eucharistic Congress and its coinciding with the third (and last) resurrected Tailteann Games that Nellie made her last important contribution to the Irish Free State. She had written, as far back as the mid-1920s, to Dudley Westropp, who was Keeper of the Art and Industrial Division at the National Museum, suggesting the desirability of collecting and preserving material relating to the Rising and the subsequent War of Independence.[2] He had agreed that it would be a good idea but nothing came of the suggestion. However, the influx of foreign visitors for both the Congress and the Games provided an international audience, and this acted as a spur to Nellie, especially after a casual meeting with an old comrade from Easter Week. They inevitably reminisced and talked of memorabilia they both had of that time. Nellie said what a pity it was that no effort had been made to conserve these mementos and, with a child's simplicity, her daughter Maeve asked, 'why don't *you* do it?'[3] The seed was sown, and though it was very close to the Congress, Nellie could see that it was an ideal time to exhibit souvenirs of Ireland's struggle for freedom.

This middle-aged lady, without benefit of either car or bicycle, and with a small daughter to care for, set out, single-handedly, to start what became the impressive collection called 'Pathway to Freedom' in the National Museum, which is now an even more impressive collection in Collins Barracks, Dublin. She began by seeking an interview with Dudley Westropp, to whom she had written many years before.[4] He still liked the idea but this time Nellie realised she had to take the initiative and that she needed support, so she approached the 1916 Club. At a specially convened meeting a resolution was passed to set up a research committee to start an exhibition of the 1916–21 struggle for freedom. At the first meeting, on 21 April 1932, Nellie was appointed Honorary Secretary. She proudly set out the full title of the committee in her minute book:

1916 Club
Cumann Saighdíurí na h-Éireann
Irish Republican Soldiers' Federation
10 Lower Abbey Street, Dublin.
Historical Research Committee.[5]

The Honorary Secretary did much of the work and never missed a meeting of the committee. Kate, much taken up by the Aonach

Tailteann, attended once and sent an excuse a second time. 'John' attended once also, and, though Grace never attended, she publicly stated her belief in the importance of such a collection and willingly gave important items on loan.

Nellie's first approaches for accommodation were to Éamon de Valera and, through him, to Minister for Education Tomás Ó Deirg, whose department encompassed the museum. She had the approval of both, and when the Minister referred her to the museum officials she was cordially received. She baulked, however, at the suggestion of Dr Adolf Mahr, keeper of Irish Antiquities at the museum, that the proposed exhibition be housed in the basement, along with the uniforms of the Napoleonic era. A compromise was reached and Nellie was offered space for three large glass cases for her exhibits, above the basement. One was furnished by J. P. Cassidy, a tailor from Pearse Street; the other two were loaned by George Messias, another tailor, from Eden Quay. Nellie called to the premises of these two men. Maeve was with her and remembered Messias pointing to a bale of dark green material on the counter which had been ordered to kilt patriotically the members of the Dáil. It had never been used.

A letter Nellie wrote to *The Irish Press* seeking exhibits was published and received a generous response.[6] She also wrote letters to known contacts and received no rebuffs. They had discussed at committee meetings the necessity of authenticity, but her knowledge of the period, and of many of the donors, stood her in good stead.

The museum authorities laid down ground rules: they would not finance the exhibition in any way, nor should their staff be asked to help in its presentation. Nellie willingly agreed to all conditions. She had her venue and her glass cases, and the exhibits started to pour in. They included precious republican pamphlets and books long out of print, the green jacket Countess Markievicz had worn in the Royal College of Surgeons and the watch (donated by Nellie herself) which was used to time the dispatches there. There was a revolver used by the same man in both the Fenian Rising of 1867 and during Easter Week, as well as a Carson rifle inscribed 'For God and Ulster', Thomas MacDonagh's MA gown and his kilt and brat, Pearse's barrister's wig and gown, Joseph Plunkett's crucifix, and the much-reported bracelet Grace had given him before he went into battle. In addition, there were anti-conscription ribbons, a Citizen Army uniform, the flag flown from the Four Courts, a Howth rifle and baton, and beautifully crafted objects from Frongoch. Nellie also selected material from Henry Sinclair, a jeweller from Nassau Street.[7] All 250 items received were authenticated and an official receipt supplied. It was a labour of love, not only for Nellie but for all those who lent their precious relics.

Everything was businesslike: duplicates of the descriptive receipts would act as indicators for any future exhibition as to from where and from whom the exhibits had come; labels were meticulously typed by Nellie in an eleventh-hour rush to beat the opening of the doors of the exhibition. It was worth it all: the visitors came, they saw, and they were conquered. One notable reaction was that of the foreign reporters who, having done this visual crash course in modern Irish history, were astonished to find that members of the professions in Ireland had been leaders and martyrs for Irish freedom.

Eulogies were the order of the day, and the role played by Mrs Eileen Gifford-Donnelly was enthusiastically acknowledged.[8] In a letter to *The Irish Press*, Mrs Kathleen Clarke questioned her in naming Pearse First President of the Republic.[9] This had been an understandable mistake made as far back as 1917, but it was true that Thomas Clarke, though not to the fore in the GPO, had been so elected. However, that aside, Mrs Clarke said, 'Mrs Donnelly deserves great credit for doing a work which will be of immense value to those who come after us.' She went on to envisage a greater collection should the museum authorities guarantee the safety of the exhibits. An enhanced exhibition, she added, would be 'a monument to one woman's energy and perseverance'.

Mr Gogan, of the museum, added his own appreciation in writing to Nellie:

> The remarkable success of your exhibition seems to me to be wholly due to the capacity and enthusiasm you brought to the task and I would regret very much indeed if your efforts and those of your Committee are thrown away. As I think I told you several times, the 1916 collection has, to my own observation, attracted an extraordinary amount of public attention and I have seen the material it contained studied with avidity by people of all ages and especially by the young.[10]

The Irish-American press also took notice, and John Devoy's paper, *The Gaelic American*, gave an enthusiastic report and concluded with the almost inevitable hope that a permanent exhibition would result.[11] Admittedly, Devoy might have been less enthusiastic had he known the exhibition contained the letter Arthur Griffith had smuggled to him, introducing Nellie, which Devoy treated casually and disinterestedly, never using it and handing it back to her as 'a souvenir'.

Having heard of the exhibition, Madge Daly wrote to Nellie from Tivoli, Limerick.[12] They had in common that Edward Daly (Madge's brother) and Joseph Plunkett (Nellie's brother-in-law) had both been shot in the early hours of 4 May 1916 in Kilmainham Gaol. This is only one example of the close ties Nellie had with exhibitors. Another shared interest was that Madge disclosed that she had a receipt for the £100 received by Liam Mellows after the surrender to enable him to escape, Nellie having helped to dye his hair. Madge offered many important articles, but there was a stipulation attached to their being given: she envisaged a permanent exhibition and wanted her items kept separately from others.

Another letter, from Bridie Clifford of Kilcoman, Killarney, reflected the heart-warming evocativeness of the undertaking:

I know how hard you worked in the museum trying to make the 1916 event such a success. I have heard several people talk of it since the Congress; they were all so glad to see their memory live once more … Kindly thanking you for your very great attention to our beloved martyrs.[13]

Bridie Clifford also promised a picture of her brother, one of Kerry's Volunteers, in the event of a permanent exhibition. Not all the items offered were confined to the twentieth century. A late offer came from the Secretary of the Pharmaceutical Society of Ireland which jolted memories for Nellie of the yellow handkerchief she had received from Bridget Hamill; it was a cannonball, fired at the battle of Clones by Bridget's hero, Owen Roe O'Neill, three centuries before.

The Irish Press, in an article on the widespread interest in the event, described Mrs Nellie Gifford-Donnelly as 'the Secretary and moving spirit'. The reporter also said, 'The collection does not purport to be in any way complete. It is, however, remarkably good, considering the fact that it was collected in three weeks. As soon as more space is available in the museum, many important additions will be made to it.'[14] The *Evening Press* repeated that report and commented that the exhibition was 'daily attracting vast throngs of both Irish and foreign visitors, who are displaying the keenest interest'.[15]

By October 1933, the temporary exhibition, which had been in existence for over a year, was being dissolved, and the obvious desirability of permanency was gaining ground, resulting in a voluminous correspondence. Assumptions were made in the early exchanges which did not materialise: the 1916 Club still saw the exhibition as theirs, and they asked Dr Mahr for a report on its success to support their plea to the Dáil for its permanent status. He willingly lent that support, as did Mr Gogan of the museum's staff. The official correspondence seemed to go along with the permanency idea. Gradually, however, that outlook was reversed, particularly when the

1916 Club pressed the point that a specialist should be appointed to take care of 'their' exhibition and that the person chosen should have taken part in the fight for freedom. It is not difficult to read between the lines that the specialist they had in mind was Nellie. In reply to a letter from de Valera's private secretary, Nellie herself explained, 'The 1916 Club have given me sole charge of the collection,' and in an article in *The Irish Press* on the matter she concluded:

> The great interest roused by the temporary exhibition has shown the necessity of making a permanent collection. The 1916 Club Research Committee, Abbey Street, asked me as their Hon. Secretary to ap- proach the government on the matter. The public will be glad to know that the government has now given permission for housing a perma- nent collection in the National Museum, Kildare Street, Dublin.[16]

In a letter to *The Irish Press* in 1935, Grace gave her views:

> The many suggestions to use Kilmainham Jail as a home for the 1916 collection brings up another side of the question. When Mrs Gifford- Donnelly conceived her idea of making the collection she had to spend months of hard, personal work interviewing possible donors, to induce them to part with their treasured possessions. As it is obvious that no building could contain all the mementos of all who fought in 1916, she was in the unique position of knowing the relative value of the mementos. Her position as sister-in-law of Thomas MacDonagh and Joseph Plunkett and her record of service in 1916 and in the Citizen Army and other branches of national affairs made collecting with discretion possible.

She argued that Nellie's personal and family ties with the movement made her invaluable. Grace referred to a letter from de Valera's private secretary regarding the inadequacy of the exhibition's accommodation and added, 'This letter, coupled with the fact that the collection is now being dealt with by museum officials who had no personal connection with the fighting, speaks for itself.'

Grace suggested optional venues: the Vice-Regal Lodge, Kilmainham Gaol or an art gallery in Harcourt Street. She concluded by declaring her intention of withholding her late husband's relics pending proper housing: they included the 'bogus' Castle Document which she stated she vividly remembered being written out as he decoded it and the much-criticised bracelet she had given Joseph.

The official door, however, had been clanged shut on the idea of Nellie being offered a paid job for managing what was obviously a rapidly growing collection. The officials with whom she had worked treated her gently: Mr Ó Cléirigh, who was to be in charge of the permanent exhibition, wrote to assure her that her request to have her name removed from the descriptive labels would be honoured.[17] Mr Westropp pledged to credit the 1916 Club with the foundation of the collection and also that in the 1935 communiqué issued through the Government Information Bureau on the matter due credit would be given to the 1916 Club and to its honorary secretary.[18] In a reply to Mr Westropp's letter containing that promise, Nellie wrote:

> Though I had a dream of building up that collection as a permanent tribute to our fighting men and women, Dr Quane gave me a rude awakening when he reminded me that I was 'only a member of the general public'. However true remarks like that are, they hurt. I have had this object so long in my heart that I feel sad that I have not the handling of it still.[19]

She ended this letter by thanking them all for their courtesy and wishing them every success with the permanent exhibition. It seems that Dr Quane was appointed to oversee the exhibition and especially to cut costs. He had spoken of her as 'only a member of the general public', but Nellie Gifford had enabled James Larkin to fulfil his promise to address the workers in Sackville Street, she had conceived and implemented the idea of the Bureau in Dawson Street to place republicans in jobs, she had instigated Alfie Byrne's very significant question at Westminster about conscription, she had served in Commandant Mallin's outpost at Easter 1916, she had drummed up enormous support for the movement in America, and she had, practically single-handedly, presented the highly successful temporary exhibition. Such involvement hardly made her fit Dr Quane's disparaging description. If Nellie were 'only a member of the general public', one may wonder what kind of person, in this context, might be regarded as unique.

How many artefacts had been destroyed or lost in the years that had elapsed since Nellie's first approach to the Department? How many more would have been lost in the passing of how many more years until officialdom awoke to the importance of the work of Nellie Gifford-Donnelly? Whatever was due to her, it was far from the scathing rejection she received.

Nellie decided to write a booklet on the exhibition. The Department of Education also vetoed this suggestion 'for the present at any rate' because such a publication was already in preparation by officials of the National Museum. It was a courteous rejection, as had been Mr Westropp's letter of 1 February 1935, in which Nellie had been assured that her part in the exhibition, and that of the 1916 Club, would be acknowledged in press reports for which the museum was responsible. There were such acknowledgements, but they gradually disappeared, and today's exhibition in Collins Barracks does not give Nellie Gifford-Donnelly any credit whatsoever.

Nellie mentioned in a letter to Mr Ó Cléirigh her intention of writing newspaper articles on the collection because, in her own words: 'As I have to fend for myself and my little girl, this business of filthy lucre counts.'[20] She published two such surviving articles, entitled 'Mementoes of Easter Week' and 'The Three Printers of the Proclamation'. The latter was a particularly excellent article, enhanced by the fact that Nellie organised a photo get-together of the three men, Christopher Brady (printer), Michael Molloy and Liam O'Brien (both compositors). All three had worked through the night in an ill-ventilated room and with the use of only a dilapidated printing press to produce the declaration of Irish freedom. Nellie's article can rightly be regarded as an important historical document in itself, presenting as it does details of that dangerous vigil in Liberty Hall and a picture of the heroic men who could have been imprisoned for this work, which they said was an honour. Another fruit of this association was that Christopher Brady gave on loan to Nellie for her exhibition the shooter and palette knife used in printing the Proclamation.

Even at this late stage it would be a fitting gesture if the authorities of the National Museum were to place a commemorative plaque on a wall of the 1916 Exhibition, now attracting a steady flow of visitors from all over the world. It could acknowledge that it had all started with the determination of a lady making her way around Dublin, seeking worthy mementos. The exhibition means that the state remembers. The plaque would mean that it does not forget.

26

GRACE'S RESTLESS YEARS

A measure of Grace's restlessness after her tragic marriage is reflected in the number of times she changed residence over the years, from when she left her childhood home in Temple Villas in May 1916. First, after the executions, she went to Joe's 'House of Larks', at his mother's invitation. Then there was the move to Kate's home in Philipsburgh Avenue. From there, it was imprisonment in Kilmainham Gaol and the NDU during the Civil War. On her release, she stayed with Mary Kelly at North Circular Road until Kate's release and then returned to Philipsburgh Avenue. After that her moves were continual, staying at first briefly, in 1923, in a Westmoreland Street flat she described as 'sub-standard'. Later addresses were at Harcourt Street, Upper Chatham Street and over offices near the Presbyterian Church corner of Parnell Square, where she had a studio on the upper floor, which was convenient for any work she did for the Gate Theatre. After receipt of the state pension awarded to her by Éamon de Valera following his accession to office in 1932, she rented two rooms in Nassau Street, overlooking the playing fields of Trinity College. Her stay there was her longest, but the stairs became too difficult, and 1950 found her in Lower Leeson Street. In 1953, she wrote to de Valera from 53 Terenure Road East. Her final address was 49 South Richmond Street. Even excluding her incarcerations in Kilmainham Gaol and the NDU, this list of moves covers twelve changes and cannot be regarded as the residential profile of a settled person. Nevertheless, Grace stoically carved out a life for herself after her personal tragedy.[1]

The award of the state pension not only made sub-standard flats avoidable but also enabled Grace to demonstrate tangibly the affection she felt for her sisters' children, especially Maeve and Donagh; she brought Donagh on a continental holiday. On a visit to France in 1924 she produced clever sketches of fellow passengers on the Rouen to Paris train – a gendarme, an old lady enjoying a glass of wine and a young *garçon* bringing home a roll of bread – pictures that captured France for those at home far more than words.

Apart from her political involvement with the movement detailed already, two other aspects of her life – social and economic – are recorded in her papers, and in those of Nellie. There is a pleasant, though indefinable, feeling that some of the men whom she met made chivalrous efforts to shelter her, economically and psychologically, after her tragic wedding. Occasionally she had lunch with Hilton Edwards and Micheál Mac Liammóir in the restaurant over the Savoy Cinema in O'Connell Street where they could enjoy not only lunch but also the music of Madame Van Allst's trio of piano, violin and cello. Another of their luncheon venues was the restaurant over the Carlton Cinema, opposite the Savoy. Edwards and Mac Liammóir gave Grace what work they could arising from their Gate productions and, in fact, she has left a detailed account – and costing – of the making of theatrical masks, requiring plaster of Paris, pieces of buckram and wood, sandpaper, Vaseline, cellulose paint and oil paint, bought in both Sibthorpe's and Lambert, Brien & Co. She shared a skill somewhat akin to that of her great-uncle, Sir Frederick, who had made the death mask of James Clarence Mangan. She also shared, with Nellie, an inventive streak and recorded such ideas as a home-brewed cough cure and a home barometer.[2]

Grace's connection with the Gate led to a misconception regarding her relationship with Blake Gifford, a young actor associated with the theatre and with Morris Davidson's first film. Davidson assumed from the comradeship between Grace and Blake, and their unusual surname, that they were brother and sister. Others shared this assumption, but the surnames were merely coincidental.[3]

Jimmy O'Dea, who had helped Grace on the beach at Skerries on the day of Muriel's drowning, gave her orders for designing posters for his famous pantomimes. Archbishop Byrne of Dublin ordered four gilt-framed certificates on vellum which Grace carefully costed for materials at £3.19 and for which she received £25. She also prepared scrolls for the Leinster School of Music, and Joseph Holloway, a legendary theatregoer, bought her pieces consistently, both before and after 1916, as well as giving her advice on commercialising her work.[4] Michael Noyek also extended the helping hand of friendship: he had been a contemporary of her brothers at the High School but, unlike them, was a supporter of Arthur Griffith and Sinn Féin. As a practising solicitor, he had worked under great difficulty in the courts of the underground First Dáil. A member of Dublin's Jewish community, Robert Briscoe, TD, also helped, and Dublin solicitor John Burke became a sort of legal guardian angel, and he and his wife welcomed Grace into their home, bought her sketches and tried to steer her towards suitable accommodation during her frequent relocations. They also did their best to nurture in her a more businesslike approach in her dealings when her generosity overcame her good sense, which was not infrequently.[5]

In listing those who reached out a helping hand to Grace, two others must be included: Hanna Sheehy Skeffington did her best to organise a woman's group in Irish-American circles to help Grace financially, and, most of all, Éamon de Valera had shown his concern as soon as he came to power, by having her included in the civil pension list.

Cathal Gannon, a fellow member of the Old Dublin Society (as were Nellie, Kate and 'John'), which had been founded in 1934 to promote the study of Dublin and Dubliners, was among those who would come round to Grace's Nassau Street flat after a lecture in the nearby premises of the society in South William Street. Cathal did odd jobs for Grace, including putting a door on the entrance to the top-floor flat in Nassau Street, thus creating a little hallway of her landing and cutting it off from the other floors. This was especially useful when she kept a Pekinese, so that the little dog would not be wandering around the offices in the building. This friendship later cooled considerably when Cathal married, because he had less free time, especially after his day's work in Guinness and new commitments. Grace felt slighted.

Gannon recalled one instance when he was doing some work in the Nassau Street flat, which Grace had leased after her pension boost. After the sound of a car drawing up outside – an unusual sound in those days – there was a ring at the door. Grace looked down from her upstairs window. She identified the caller and said, 'It's Eddie de Valera. I'm not going down.'[6] So the Taoiseach of Ireland went back to his chauffeured car. It was not that she was ungrateful for her civil-list pension – quite the contrary – but she found his intellectualism daunting, and, perhaps, at the back of it all, there was the anti-Treaty feeling that even Fianna Fáil had sold out Northern Ireland.

Before taking his seat in the Dáil, de Valera had confided in Grace his indecision as to the best course to take and concluded his arguments by the very human rhetorical question: 'Grace, what am I to do?' There is the possibility, of course, that he was sounding her out. If he was seeking her reassurance, he got none, though she respected him as the only surviving commandant of Easter Week, saved from execution with the others only by an accident of birth. He respected her stand also; after all, it had been his for over ten turbulent years. In fact, he never gave up his solicitude for his young fellow commandant's widow. Yet even when de Valera later visited Grace in hospital, though she appreciated the kindness, she still found it less than easy to cope with him conversationally, which was not characteristic of her. Nevertheless, that she trusted this most famous of her caring circle of sympathisers is best illustrated by the fact that it was to de Valera she wrote in 1953 when she was ill, letting him know of her wish to dispose of such important papers as the famous Castle Document. F. Bowyer Bell and other biographers have noted this conciliatory vein in de Valera's political make-up: there were those in his party who would have been militant against the diehards, but de Valera still found it difficult to condemn out of hand the old friends of the glory years.

A friend of the Gannon family, Denis Sexton, was told that Cathal had seen a scrapbook of Joseph Plunkett in the refuse bin at Nassau Street, along with a bronze medal relating to him.[7] In an interview, the late Eilís Dillon used this incident, possibly from the same source, to illustrate what she called 'Grace's improvidence'.[8] The criticism seems valid, but because Grace is not here to defend herself, several points need to be made to explain this seeming indifference. First, it was out of character. She kept bills for thirty years, as her sister Nellie ruefully recorded; she had all Joseph's other papers, the historically important ones, and, as was disclosed in her letter to the press, she thought too much of her husband's keepsakes to lend them to a permanent exhibition until a suitable premises could be found. Second, she prepared a scrapbook relating to Joseph which almost certainly incorporated everything she felt was important from the discarded book. Third, in Nellie's careful notes of material received for her museum exhibition, Grace's contributions, all carefully noted, include Joseph's GPO diary, his crucifix, rosary beads, prayer book, signed books, photographs, one of his poems and the bracelet she had given him. Fourth, she may have excluded from the old scrapbook any pictures of the Plunkett family and any allusion to Joseph's first love, Columba, his 'white dove of the wild, dark eyes' – leaving out his family perhaps because of deteriorating relationships and his first young love for obvious reasons. The National Library wrote to Grace asking her if she had seen or heard of the publication of *Sonnets to Columba*.[9] She replied, 'I have not seen or heard of the publication of *Sonnets to Columba*. All other Mss. by my husband are in my possession – with the exception of some which have recently been presented to an American Jesuit College.'[10]

Grace thus excluded the scrapbook from deserving to be categorised as a manuscript. Certainly the revised scrapbook, edited by Grace, would afford less academic interest than Joseph's, but might be sturdier and more artistically assembled.

Grace had been indicted for another seeming indifference – wanting to throw out Joseph's love letters before Cathal Gannon persuaded her to give them to the National Library[11] – but the library's records show otherwise: she held them to her dying day, having bequeathed them to Maeve, who arranged for their final deposit in the library. As for the discarded medal incident, this was certainly not the only rejection of honours by families of the executed, who, like Grace, saw the truncation of Ireland as a 'sell out' – not a matter of celebration by those responsible.

Over the years, despite Countess Plunkett's initial kindness, there had been a lessening of and finally no communication between Grace and her husband's family. In her leaner years, despite the fact that others seemed anxious to help her, there were no such offers coming from her in-laws. Their steadily worsening relationship went back to the 1920s when Grace was living in poor circumstances in Westmoreland Street.[12] Joseph Plunkett had wanted his family to give Grace her wife's share of 'everything of which I am possessed or may become possessed'. At that stage, he must have known that under the terms of the will of his great-uncle, Dr Cranny, who died in 1904, he was entitled to a part of the inheritance, after accumulated debts were paid and after due recognition was given to Dr Cranny's widow, who died in 1930. Grace made efforts to have her husband's wishes honoured, but to no avail.

Of course the will was not binding, being prenuptial and having only one witness' signature, but there was a moral imperative there, a son clearly providing for his widow while facing execution. Geraldine Plunkett Dillon surprisingly stood up for her sister-in-law in the matter, but the Countess was adamant. It must be remembered that she had so disapproved of the marriage that she refused her son the £100 he requested for his wedding-day expenses, when the ceremony was to have been in Rathmines church. Nevertheless, one might have expected what was in effect her son's 'deathbed' wish to be fulfilled. Apparently the Countess did not feel conscience-bound to honour the will and refused to bend on the matter. She was taken aback, however, when Grace publicised her stand by taking her mother-in-law to court.[13] To avoid further gossip, the Plunketts decided to settle out of court. Mr V. Rice, Grace's senior counsel, explained that she had been trying for years to get an account of an estate which included many houses on the Elgin and Marlborough Roads in Ballsbridge and Donnybrook. Despite even Geraldine's support, the estate was heavily encumbered, and provisions had to be made for Dr Cranny's widow, apart from the heavy debts. Grace was awarded £700. Justice Johnson's observation was: 'I am very glad the Countess has seen her way to take over these assets and pay off this young lady.'[14]

The 'young lady' was then forty-seven years of age. The Count was co-defendant, but the justice apparently saw his status as nominal only. Grace really needed help when she pursued the matter in the 1920s, but at least part of her motivation was a doggedness to see her husband's dying wish fulfilled. On the Countess' part, it could be conceded that the estate was tied up financially for years, but an explanation to that effect might have calmed the troubled waters.

It would be a mistake to assume, however pleasant the seeming gallantry of many to help this tragic young woman, that the orders she got for her artistic output were based on sympathy alone. She had, in fact, become increasingly competent in her work. As far back as 1918 she had made a little money on a book of her cartoons called *To Hold as 'Twere*. It was warmly received everywhere, with one dissentient voice from a reviewer in *The Irish Book Lover*:

> Readers who used to take delight in the clever cartoons that some-times adorned the numbers of *The Irish Review* signed *Grace Gifford* will welcome a handsome quarto just issued by Mr William Tempest of the Dundealgan Press, Dundalk, at the price of half a crown … The likeness in many is well caught, the drawing is excellent, but the whole spirit of the work is too satirical.[15]

Grace's satire was, in fact, variously described as gentle, impish or even 'mischievous'. In any event, it had made her a little money. The impishness surfaced in recent years in one of Grace's cartoons at Taylor de Vere's gallery in Kildare Street: it was called irreverently *On Board the HMS Hi You!*[16] Another signed, pen-and-ink cartoon, *The Abbey Players*, sold at Adam's in 1996.[17]

In complete contrast had been Grace's cartoons of the Simon Enquiry into the murder of Francis Sheehy Skeffington during Easter Week 1916. These had reflected the artist's contempt for that enquiry. For some, her most interesting piece of work was a page of sketches, a sort of potted Irish history, to counteract conscription for the First World War. These were not money-spinners, but she did derive a small income from commercial advertising of such commodities as soap, Clarke's shoes, the Irish Sweepstakes, biscuits and Gaeltacht industries. Grace was very businesslike in her approach and made out a schedule of deadlines for the various publications and the exact space she would require.

Between them, *Irish Life* and *Irish Fun* published over eighty of Grace's cartoons, and other publications which used her work included some still known, others long since gone:

Bystander	*Irish Radio Journal*
Catholic Pictorial	*Irish Sketch*
Éire	*Irish Women's Weekly*
Herald	*Punch*
Honesty	*Sunday Independent*
Ideal Irish Homes	*Tatler & Sketch*
Irish Independent	*The Studio*

It is estimated that her cartoon output was in the hundreds, possibly a thousand pieces. None of her work looked as if it were 'dashed off'. There is sometimes not only the mischievous element and the clever likenesses but also a delicacy of colour, never crude – particularly the use of a soft mauve, not usually associated with the more strident colours of many cartoons.

Colm Ó Lochlainn had worked with Joseph Plunkett before Easter Week in the disclosure of the Castle Document. Now his publishing firm, The Sign of the Three Candles, published a series of Grace's cartoons of Abbey actors and actresses in a book called *Doctors Recommend It*. Its 200 subscribers had backed a winner. It was, deservedly, very well received, but Grace decided against a second edition in favour of another set of cartoons, equally successful. The editions were called respectively *Twelve Nights at the Abbey Theatre* and *An Abbey Tonic in Twelve Doses*. *Drama*, an English journal, republished the first of these two in 1949.[18]

Grace dabbled in poetry, more successfully, it has to be said, than Nellie. Her love for and admiration of her niece Maeve is immortalised in verse, and Joseph would have admired the poem she published on the humble animal who bore Christ to his Passion:

'*The Entry into Jerusalem*'
Pace slow in mournful tread of humble beast.
Heed not the shouts of joy, the palm-strewn road.

Reluctant move, suffer the stinging goad,

lest you should speed the horror in the East.

Lest you should see, beneath the rising sun

the knout, the crown of thorns, the awful tree:

Oh humble beast, forever honoured be

for on your back there rides the Holy One.[19]

She signed herself 'Grace Plunkett' on this occasion but she also sometimes used Gráinne Uí Phluncéid, Grace Gifford-Plunkett and Grace Vandeleur Gifford Plunkett, still proud of her kinsman's name, Vandeleur, because of his nineteenth-century association with the founding of the Ralahine Commune experiment in County Clare, where there was thought for the tenantry as well as for the landlord's profit – not the more usual exploitation and indifference. It was another Plunkett, Horace, who initiated the cooperative movement in Ireland. So the juxtaposition of the two names in Grace's signature – Vandeleur and Plunkett – however coincidental their closeness, forms an odd linking up of two of the landlord class who cared.

A shared prayer with Joseph was the 'bookmark' of St Teresa of Ávila, found among Grace's memorabilia:

Let nothing disturb thee;

Let nothing affright thee.

All things pass away;

God only is changeless.

Patience wins all things.

To him who possesses God

nothing is wanting.

God only sufficeth.

It is written on the back of her poem 'The Entry into Jerusalem' in her own handwriting, and the first letter of the word 'patience' is written with her distinctive P – a hallmark of her work, like a circle with an upright sword through it, a sort of pictorial representation of the title of Joseph's book of poems.

During the 1920s and 1930s we get brief glimpses of Grace about Dublin, sketching, attending meetings of the Old Dublin Society, visiting friends – the Kellys on the North Circular Road and the Burkes in Rathgar, calling on her sisters, especially Nellie in Drumcondra, and visiting the cinema.

Lest there be any doubt as to Grace's political leanings during this time, there is no better way to show her being a 'sea-green incorruptible' than the recollections of her niece Maeve during her late childhood and early adolescent years. Grace often brought Maeve on visits to the cinema or theatre. In those days the National Anthem was played after every social event, and the audience all stood silently and respectfully during its performance – honouring their hard-won freedom: all except one member of the audience that is, because Grace Plunkett refused to stand for a state for which her husband did not die – a truncated twenty-six counties. Maeve recalled that she enjoyed the outings but dreaded the finale when she stood with everyone else for 'Amhrán na bhFiann', while her aunt remained determinedly seated, an embarrassment to self-conscious adolescence.[20]

271

27

A State of Emergency

The Gifford daughters had been involved with all the major episodes of Ireland's twentieth-century bid for freedom: the catalytic strike of 1913, the anti-conscription campaign, the insurrection of Easter Week, the War of Independence and the Civil War. The shambolic Boundary Commission ended with the signing away of the six northern counties by W. T. Cosgrave, Kevin O'Higgins, Ernest Blythe and John O'Byrne, leaving the nationalists in the north of Ireland still socially imprisoned, without votes and often without houses or jobs.[1] After the Civil War, Kate, Nellie and Grace stopped being hands-on involved with any turbulent rejection of the Treaty: only 'John' remained an active republican, partly through her writing but partly also because her friends were not only from the 'arty' stratum of Dublin society but also from the more persistently republican elements. In fact, Maeve Donnelly recalled a visit she and her mother made to Wicklow town where 'John' was acting as substitute editor to *An Phoblacht*, its editor, Frank Ryan, having gone to fight in the Spanish Civil War.[2] This would have been in the mid-1930s, when de Valera was coming down heavily on extremists.

The Treaty ended only armed conflict with Britain: the Economic War started with de Valera's refusal to pay any more land annuities. Britain retaliated by rejecting Irish cattle; de Valera replied by rejecting British coal, leaving Irish householders with the doubtful joy of sodden turf. The Economic War ended with Ireland paying, in full and final settlement, £10 million for land annuities. The Irish ports, still held by Britain under the Anglo-Irish Treaty, were given back to Ireland. The return of these crucial ports enabled de Valera to opt out of the Second World War, when Britain declared war on Germany on 1 September 1939. Britain's use of these ports would have made Irish neutrality impossible.

There is no mention anywhere during these years of Ernest Gifford, but the four sisters living in Ireland – Kate, Nellie, Grace and 'John' – kept in touch with him. They were now coping with the strictures of the Emergency. Nellie has left a pencilled note jotting down home details of her stringent day-to-day living during this time: Grace, obviously not as economically restricted as she had been before receiving her state pension, tried, on her visits to Nellie and Maeve, to bring food that would then have been rationed. A note records that Kate took them to a Local Defence Force concert and a show called *Signal Fires*. Mention is made of helping out 'John' with a rent problem. A footnote to the pencilled jotting gives a brief look at what the family were engaged in:

Summary, 1943

Kate at Hospitals Commission.

John at Views and News (Roleograph)

Finian mending films at Paramount Reuters' Office, Middle Abbey
    Street.

Maeve advanced at last … to pen and ink illustration.[3]

There is a further note which lists prize money Maeve had won for artistic endeavours, one in Belfast on 9 February and two on 21 July – one first prize and another 'special prize'. She was now illustrating books and obviously doing well.[4]

Muriel's son and daughter, Donagh and Barbara, were also leading contented lives, as was Eric, Claude's son, and 'John's' son, Finian. In fact, all the children of the Temple Villas Giffords were making their way in the world. In contrast to the twelve offspring of Frederick and Isabella and the twenty-three children of Isabella's grandmother, Emily, these Irish grandchildren numbered only six. Claude's son, Eric was the eldest grandchild. He had been born in 1906 and spent some time living with his grandmother, Isabella. He also remained in contact with his Aunts Kate and Nellie over the years. Some time after Claude's death Kate visited Eric and his mother in London. Ernest simply fades out of the family news. It is very interesting, however, to see family traits carried on down the generations: the old ability in art keeps cropping up, and also the love of animals. The following excerpt from the *Cork Weekly Examiner*, accompanying a picture of Eric, publicised his London exhibition of paintings:

> Thirty-one-year-old Dubliner, Eric Gifford, nephew of Mrs Gifford-Wilson, Secretary of the 1932 Tailteann Games, and of Dublin artist, Grace Plunkett, whose first 'one-man' show of paintings is now at the Wertheim Gallery, London.
>
> Mr Gifford spent six years in the Near East and most of his pictures were painted in Greece and Cyprus. He has vivid memories of Easter Week, 1916; a sniper was killed on the roof of his parents' Baggot Street house. He left Ireland in 1920 to study in Rome.
>
> He was in Madrid and Barcelona when Alfonso was driven from Spain in 1931. When he arrived in Cyprus the following year he witnessed the rebellion there, when the government house, occupied by Sir Ronald Storrs, the governor and commander-in-chief, was burned. He was at Athens at the time of the Venezilist revolt a few years later, and was in Spanish Morocco when last summer's Franco revolt began. He just managed to escape through Tangier with his mother, but many of his paintings had to be left behind, as well as his personal belongings.[5]

Eric's work in Morocco was originally as a civil engineer, but in 1957 he wrote to his Aunt Nellie to tell her that, though the newspaper he had been working for had closed down, its editor had recommended him to Radio Africa, and a new career took him to South Africa. It was part of the Radio Andorra/Madrid/Lisbon chain of commercial radio stations, and Eric was the only English speaker. He was stationed in Tangier, where he had a circle of friends, and liked it there, so he resisted an official inclination to place him in Casablanca. Eric's droll description of his lifestyle is worth recording: 'where there's a revolution, I'm there!'[6] Five revolutions, beginning in Ireland and ending in Morocco, support his claim.

The second Gifford grandson (Muriel's son Donagh), who remembered May 1916 only vaguely, when his father was executed in Kilmainham Gaol, grew up to be a judge, a poet (like his father) and also a playwright: his *Happy as Larry* production was very successful. Although the MacDonagh family effectively abducted him from his Aunt Kate's home in Philipsburgh Avenue, there seemed never to have been any animosity or ill-feeling as far as he was concerned between the two families. He became a district justice, but we get an insight into the man who was Muriel's firstborn from his verse on the card sent one Christmas from him and his wife Nuala. It must be one of the most arresting word pictures of the Annunciation:

In no rich robes of Babylonian stuff the maiden walks the simple garden dreaming of quiet marriage to her Carpenter. From her still beauty tree flower and gilded bee borrow new loveliness and the courtly fountain mirrors her grace; tuned to her steps, the music of all nature is grown sweet until from the magnificent heaven falls a shining Messenger dazzling the earth, announcing tidings more terrible than ever brazen trumpet sounded in peace or war. The maiden bows in obedience to that awful word and in the garden spring light is blasted and the air is rank with smoky torches; dim with presage of a Saviour betrayed.[7]

Donagh remained in touch with his mother's family. He was a special favourite of his Aunt Grace, and that affection was obviously reciprocated in the way he looked out for her when her health failed.[8] Grace and Kate had been the surrogate mothers of Donagh and Barbara in the immediate aftermath of their mother's death.

The only other Gifford grandson was Finian, whose artistic bent lay in photography, which materialised into cinematic reproductions, and he not only cared for Reuter's newsreels at Paramount's Abbey Street office but was also a cinema projectionist. His love of animals is reflected in numerous snapshots of his dog, but he had a more practical view of the more mundane aspects of daily living than his mother: it was his practicality that steered their domestic ship through economic storms with which the captain, 'John', was less able to cope.

Barbara, Donagh's young sister, was the oldest granddaughter. Her marriage to Liam Redmond, the Abbey actor, was a happy one, and they had four children. Their home welcomed Muriel's sisters, and Kate was a particularly welcome visitor always – a great favourite of Liam.

The second granddaughter, Maeve, grew to be a lady of great charm and integrity, twinning the genetic characteristics of art and love of animals. Even in her senior years she was beautiful, yet there was almost a complete dearth of photographs of her. In correspondence, Nellie described, nonchalantly, that Maeve got up at 6.30 a.m. so that she could walk the dogs. There is a word picture left by the late Frances White, who was Secretary to the North Dublin Society for the Prevention of Cruelty to Animals.[9] Frances said it was 'something to see' this beautiful young woman with long, curly hair, walking a bevy of small dogs along Carlingford Road in Drumcondra in the earlier hours of the morning, before going to work. Maeve became Assistant Secretary of Arks Advertising Agency. She took part in amateur dramatics and had her share of admirers. Animals were a particular love of hers, and she gave her services unstintingly to the North Dublin SPCA for most of her adult life. She was its treasurer for more than twenty years and its representative on the Dublin SPCA Committee. I can vouch for her unfailing and punctual attendance at their meetings. She listened to the points made in any relevant discussion, said very little, but cast her vote decisively. At one meeting, however, a matter arose concerning bloodsports which touched a nerve, and this quiet lady vehemently made known her abhorrence of such activities. Her words were concise, forceful and fruitful. She was also Honorary Secretary of the Shetland Sheepdog Club and, later, of the Japanese Chins Club, of which breed she had four – Alannah, Joy, Serena and Suki – as well as a grey parrot called Rocky who lived to be forty-three. Apart from art and love of animals, Maeve Donnelly had a third, very charming, genetic characteristic: like her Aunt Kate she had a most musical speaking voice and sang very sweetly.

The youngest Gifford granddaughter, Geraldine, was born in the USA to Gabriel and his wife Mary. She was said to resemble Maeve in her good looks. She pursued a successful professional career and married a chemist named John Topliss from Nottingham, England, in 1958.

In 1949, 'John' published a series of articles called 'Dublin Fifty Years Ago', in the *Irish Weekly Independent*. They were directed at Irish emigrants and brought Gabriel, on his reading them, in touch with 'John' again. In 1950 he and Nellie started writing to one another after Ada's death. Nellie retained copies of her correspondence, and from these letters can be traced the receding tides of the lives of the children who had played in the top storey of the house in Temple Villas and the incoming tides of the next generation: the normal ebb and flow of family life.[10]

28

FOR WHOM THE BELLS TOLL

The only Irish grave of the sons of Frederick and Isabella as recorded in Nellie Gifford-Donnelly's papers is that of Gerald, with whom his mother elected to be buried, in Mount Jerome Cemetery. Edward Cecil and Liebert almost certainly lie buried in North America, Claude in London, with no record in available data of Ernest's resting place. By 1950, Gabriel seemed to have been sole survivor of the six Gifford sons, and he was still living in America.[1]

After Muriel's tragic death in 1917 there was a gap of over thirty years before Ada, the next Gifford sister, was to die. With her death a bright, vivid light was extinguished. It would have been fitting had her coffin been draped with the Tricolour, to acknowledge the passing of Ireland's first self-appointed spy and to commemorate her joyful ride on top of the New York trolley in 1916, waving the new Irish flag. It is highly unlikely, however, that such an honour was accorded. Family papers indicate that she died in 1949 at the age of sixty-seven, and one of the fruits of her passing was renewed contact through correspondence between Gabriel and his sisters in Ireland, and in particular Nellie, these two especially drawn together by Ada's passing, the third of their nursery trio who had been like a separate family within a family.

In the exchange of letters between Gabriel and Nellie he emerges as a pleasant, loving husband and father. His comment, written on the back of a snap of himself, suggests that he inherited some of his

278

father's humour. In his straw hat, he bears a resemblance to Winston Churchill, and this is what he has to say:

Aug 6: Ah, here he is, not Winston as you might think at first glance. I am forbidden to send this but I am taking the law into my own hands. I meant it to be me making a sketch but they say I look more like a cop taking someone's license number. This farmer-like hat is really a smart new panama let me tell you.[2]

In another letter he describes his meeting with Mary, who was to become his wife:

Mary, when I first met her, was acting in one of Synge's plays under the direction of J. Campbell. She was then in her late twenties, not much of an actress, but otherwise very sweet, a little woman with brown eyes and black hair. I used to take her to dinners and shows, etc. We began to like each other and got married. It has been a great success. We went through times bad enough to ruin any temper but she never was anything but cheerful, even when I wasn't. It is hard to say what it is makes a person lovable but she has it in the highest degree.[3]

Nellie and Gabriel began to exchange gifts at Christmas and in the course of correspondence hopefully envisaged their two families making visits to America and Ireland. They recalled their nursery days and wrote of their early, haphazard education by Isabella's Mission Society friends. Gabriel lauds his St Andrew's school education and Protestant education generally in Ireland for its 'slovenliness' and contrasts it with the rigid disciplines of Protestant education in England and Catholic education in Ireland. To support his argument, he instances great minds from Irish Protestant education: Hamilton for mathematics, Boyle for chemistry, Berkeley for philosophy, Burke for statesmanship and Wellington for military prowess. Obviously never touched, as his sisters were (and two of his brothers-in-law), by the spirit of Irish Ireland, Gabriel is dismissive of the Irish nation's determination to promote the Irish language.

His correspondence also reflects that his art became less financially rewarding than it had been, and his letters also reveal a twin interest with Nellie in their Huguenot ancestry, with his more focused historic interpretation of the purge that sent the Bissets to America. He makes a jocose claim that he should be a member of the peerage through some fault in the Cole-Hamilton Walsh line, and, though he is only four years younger than Kate, observes, 'dear Kate. What a great old girl she is. Her handwriting is as firm as ever and her mind as clear. She is the one who should have come to America. She would have been Secretary to the President.' But he is not being patronising to someone so close to his own age because he explains how he has always seen her 'as something like an aunt or deputy mother'. Nellie's childhood concept of Kate is even more exclusive as 'a vague and rather terrifying elder sister distantly immersed in books in college'.[4]

A copy of the first extant letter Nellie sent to Gabriel, dated 10 February 1950, contains a word picture of Kate. She has 'a complexion like a rose' and her hair has faded from the old 'carrots' to 'golden'. Nellie asks Gabriel not to share their exchanged letters with other members of the family: 'cut my small personality free' is how she phrases her request.[5]

It was clear that Ada's death had brought the family closer together, but it also produced the problem of Charlie Constant, who seems to have been in a long-term relationship with her. He claimed they had been married (and that he was, therefore, entitled to her estate), but Nellie challenged this allegation. She says in her letter to Gabriel:

Ada's money, which is in the bank's care, will, I imagine, be for her brothers and sisters. But the point of the marriage must be clear. Charlie has only written the one letter to me, the one which I answered and which you saw. Could you not face Charlie, get his marriage date (if any) and verify it by a phone call to the Bureau of Marriage Licences, or whatever they call the Department. Maybe the Irish Consul could tell you the proper procedure. As the USA and Ireland both come into the picture, one end of the story must be unravelled before anything can be done with the other. Katie says she does not mean to take any steps except to cable CC and ask him again.[6]

It is not clear what relationship there had been between the said Charlie Constant and Ada Gifford but, though Gabriel and Kate show a reluctance to pursue the matter, Nellie persevered, and the Irish Consul to America finally solved the problem. Constant's claims that his birth and marriage certificates were burned were declared to be false, and Nellie referred scathingly to 'Constant's dull tricks'.[7] The estate amounted to very little, and Gabriel wrote and said that his share was to go to Nellie and Maeve, for a holiday (as was decided in family conference).

Nellie shares in her letters, joyfully and nostalgically, her brother's memories of their nursery days, much to the delight of his daughter Geraldine, who loved to hear of what her respectable father had been up to in his youth. He is metaphorically brought back to Rathmines via memory lane and was assured that many of the shops are still there – Lee's drapery, the Lucan Dairy and even the one 'with the brownish red paint with no shine in it as you saw it last'.[8]

Nellie's pride and joy in Maeve are reflected in the correspondence: her responsible post in Arks Advertising Agency, her clear soprano singing voice, her rising so early to walk her beloved dogs, her partaking in amateur dramatics, the ease with which she took to driving her first car, the fact that the two of them had never a cross word and that Nellie worried, sometimes, that she may take too much of Maeve's companionship. As against that, she mentions Maeve's 'admirers' and the deep affection she holds for her.

Typical of those who enjoy rude health, Nellie is not wholly sympathetic about Grace's stays in nursing homes and shares her feelings with Gabriel that Grace's ill health is due to 'too much smoking, and too little exercise'.[9] A greater complaint, however, shared in this correspondence with Gabriel, is reflected in her observation that the municipal libraries are prone to have books by 'quaint Irish priests' whom she criticises for having 'quashed' the Mother and Child Scheme proposed by Dr Noel Browne, TD.

It is obvious that Gabriel has agreed with her as she confides in him her distaste of hierocratic jurisdiction:

> I am the only one of the family now who is not swamped with Ortho-
> dox Catholicism. It makes it a little sad for me that in my own family
> I have no confidence in their opinions as they are merely the opinions
> they are told to have … Kate offends least. Grace lays it on 'with a
> shovel'.[10]

Nellie gets really angry, however, describing how Grace started to tell her of St Jude, the saint Catholics see as the solver of lost causes. When 'John' converts to Catholicism, Nellie expresses the hurt she felt that it had appeared in the press as a news item before Grace told her it was 'rumoured'. There is even a little touch of Nellie's feeling about Catholicism, as she tells Gabriel in a letter written in 1958: 'Maeve is out with the "boy" at the moment, a nice lad and nice-looking but alas of the majority.'[11] That 'alas' tells it all, but may have been coloured by her own failed marriage.

Very diplomatically, Nellie observes to Gabriel in one of her letters, 'I think from your Christmas card that your drawing has changed a lot.' Copies of his work he had sent her make it obvious that he had bowed to the Irish-American market, and his cards are much given to images of leprechauns. There is, however, in Nellie's papers, a clever sketch by him of a man looking rather like himself, battling the wind on a stormy day. There is also extant a very pleasant picture of a lady resting, with a small dog on her lap.[12]

Asthma and heart trouble eventually took their toll on Grace. She died on 12 December 1955. Despite Nellie's impatience with her sister's small Catholic pieties, she wrote nostalgically:

> I still find it hard to believe she is gone. She had many of the qualities attributed to songbirds, singing aggressively in her own patch ... We miss her and will always miss her for the excited interest she took in the little things many people would not think worth a thought.
>
> Even today a little pang went through me that I could not see her surprise at the six-inch high sweet pea in the garden. I had nursed the seed in a shed and set it out to brave the frost, which they did. Moreover, the seeds had lain in a bureau two years. She loved any young, growing things, whether children, animals, cultures or ideas ... Asthma over five or more years wrecked her health.[13]

It was obvious that Grace's affection for her favourite niece and nephew, Maeve and Donagh, was reciprocated, and there is evidence that Donagh, as well as Mr Burke, her solicitor friend, kept an eye on things for her.[14]

Grace's death was a lonely one. Maeve left the following, brief note on what transpired:

> At that time I was working in Harcourt Street so it was very conveni-ent ... Her doctor rang me to say he could not gain admission (he visited her constantly). I rang the landlord and John Burke. Land-lord met us at the flat and opened the door. We found Grace (fully dressed) on the floor, slumped against the side of the bed. The gas fire was lit. Her death was clearly sudden and unexpected.[15]

So the bride with the great, sad eyes looking into a futureless marriage would no more smoke her forbidden cigarettes, no more defiantly sit out the national anthem. There is evidence that she had become reclusive in her declining years, and even somewhat asocial. She died the poorest of the Giffords, had never owned a house and left assets of less than £200, which, even in the 1950s, was no fortune. Her generosity, ill health and a diminishing ability to practise her craft had affected her economically. Her few effects included a sewing machine, with which she made many of her clothes, a talent she no doubt inherited from her mother. In a roughly pencilled note dated 8 May 1956, Nellie has recorded, 'Gave Fiona circle and sword ring – and loose stone cross (for Jack Plunkett). Rosary beads and Joe's Confirmation prayerbook.'[16] So the scrapbook and bronze medal may have been deemed by Grace fit for rejection, but these other very personal items, apart from the major items on loan to museums, were carefully preserved for a period of almost forty years. Grace left also her clever, insightful sketches and some evocative poems that expressed her conviction that the troubled times, the gentle term used in Ireland to describe those difficult years, would eventually bear good fruit:

To the Leaders
Little we thought who watched your strength and power
That you would be 'defeated' 'neath the sod;
The flag is furled that knew your glorious hour,
Your eyes are closed now by the hand of God.
(And yet from age to age remember we
Christ did not die in vain on Calvary.)
　　Grace Plunkett,
　　Larkfield, Kimmage,
　　County Dublin, 1916

This had been written in Joseph's old home after his execution in

1916 and before the ensuing War of Independence. When Grace died, a healing branch was extended to her sisters by the Plunkett family, who offered a place in the family burial plot. It was Joseph's younger sister, Fiona, most close to Grace during her stay in Larkfield, who initiated this arrangement.[17]

Archdeacon Sherwin had received Grace into the Catholic Church before her marriage, and it was he who celebrated her Requiem Mass in St Kevin's church, Harrington Street. It was not a huge, public funeral – Eddie Kelly said there were only about twenty members of the public there, apart from the Gifford and Plunkett families and veterans from the War of Independence, including the President Seán T. Ó Ceallaigh, Éamon de Valera, Seán MacBride, Dr James Ryan, Oscar Traynor and Harry Colley. Despite her expressed distaste for a truncated Ireland, Grace was accorded full military honours, with a firing party and a bugled last salute. The Irish newspapers gave ample coverage to the funeral. Appropriately, the comprehensive and moving obituary in *The Irish Press* was written by Anna Kelly, the name used by May Kelly, the oldest of the Kelly children, who had metaphorically jumped over the gate of Kilmainham Gaol on the back of Grace's magnified Rex. Another obituary included an observation by her nephew, Donagh MacDonagh, who had helped her look after her business affairs and her medical expenses:

Thirty-five years ago I remember as a very small child hearing a ballad maker in the County Clare singing a song of his own composition:

'I loved Joe Plunkett and he loved me,
He gave his life to set Ireland free.'

That was a very few years after the Easter Rising of 1916, and my aunt Grace Plunkett had already entered the most secure of all National Parthenons: the world of the ballad.[18]

When Kate Gifford-Wilson died in 1957, at the age of eighty-two, she was not accorded state honours, and was buried with her husband, Walter, though there is no inscription on the tombstone to record her passing. She left behind a remembered glow; you could see eyes light up in the remembering. For instance, the late Frank Cleary, who was to found Scoil na Ceathra Maistrí in County Donegal (one of the then much-needed secondary schools founded by private individuals in rural Ireland), remembered Mrs Kate Wilson as a respected teacher of French before she left the teaching profession in 1924. Eddie Kelly's description of Kate came in staccatoed remembrances: distinguished, kind, gentle, dignified, sincere.

It is to the Scott family, close friends of Kate, that we owe the most detailed word picture of their 'Aunt Katie', an honorary title. Dymphna, Eithne and Frazia had their respective contributions. There was her physical presence: with the arrival of other adult visitors, the Scott children would leave the grown-ups and resort to the garden; with Aunt Katie, it was different. 'Elegance' and 'fascination' were words used to describe her presence, but certainly not beauty, she had a square jawline and straight reddish-grey hair. The youngest sister, Frazia, said she sat 'entranced' listening to their visitor's words, not always fully understanding them; they were spoken in a clear, very musical voice and were usually about family matters and politics. Her words were enhanced by her beautifully beringed hands with which she gestured. She smoked through a long cigarette holder. Her other jewellery was also remembered: long, dangling earrings and amber beads.

Above all, the girls remembered the personality that shone through the words: Kate had definite views but was never aggressive about them, and, in an era when it was considered that 'children should be seen but not heard' they remembered her listening to them and never making them appear 'gauche or stupid'.[19] There were eight children in the Scott household and therefore sixteen godparents. Kate was godmother to the lucky Walter, who was the envy of his siblings because of her generosity. When the Royal Dublin Golf Club burned down, Aunt Katie offered to replace the golf clubs of Larry, the eldest of the Scotts. As it happened, his clubs were unharmed, but the kind thought was there.[20]

In 1957, this gentle lady passed on, having been in her time a standby for her parents, a surrogate mother to her younger brothers and sisters, a teacher in Germany and in Parnell Square, Registrar of the First Dáil, a prisoner in Kilmainham Gaol whose release would mean, according to the Minister for Defence in 1923, 'that the public safety would be endangered', General Secretary of the revised Tailteann Games in 1924, Assistant Director and Woman's Organiser in the initiation of the new Irish broadcasting service which was to become 2RN and, finally, an employee of the Irish Hospital Sweepstakes.

The three sisters lie close together in Glasnevin's Mount Prospect Cemetery: Muriel, buried with her daughter Barbara and her son-in-law Liam Redmond; Grace in the Plunkett family grave; and Kate, buried with her husband Walter.

29

Their Entrances and Exits

After the deaths of Ada, Grace and Kate, the surviving sisters, Nellie and 'John', were inevitably brought closer together. Their lifestyles were still very different, 'John' fraternising with her more 'arty' friends and Nellie, described by Eddie Kelly as 'down to earth', contentedly living with her daughter Maeve and engaging herself in such a variety of activities as to exclude any suggestion that she had 'settled down'. Apart altogether from housekeeping and her beloved garden, among her more sedentary occupations was a keen interest in her forebears, though even this involved some footwork. There was nothing to glean from her father's 'only child' status, but her mother's colourful background was a rich field to harvest.

Meanwhile, Nellie continued to correspond with Gabriel and signed off a letter of 19 April 1958 with the phrase 'Till next week – Love to you three, Nellie'.[1] There is a gap in the correspondence – Gabriel has moved house. Finally, there is a copy of a letter Nellie sent to Mary dated 15 December 1960. It is, sadly, addressed to Gabriel's widow. Nellie speaks, among other things, of how her brother always loved children and they him. So, as far as records are available, the last of the Gifford Palatine Pact sons, baptised Catholic but Protestant and unionist each one to his life's end, had passed on. All that remained now of the Temple Villas Giffords were Nellie and 'John'.

Though Nellie had written to Gabriel about her diminished sense of patriotism, there is no indication of that diminution in another of her hobbies – preserving newspaper cuttings. They represent, in fact, a sort of history of pre- and post-Treaty Ireland and are a treasure trove for researchers. The 1930s' and 1940s' letters and articles constitute a mini-history of the Rising and the exhibition. Apart from the press reports on Grace's funeral, there is a lull for the 1950s. With the approaching advent of the half-century anniversary of the Rising, however, Nellie's patriotic feeling, never dead, is obviously rekindled, with family interest also appearing now and then.

In this mélange of 1916 memorabilia, Nellie has also cut out from some newspaper a short, illustrated article on the symbol chosen by the Government for the 1916 commemorative events: the sword of light.[2] On 11 April, three days before District Justice Donagh MacDonagh was conferred with an honorary doctorate, his sister, Barbara, had opened the Thomas MacDonagh Memorial Hall in Cloughjordan, County Tipperary, where her father had been born. *The Irish Times* published a picture of Barbara and beneath detailed her relationships with Pádraig Pearse (her godfather) and her aunts, Grace Plunkett and Helen (Nellie) Donnelly, mentioning Nellie's active service in the insurrection and stating that it was she who had initiated the 1916 collection in the National Museum. An *Irish Independent* article on Britain's failed Irish Conscription Bill for the First World War had also caught Nellie's attention, as did an article in the *RTÉ Guide* entitled 'Insurrection', the eight-part series on the Rising. An *Irish Times* 'London Letter' dealt with Lady Lavery's picture on the Irish £1 and 10-shilling notes and, in the same issue, Grace's sojourn in the Metropolitan School of Art is covered in 'An Irishwoman's Diary' by 'Candida'. *The Irish Times* elsewhere celebrated the publication by Corgi Books in paperback of Dorothy Macardle's masterpiece, *The Irish Republic*, of special interest to Nellie because Grace and Kate had been imprisoned with the author. Preserved also by Nellie, whose patriotism was obviously still very much alive, was an article on James Connolly by Frank Robbins.

Another bit of memorabilia Nellie preserved is her description of 'The last concert held in Liberty Hall'. This story relates how James Connolly heard of an unfortunate group of homeless people, stranded on Dublin's quays. Nothing would do for Connolly, beset by problems regarding the insurrection, but to help this wretched group, which included children. There was no cash in hand, so a concert would have to be organised to make some money. Nellie volunteered to run this fund-raising event, and she sought the help, willingly given, of her friends, Máire Perolz and Helena Molony. They had no problem finding vocalists and musicians in Dublin, but Nellie decided that a band would give the concert an artistic flip, so she wrote to two bands, including St James' Brass and Reed Band, who agreed to do the concert. The name of the secretary of that band happened to be James Connolly, and Seán Connolly, a member of the Citizen Army and Abbey actor, was also involved. Furthermore, Commandant Connolly gave them a play he had written, so it might have been called *The Connolly Concert*. Held in Liberty Hall, it was a great success, and the stranded family was rescued – all through the offices of a great labour leader and a caring family man. Nellie has left this extraordinary glimpse of Connolly, of his deep compassion for the down-at-heel, even in the extremely difficult preparations for that Easter Week. Was there ever a general, anywhere, who took the trouble, just before a major conflict, to reach out a helping hand to a poor, unimportant, miserable group?

Nellie was also interested in saving pictures and film of historic interest and received acknowledgement of a series of photographs of Countess Markievicz from the curator of Sligo County Library and Museum. Her interest in locating historic film surfaced in her search for a 1915 film recording that year's Wolfe Tone Procession to Bodenstown. In 1913, Thomas Clarke had requested (for John

Devoy's propaganda efforts in the USA) James T. Jameson of the Irish Animated Picture Company to record the 1913 event. Though fearful of its not being popular, Jameson complied. Captured on film were the thousand-plus pilgrims, with Pádraig Pearse giving the oration. Shown initially in the Round Room of the Mansion House and in the Town Hall, Rathmines, it would then have been shown in Jameson's cinemas, on the Curragh and in Cobh, Galway and Tralee, as well as on Jameson's touring shows. It was an unqualified success, and Thomas Clarke reported 'no picture Jameson had ever shown had received such tremendous applause'. The following year, 1914, that success was repeated. Filmed this time were The O'Rahilly, Seán Mac Diarmada, P. H. Pearse, Éamonn Ceannt and Countess Markievicz marching with Na Fianna and also James Larkin with the Irish Citizen Army. *The Freeman's Journal* had this to say of it:

> The picture was received with possibly the greatest applause yet extended to any film previously shown in this house and especially the portion containing the march of the Irish Volunteers to the graveside. Much enthusiasm was expressed at the announcement that the Irish Ladies String Orchestra under the able direction of Miss May Murphy would play *The Volunteers' March*.

In fact, Nellie's worthy search for a 1915 film of the Bodenstown Commemoration was futile, because there was no repetition of the event in that year.[3] The Volunteers' split had ensured that and, on the day, resulted in Redmond addressing a meeting at the Parnell monument in Sackville Street on the advisability of joining the British army, while further up Sackville Street, at its junction with Abbey Street, Pearse urged the rejection of such recruitment. Meanwhile, in the Phoenix Park, the anti-Redmondites were training in manoeuvres.

Nellie contacted several people who might have known something of a 1915 film's whereabouts, including Maurice Gorham of Radio Éireann, Gearóid Ó Lochlainn, Vice-Chairman of Equity, Nancy Wyse-Power, Donagh MacDonagh and Owen Sheehy Skeffington. Nellie's efforts were indeed futile, but they show her commitment and her usual thoroughness.

In June 1966, she wrote to Ida Grehan regarding, amongst other things, the desirability of including in a tourist guide a note on No. 2 Dawson Street, headquarters of the Irish Volunteers and, incidentally, of her very useful Bureau of Employment, 'The Burra'. She also urged that a note on the bust of James Clarence Mangan by her great-uncle, Sir Frederick, be included.

Nellie's newspaper clippings tell the tale: there were no knitting patterns, no recipes. Most of them reflect the nationalism which she alleged to Gabriel had lost much of its interest.[4] This very alert lady seems not to have been assessed accurately as a person who would not benefit from schooling after the age of fifteen. Perhaps her own explanation was right: she was a 'book under the desk' student with an educational independence learned at the Miss Fitts' 'academy'. Neither does all this reflect her alleged loss of interest in things patriotic. She might better have explained to Gabriel, perhaps, that while Grace and Kate were imprisoned during the Civil War, she, on her return to Ireland in 1920, had been absorbed in marital problems and in the care of her daughter. As well as that, her friends, unlike many of those of her Catholic sisters, might have met her in the church and been less likely to have had republican political thinking. She most certainly was less involved politically than her sisters in Ireland but still commemorated the movement in her drive for a museum.

So, in her later years, Nellie kept house, did the garden, cooked, decorated rooms, read avidly, watched documentaries on TV, corresponded happily and at length, looked after household pets, prepared scripts for radio and engaged in freelance journalism. As well as all that, during the 1966 commemoration of the Rising, when she received her well-earned gold medal, she met many interesting personalities from abroad.

Her agile mind was a veritable factory for ideas: in 1949, one of her inventions, the 'toy book cover', won a bronze medal at the Third Exhibition of Irish Inventions, Ideas, Handicrafts and Designs, her exhibit being featured at the Mansion House Exhibition of that year. Nellie contacted Fine Art Plastics in Middle Abbey Street and had them fashion clear plastic cylinders to fit the spines of children's storybooks. A suitable toy teddy bear, a 'Cinderella' or 'Little Red Riding Hood' could be inserted into the cylinder, adding enormously to the young reader's enjoyment. Unfortunately, the idea was not economically viable – the 1940s and 1950s were not exactly a boom time financially, so Nellie had to be content with the honour awarded.

Her radio contributions under the heading 'Suggestions' included a feature on swimming, which embodied a programme for safety, including rafts at swimming places, lifebelts, a rowing boat (preferably with an engine) and the organisation of a life-saving Congress to include the Royal Lifeboat Institute, St John's Ambulance, rowing and yachting clubs, swimming clubs and athletic clubs. Other ideas included more leg room in cinemas and a cloakroom for wet coats after patrons had queued in the rain; a law against despoiling the countryside and its wild flowers; an ingenious birds' nesting place and a suggestion that visitors to Ireland be invited to 'plant a tree'; school libraries stocking films to record Irish events; rubbish providing steam power or being recycled, thus providing jobs; kerbless frontage on paths to allow for transit of wheelchairs and prams. Nellie was ahead of her time – her ideas were all comprehensive and excellent. One sees two ghosts, perhaps, hovering behind her idea for life-saving: 'the swimmin' woman' of the Gifford childhood holidays at Greystones and the tragic drowning of Muriel in 1917.

Nellie's stories show most of their subject matter to have derived from her Meath sojourn; there is the whiff of the turf fire, the sound of the melodeon, the hand-to-mouth economy demanding that a little girl be 'sold' into service in 'the big house'. There is also the tragedy of emigration, the *fleadh*, the empty pot, and Irish dancing. She even contrived a kitchen ballet.

Inevitably, however, the machine wore down a little, and her final months had to be spent in a retirement home. The picture taken there shows a woman of contentment. She left this life, to which she had given so much, on 24 June 1971. The records of the cemetery where Nellie lies at rest with her daughter Maeve, at Balgriffin, Malahide, show Maeve's religion as Presbyterian. Nellie, irritated by Catholic pieties as she was, is recorded as 'RC', a sobering indication that what one finds in the records is not always true.

Now 'John' was the only living graduate of Bridget Hamill's nursery. Appropriately, the youngest was the last to die. She had always been somewhat apart: the only girl with a brown head of hair among all the golden redheads. She was always rather isolated, being the baby of the family, and she was the first to take an active part in republicanism, using her pen.

'John' ploughed her own furrow, even in America, and John Devoy's contemptuous dismissal of republican women, not unlike the viewpoint expressed later by Kevin O'Higgins, left her unfazed as she made her own way in republican circles. She left a little gem of a book, covering her Victorian childhood, her American sojourn and the troubled times. It is episodic and not, therefore, by its very nature, a comprehensive study, but it offers illuminating insights into events, family and friends. The debt for rescuing this material is owed to Gifford and Craven who published it under the title *The Years Flew By* shortly after 'John' died. In 2000 Arlen House republished an enlarged edition with a comprehensive essay on the six Gifford sisters written by Alan Hayes. In the book 'John' has captured pithily 'the troubled times'.

Apart from being the youngest and the only brown-haired member of the family, it became obvious from the reactions of those who met her that 'John' was the most volatile of the sisters, Ada perhaps excepted. Though she had her father's sense of fun, coupled with a gift of mimicry, her reactions to others varied between charming approval and somewhat contemptuous dismissiveness. A letter she wrote to a friend, still extant, could be termed gushing, yet her niece Maeve did not speak much of her and indeed seemed to treat her rather distantly, confessing that she and 'John's' son, Finian, opted out of conversations between their mothers, because the talk was almost invariably political. Kate had considered sharing accommodation with her youngest sister, but it was felt that 'John's' artistic friends and irregular hours would not make them suitable housemates.

The charming portrait of 'John' and Grace in early childhood had not been a harbinger of a close relationship in later years between the two. The distinctions made by the Plunkett ladies of charming Kate and Muriel, and 'John' and Grace of 'sharp' wit did not allow for the fact that Grace was quieter than her younger sister, losing contact with the more prominent women of the movement. 'John' was socialising with Helena Molony, Máire Perolz and Kathleen Lynn, but Grace's friends, like the Burkes and the Kellys, were not in that category.

In fact, 'John's' contacts over the years were less with family than with artistic people and old friends from political affiliations. Jimmy O'Dea produced some of her plays, and she was pictured with two celebrity comedians: Noel Purcell, who captured our childhood hearts as the pantomime 'Dame' ('Oh no, he didn't; oh yes, he did') and none other than Stan Laurel when he and Oliver Hardy played in the Olympia Theatre, Dublin, in the 1950s. She was a regular visitor to Maud Gonne MacBride's house, where she played the planchette board with Maud and her daughter Iseult. Helena Molony was another 'old faithful' from the troubled times who remained a friend.

'John' also remained close to Kathleen Lynn, and she and Finian stayed with Dr Lynn during one of their residential problem periods before they bought the house – in Finian's name – at Chester Road, Ranelagh, the final address for both of them.

Apart from appearing to have inherited her father's sense of humour and aside from whatever influence Bridget might have had, 'John' herself recalled that her father, though a unionist, felt chagrined to see Irish Catholic peasants doff their caps to the landlords who had acquired, by conquest, their forebears' land. Like Nellie in County Meath, Frederick's work brought him face to face with all that was socially wrong in Ireland.

A more assertive personality than either Kate, Grace, or Nellie, 'John' can be seen to have inherited much of her mother's nature, though she, too, in *The Years Flew By*, conveys, however tentatively, Nellie's more outspoken reservations about Isabella's lack of motherliness. This was somewhat at odds with the recollections of Maeve and Finian, who had good memories of their grandmother on their visits to her home.

It took moral stamina for 'John', as it did for Nellie and Grace, to struggle through the years of economic difficulty. Her journalism reads today as pungently as for her then audience, the more extreme republicans. Gradually, apart from her own *News and Views* publication, her work found its way into more politically subdued channels, even finding acceptance in the conservative *Irish Times*.

As well as writing about her beliefs, 'John' also passed on her views in person, both in the 1930s and 1950s, to obviously enraptured audiences of children in the various public libraries around Dublin. It made all the difference to hear Ireland's history from someone who had been so close to its emerging freedom.

She threw herself, wholeheartedly, into any cause she espoused and was involved in commemorative celebrations for both Maud Gonne MacBride and Dr Lynn. It has to be said that most of her causes, as well as being philanthropic, were also anti-British: she argued in an article in *An Phoblacht* that Ireland had shown India the way to freedom, and she marched with Maud Gonne MacBride, both of them carrying banners, with the 1932 Indian–Irish League; during the Second World War she was involved in homing about 400 German children in Ireland, to save them from British bombs.

Her son Finian thought of her not only with affection but also with pride. He had lived with her in poverty as well as in better times, and both he and his Aunt Kate had helped her lack of economic worldliness.

Sidney Gifford-Czira died on 15 September 1974, the last of the Temple Villas Giffords, a determined republican to the very end.[5]

May they all rest in God's peace, those with their pygmy army and also their mightier opponents from whom they wrestled Ireland's long-sought freedom. Their entrances and exits, all of them – now a part of time.

NOTES

INTRODUCTION

1   Kilmainham Gaol Records: 1916 Political Prisoners.
2   Grace Gifford's description of the wedding is recorded by her friend R. M. Fox in his *Rebel Irishwomen*, Dublin: Talbot Press, 1935; National Library (MS 21593); her statement to the Bureau of Military History in 1949.
3   National Library, MS 25913.
4   *The Irish Times*, 5 May 1916.
5   National Gallery of Ireland, Dublin.

1 FOREBEARS

1   Irish Records kept at Irish Family History Centre (Mormon), Finglas Road, Dublin.
2   Nellie Gifford-Donnelly's papers, hereinafter called NGDPs (private collection).
3   Church of Ireland Records, Dublin, under heading 'Vicars, Nineteenth Century'.
4   NGDPs.
5   This strange pact, introduced to accommodate 'mixed' marriages between Catholics and Protestants, decreed that the boys of the union would follow their father's religion and the girls that of their mother. It had no papal approval, and, in fact, Pope Leo XIII vetoed it.
6   NGDPs; Sidney Gifford-Czira, *The Years Flew By*, 2nd edn, Galway: Arlen House, 2000.

2 THE GIFFORD PARENTS

1   NGDPs.
2   In conversation with Nellie's daughter Maeve Donnelly in the early 1990s.
3   NGDPs.
4   W. F. Butler, *Sir William Butler: Autobiography*, London: Scribner's, 1911; National Library (IR 92 B 303).
5   This was when Parnell (Home Ruler), Michael Davitt (agrarian socialist) and John Devoy (ex-insurrectionist) united.
6   Details from Simon Kelliher, BL.
7   NGDPs.
8   Gifford-Czira, *The Years Flew By*, p. 4.
9   NGDPs.
10   *Ibid.*

11   *Ibid.*
12   *Ibid.*
13   *Ibid.*
14   In conversation with Maeve Donnelly in the early 1990s.
15   Baptismal records of Sandford parish church, Holy Trinity, Rathmines; St Philips, Milltown, Donnybrook Church and Church of the Three Patrons, Rathgar.
16   NGDPs.
17   *Ibid.*
18   *Ibid.*
19   *Ibid.*
20   *Ibid.*

3   VICTORIAN CHILDHOOD

1   Details from Irish Family History Centre (Mormon), Finglas Road, Dublin; NGDPs.
2   Dr Jacinta Prunty, *Dublin Slums, 1800–1925: A Study in Urban Geography*, Dublin: Irish Academic Press, 1988, Chapters 1, 2, 3 and 8.
3   NGDPs.
4   *Ibid.*
5   William E. H. Lecky, *A History of England in the Eighteenth Century*, London: Longman, Green & Co., 1878.
6   This was a phrase used to describe bad behaviour.
7   Gifford-Czira, *The Years Flew By*, pp. 6–7.
8   NGDPs.
9   *Ibid.*
10   *Ibid.*
11   *Ibid.*
12   Census of Population, 1901 and 1911.

4   GROWING UP

1   NGDPs.
2   *Ibid.*
3   *Ibid.*
4   Pupils Address Book, 1877–1908 (The High School), ref. MS 9b/12; material from David Edwards, archivist to the Erasmus Smith Trust.
5   NGDPs.
6   *Ibid.*
7   *Ibid.*
8   *Ibid.*
9   *Ibid.*
10   Gifford-Czira, *The Years Flew By*, pp. 10–11.
11   NGDPs.
12   *Ibid.*
13   Gifford-Czira, *The Years Flew By*, p. 9.
14   NGDPs.

5 INTO THE WORLD

1 Nell Gay, 'The Pretty Ladies', *The Monitor* (undated), p. 10.
2 In conversation with Maeve Donnelly in the early 1990s.
3 NGDPs.
4 Nell Gay, 'The Pretty Ladies', *The Monitor* (undated), p. 10.
5 Robert Lynd, *The Times* (London), 5 October 1892.
6 Gifford-Czira, *The Years Flew By*, pp. 12–14; NGDPs.
7 In conversation with Maeve Donnelly in the early 1990s.
8 *Ibid.*
9 Courtesy of Margaret Byrne, Librarian, Incorporated Law Society.
10 NGDPs.
11 Courtesy of Madeleine Cooke; NGDPs.
12 NGDPs.
13 Jack Fitzsimons, *Parish of Kilbeg*, Kells Art Studios, 1974. By kind permission of the editor.
14 NGDPs.
15 *Ibid.*
16 *Ibid.*
17 *Ibid.*

6 REVIVING AN OLD CULTURE

1 Gifford-Czira, *The Years Flew By*, pp. 30–31.
2 NGDPs.
3 Joseph F. Foyle, *Using Our Gaelic Games*, Thurles: The Nationalist Newspaper Co. Ltd., 1968, pp. 5, 40.
4 In conversation with Maud Clare.
5 Gifford-Czira, *The Years Flew By*, pp. 54–55.
6 In conversation with Eileen Walsh's daughter.

7 THE MIGHTY PEN

1 Gifford-Czira, *The Years Flew By*, p. 44.
2 Ed Dalton, 'Robbery Under Arms', *The Spark*, vol. III, no. 60, 2 April 1916, pp. 1, 4.
3 *Ibid.*
4 *Ibid.*
5 NGDPs.
6 *Ibid.*
7 Gifford-Czira, *The Years Flew By*, p. 35.
8 *Ibid.*, pp. 44–45.

8 DARKER DUBLIN

1 Nora Connolly O'Brien, *Portrait of a Rebel Father*, Dublin: Talbot Press, 1935, p. 119.
2 Gifford-Czira, *The Years Flew By*, p. 46; NGDPs.
3 Prunty, *Dublin Slums, 1800–1925*.
4 NGDPs.

5   *Ibid.*
6   Gifford-Czira, *The Years Flew By*, pp. 38–39.
7   James Larkin, address to enquiry chaired by Sir George Asquith, Dublin Castle, 5 October 1913.
8   Sean O'Casey, *Drums Under the Window*, London: Macmillan, 1945.
9   Gifford-Czira, *The Years Flew By*, pp. 61–62.
10 *Ibid.*, p. 63.
11 George Russell (Æ), 'Open Letter to the Dublin Employers', *The Irish Times*, 7 October 1913.
12 NGDPs.

9 INTRODUCTIONS

1   Gifford-Czira, *The Years Flew By*, p. 19.
2   NGDPs.
3   *Midland Tribune*, 1916 Jubilee Supplement (undated).
4   Donagh MacDonagh, 'Thomas MacDonagh', *An Cosantóir*, vol. V, no. 10, p. 525.
5   Donagh MacDonagh, 'A Poet and Scholar Died', *The Irish Press*, 6 April 1956, p. 4.
6   NGDPs.
7   Gifford-Czira, *The Years Flew By*, p. 19.
8   NGDPs.
9   Gifford-Czira, *The Years Flew By*, p. 19.
10 Eilís Dillon, 'A Victorian Household', in *Victorian Dublin*, edited by Tom Kennedy, Dublin: Albertine Kennedy Publishing with Dublin Arts Festival, 1980, pp. 64–65, 71.
11 Conversation with Eoghan Plunkett, Countess Plunkett's grandson.
12 Dillon, 'A Victorian Household', pp. 69–70.
13 *Ibid.*, pp. 68–69.
14 *Ibid.*, p. 67.
15 *Ibid.*
16 Conversation with Mimi Plunkett's son, Colm Ó Laoghaire.
17 Dillon, 'A Victorian Household', p. 69.
18 NGDPs.
19 *Ibid.*
20 Undated newspaper cutting.
21 Joseph Mary Plunkett, *The Poems of Joseph Mary Plunkett*, Dublin: The Talbot Press (undated), p. xii.

10 A QUESTION OF GUNS

1   Gifford-Czira, *The Years Flew By*, p. 40.
2   Conversation with Fr Dermot Brangan, SJ, Hong Kong Mission (grandson of Superintendent Brangan).
3   Conversation with John Murphy, Molly Brohoon's grandson, librarian in All Hallows library.
4   A lady to whom I spoke was there that day and remembered the hushed atmosphere as the words rang out in the clear air, with the accompaniment

of faint twittering of birds and the slight, but audible, shift of gravel near the graveside.

11 ENTER CUPID BEARING ARROWS

1 Sir William Orpen, Art Gallery, Mayfair, London.
2 In conversation with Maeve Donnelly in the early 1990s.
3 Geraldine Plunkett, 'Foreword', in Joseph Mary Plunkett, *The Poems of Joseph Mary Plunkett*, pp. ix, x.
4 *Ibid.*
5 *Ibid.*, p. x.

12 NELLIE'S *BURRA*

1 NGDPs.
2 *Ibid.*
3 *Ibid.*
4 *Ibid.*
5 *Ibid.*
6 *Ibid.*

13 HER EXILED GIFFORD CHILDREN

1 Andrew J. Kettle, *The Material for Victory: Being the Memoirs of Andrew J. Kettle*, Dublin: C. J. Fallon, 1958, p. 119.
2 NGDPs.
3 *Ibid.*
4 Arthur Read and David Fisher, *Colonel Z: The Life and Times of a Master of Spies*, London: Hodder & Stoughton, 1984.
5 NGDPs.
6 Gifford-Czira, *The Years Flew By*, p. 67.
7 *Ibid.*, p. 68.
8 *Ibid.*, p. 71.
9 *Ibid.*, p. 73.
10 *Ibid.*, p. 74.
11 *Ibid.*, p. 75.
12 *Ibid.*, pp. 75–76.
13 In her 1949 statement to the Bureau of Military History (1913–21), Grace stated that Joseph told her very little of his military affairs: WS 257, file no. S.395.

14 ROMANCE AND REBELLION

1 Bureau of Military History (1913–21): WS 257, file no. S.395.
2 The National Library, MS 21590.
3 Joseph Mary Plunkett, Letters to Grace Gifford, National Library of Ireland. Many thanks to Maeve Donnelly for her assistance in gaining access to these papers and permission to use them. All the quotations in this chapter from Joseph come from the same source.
4 The Red Bank was a Dublin restaurant.

5   'Rath' is probably a reference to the MacDonagh home in Rathmines.
6   The gun is housed, inscribed with identification, in Collins Barracks Museum, Dublin.

15   AN UNEASY CITY

1   Lieutenant Colonel J. P. Duggan, '1916. Overall Plan: A Concept of Operations', *An Cosantóir*, April 1991, pp. 23–29.
2   *Ibid.*, p. 27.
3   *Ibid.*, pp. 27–28.
4   J. Little, TD, Minister for Posts and Telegraphs, 'A 1916 Document', *The Capuchin Annual*, 1942, pp. 452–462.
5   Bureau of Military History: WS 257, file no. S.395.
6   Extract from logbook of HMS *Bluebell* for 22 April 1916: '9.28 a.m. Closed on S.S. Aud who blew ship up. 9.40 a.m. Vessel Aud sank.'

16   IN THE GARRISONS

1   Alfred Dennis, 'A Memory of P. H. Pearse', *The Capuchin Annual*, 1942, p. 260.
2   Thomas Coffey, *Agony at Easter: The 1916 Irish Uprising*, London: Harrap, 1969, pp. 5, 6, 12.
3   Charles Duff, *Six Days to Shake an Empire: Events and Factors Behind the Irish Rebellion of 1916*, London: J. M. Dent, 1966, p. 177.
4   Ruth Dudley Edwards, *James Connolly*, Dublin: Gill & Macmillan, 1981, p. 138.
5   Kenneth Griffith and Timothy O'Grady, *Curious Journey*, Cork: Mercier Press, 1998, p. 49.
6   Desmond FitzGerald, *Memoirs*, London: Routledge & Kegan Paul, 1968, p. 138; W. J. Brennan-Whitmore, *Dublin Burning*, Dublin: Gill & Macmillan, 1966, p. 36.
7   Conversation with Seoirse Plunkett.
8   Desmond Ryan, *The Rising*, Dublin: Golden Eagle Books, 1957, pp. 151–152.
9   *Ibid.*, pp. 151–152.
10 *Ibid.*, p. 157.
11 Lieutenant P. B. Brennan, 'J. M. Plunkett, The Military Tactician', *An Cosantóir*.
12 NGDPs.
13 Nellie Gifford-Donnelly, *An Phoblacht*, 18 April 1930.
14 NGDPs.
15 *Ibid.*
16 *Ibid.*
17 *Ibid.*
18 *Catholic Bulletin*, February 1917.
19 NGDPs.
20 *Ibid.*
21 *Ibid.*

17 SURRENDER

1   Nellie wrote 'Wolfe Tone' in her description, but others recorded 'Emmet'.

2   These facts are in a privately published booklet, *A Fragment of 1916 History* (undated) and include statements by the widows and neighbours of the murdered men and two teenagers: Ann Fennel, Kate Ennis, Mrs Byrne, Mrs Hickey, Kate Kelly, Mrs Connolly, Sally Hughes, Ellen Walsh, Mrs Healy, Mary O'Rourke, Roseanna Knowles and Elizabeth Beirnes, p. 19. Bureau of Military History (1913–21): CD 227/3/5. Used courtesy of the Military Archives, Cathal Brugha Barracks.

3   *A Fragment of 1916 History*, pp. 27–28.

4   Captain Wilson paid with his life for his ridicule. During the ensuing War of Independence, which was born of Easter Week, he was shot dead, by order of Michael Collins it is believed, who had been there, smouldering with resentment, in the grounds of the Rotunda, watching Wilson's iniquities.

5   R. M. Fox, 'Women of the Rising', *The Irish Press*, 9 March 1966.

18 SIXTEEN FUNERALS AND A WEDDING

1   James Connolly, *Labour and Easter Week*, Dublin: The Three Candles, 1949, p. 21.

2   Public Record Office, document no. 33/65 (or 35/65) 17858.

3   *Ibid.*, marked 'secret': letter to headquarters from Captain Arthur N. Lee, 17th Infantry Battalion dated 9.50 a.m., 3 April 1916.

4   James Stephens, 'Preface', in Thomas MacDonagh, *The Poetical Works of Thomas MacDonagh*, Dublin: The Talbot Press, 1916, p. xi.

5   Piaras F. MacLochlainn, *Last Words: Letters and Statements of the Leaders Executed After the Rising at Easter 1916*, Dublin: Stationery Office for the Office of Public Works, 1990, p. 89.

6   'Events of Easter Week, Mrs Joseph Mary Plunkett' *Catholic Bulletin*, February 1917, p. 127.

7   Grace Plunkett papers, National Library, MS 21, 593, 1 vol. (c. 1922).

8   *Ibid.*

9   Dillon, 'A Victorian Household', p. 69.

10 Brendan Kennelly, 'Joseph Plunkett', *Dublin Magazine* (spring 1966), p. 35.

11 MacLochlainn, *Last Words*, p. 151.

12 Correction in *Evening Herald*, 1 June 1916.

13 MacLochlainn, *Last Words*, p. 121.

14 *Ibid.*, pp. 137–138.

15 *Ibid.*, p. 111.

16 *Ibid.*, pp. 121–127.

17 *Ibid.*, p. 156.

18 *Ibid.*, p. 173.

19 Hubert O'Keeffe, *Centenary Booklet for Parish of St James*, 1944.

20 MacLochlainn, *Last Words*, p. 213.

19 FRONGOCH

1   Kenneth Griffith and Timothy O'Grady, *Curious Journey*, Cork: Mercier Press, 1998, p. 8.
2   Tomás MacCurtain Papers, Cork Public Museum, Memo to Staff Officer, Room 2, June 1916.
3   Seán O'Mahony, *Frongoch University of Revolution*, Killiney: FDR Teoranta, 1987, p. 83.
4   *Ibid.*, p. 133.
5   *Ibid.*, pp. 80–82; Kilmainham Gaol Archives.
6   Recorded in Pádraig Ó Baoighill, *Óglach na Rosann, Niall Pluincéad Ó Baoighill*, Annaghmakerrig: Johnswood Press, 1994, p. 53.

20 IMMEDIATE AFTERMATH

1   NGDPs.
2   The rejection in these words is recorded in Nellie's diary and was narrated by her daughter Maeve to the author.
3   NGDPs.
4   Undated cutting from *The Irish Press* (Reader's Views).
5   Gifford-Czira, *The Years Flew By*, p. 79.
6   NGDPs.
7   *Ibid.*
8   Grace Plunkett Collection, National Library, M521, 595.
9   Máire Comerford, *The First Dáil, January 21st 1919*, Dublin: J. Clarke, c. 1969, p. 42.
10   *Catholic Bulletin*, August 1917.
11   In conversation with Paddy Halpin in 1991.
12   In conversation with Maeve Donnelly in the early 1990s.
13   Narrated to the author by Greta Ó Lochlainn, whose family, like many others, had to flee Northern Ireland to avoid persecution by unionists.
14   NGDPs.
15   Recorded in the Ó Brolcháin interview.
16   In conversation with Maeve Donnelly in the early 1990s.

21 THE GIFFORDS CONFRONT THE VIGILANTES ... AND CLAN NA GAEL

1   Letter to *An Phoblacht*, 21 October 1932.
2   NGDPs; in conversation with Maeve Donnelly in the early 1990s.
3   Gifford-Czira, *The Years Flew By*, p. 80.
4   NGDPS.
5   Gifford-Czira, *The Years Flew By*, pp. 88–89.
6   NGDPs.

22 THE WAR OF INDEPENDENCE

1   David Neligan, cited in Kenneth Griffith and Timothy O'Grady, *Curious Journey*, Cork: Mercier Press, 1998, p. 135.

2 *The Irish Press*, Commemorative Supplement, 9 April 1966.

3 Comerford, *The First Dáil*, p. 58.

4 Myles Dungan, *Conspiracy: Irish Political Trials*, Dublin: Royal Irish Academy, 2009.

5 Kevin Haddick Flynn, 'Soloheadbeg: What Really Happened?', *History Ireland*, vol. 5, no. 1, 1997.

6 Kevin Haddick Flynn, 'Review of *Dan Breen and the IRA*', *History Ireland* vol. 15, no. 3, 2007.

7 Griffith and O'Grady, *Curious Journey*, p. 182.

23 THE TREATY AND ITS BITTER FRUIT

1 R. M. Fox, *Rebel Irishwomen*, Dublin: Talbot Press, 1935, pp. 75–89.

2 In conversation with Maeve Donnelly in the early 1990s; *An Cosantóir*, August 1945, vol. V, no. 10, p. 534.

3 In conversation with Maeve Donnelly in the early 1990s.

4 *Ibid.*

5 'The White Flag of the Republic', *The Republic*, March 1922. Grace published a similar argument in the *Irish Independent*.

6 T. Ryle Dwyer, *Michael Collins and the Treaty: His Differences with De Valera*, Cork: Mercier Press, 1981.

7 Tom Barry, *Guerilla Days in Ireland*, Dublin: Anvil Books, 1981, pp. 168–169.

8 In conversation with Maeve Donnelly in the early 1990s.

9 Grace has used a different spelling for Ciarán's name. 'Gus' was the pet name for Gabrielle, whose daughter, Aoife, preserved the sketch in Australia.

10 NGDPs.

11 Material supplied by Niamh O'Sullivan, Archivist, Kilmainham Gaol, where many of the autographs are held.

12 This extract is taken from Dorothy Macardle, *The Kilmainham Tortures*, courtesy of Kilmainham Gaol Archives. There is also a script in the National Library of Ireland headed 'Farewell to Kilmainham' by Dorothy Macardle which is almost the same but there are very slight, insignificant word differences in the last few lines of these accounts. The author is grateful to the National Library for providing her with a copy of this account.

13 *Ibid.*

14 *Ibid.*

15 National Archives, ref. no. NA 999/951, pp. 110–13.

16 Courtesy of Niamh O'Sullivan, Archivist, Kilmainham Gaol.

24 PICKING UP THE PIECES

1 Copies of this, and 'John's' following contributions are filed in Military Archives, Cathal Brugha Barracks, Dublin.

2 In conversation with Maeve Donnelly in the early 1990s.

3 NGDPs.

4 *Ibid.*, Isabella's will.

5   Comerford, *The First Dáil*, pp. 96–97.

6   Details of games furnished by GAA Museum, Croke Park, Dublin; NGDPs.

7   Richard Pine, *2RN and the Origins of Irish Radio*, Dublin: Four Courts, 2002.

8   P. S. O'Hegarty, 'The Early Days of Irish Radio', *Sunday Independent*, 8 August 1948.

9   *An Phoblacht*, 2 January 1926, p. 6.

10   EGD (Eileen Gifford-Donnelly), Nellie's name in the USA (NGDPs).

11   *Whistling Michael* had also been accepted for publication by the Educational Company of Ireland in July 1927.

25   THE NEW STATE REMEMBERS ... AND FORGETS

1   NGDPs; in conversation with Maeve Donnelly in the early 1990s.

2   NGDPs.

3   *Ibid.*; in conversation with Maeve Donnelly in the early 1990s.

4   NGDPs.

5   *Ibid.*

6   *Ibid.*

7   *Ibid.*

8   Nellie sometimes used the English 'Eileen' bestowed on her by Americans and sometimes the Gaelic 'Eibhlín'.

9   Mrs Clarke's letter appeared following Nellie's article on the exhibition in *The Irish Press*, 4 April 1934, entitled 'Mementoes of Easter Week'.

10   NGDPs.

11   *The Gaelic American*, 9 July 1932.

12   NGDPs.

13   *Ibid.*

14   'Relics of 1916 Rising', *The Irish Press*, 25 June 1932.

15   'Widespread Interest in Growing Collection', *Evening Press*, 25 June 1932.

16   NGDPs; Gifford-Donnelly, 'Mementoes of Easter Week'.

17   NGDPs.

18   *Ibid.*

19   *Ibid.*

20   *Ibid.*

26   GRACE'S RESTLESS YEARS

1   NGDPs.

2   *Ibid.*

3   Letter from Robert Monks, Liam Ó Laoghaire Archives, National Library of Ireland.

4   NGDPs.

5   In conversation with Maeve Donnelly in the early 1990s.

6   In conversation with Denis Sexton in the 1990s.

7   *Ibid.*

8   In conversation with Alan Hayes and Eilís Dillon, 1992.
9   Letter to Grace from National Library of Ireland, 29 August 1938.
10   Grace's reply to National Library letter, 30 September.
11   Charles Gannon, *Cathal Gannon: The Life and Times of a Dublin Craftsman (1910–1999)*, Dublin: The Lilliput Press, 2006, pp. 118, 149.
12   Letter dated 16 January 1923, NGDPs.
13   High Court Case 3787 (1934) National Archives.
14   *The Irish Press*, 2 March 1925.
15   UCD Archives, Belfield, vol. XI, J010.
16   Taylor de Vere Gallery.
17   Catalogue, Adam's, Blackrock, 25 March 1996.
18   Letter to Donagh MacDonagh from Assistant Editor, *Drama*, 13 January 1949.
19   National Library Archives, MS 21597. It was published in the *Catholic Bulletin*, 1928.
20   In conversation with Maeve Donnelly in the early 1990s.

27   A STATE OF EMERGENCY

1   Arthur Mitchell and Pádraig Ó Snodaigh, *Irish Political Documents 1916–1949*, Dublin: Irish Academic Press, pp. 164–169.
2   In conversation with Maeve Donnelly in the early 1990s.
3   NGDPs.
4   *Ibid.*
5   *Cork Weekly Examiner*, 6 March 1937.
6   NGDPs, press article.
7   Given to the author by Finian Czira.
8   Letter from the Assistant Editor of *Drama* to Donagh MacDonagh, regarding *Twelve Nights* at the Abbey Theatre, 13 January 1949; NGDPs; receipts from St Vincent's Hospital.
9   In conversation with Marie O'Byrne, North Dublin SPCA, 2007.
10   Nellie's correspondence with Gabriel, NGDPs.

28   FOR WHOM THE BELLS TOLL

1   In Nellie's letter to Gabriel, dated 10 February 1950, she refers to Ada's *brother* and sisters, NGDPs.
2   NGDPs.
3   *Ibid.*
4   *Ibid.*
5   *Ibid.*
6   *Ibid.*
7   *Ibid.*
8   *Ibid.*
9   *Ibid.*
10   *Ibid.*
11   *Ibid.*
12   *Ibid.*
13   *Ibid.*

14   MacDonagh's letter to the publisher of Grace's *Nights at the Abbey*.
15   Maeve Donnelly's written notes. NGDPs.
16   NGDPs.
17   Interview with Colm Ó Laoghaire.
18   *The Irish Press*, 14 December 1955.
19   Frazia Scott, in conversation.
20   In conversation with members of the Scott family, late 1990s and early 2000s.

29   THEIR ENTRANCES AND EXITS

1   NGDPs.
2   The work of the late Una McDonnell Watters.
3   Robert Monks, Liam Ó Laoghaire Archives, National Museum.
4   NGDPs.
5   The material in this chapter derives, almost exclusively, from NGDPs and from an interview with Finian Czira.

Acknowledgements

I would like to express my sincere thanks to everyone who helped me with the writing of this book. To Maeve Donnelly for lending me the papers of her mother, Nellie Gifford-Donnelly.

To Alan Hayes of Arlen house for his great help and support always. To Jim Larkin and Madeleine Cooke for their excellent research.

To the staff of the National Library, Niamh O'Sullivan, archivist at Kilmainham Gaol, the staff of the Military Archives in Cathal Brugha barracks and the Gilbert Library, Sister Maria Consilio, librarian of St Mary's Secondary School, Glasnevin, and the staff at Ballymun and Drumcondra local County Council libraries, the Mormon Family Archives, the Church of Ireland Records Office and Brian Crowley at St Enda's Archives.

My thanks also to Dr Jacinta Prunty, David Edwards of the Erasmus Smith Trust, Simon Kelliher BL, Dermot Bolger, Margaret Byrne, Maureen Kerr, Ann Ryder, Eithne Diggins, Greta Ó Lochlainn, Padraig Ó Baoghail, Dymphna Scott Murray, Frazia Scott Statham, Walter and Michael Scott, Robert Monks of the Liam Ó Laoghaire Archives, Father William King PP, without whose encouragement this book would not have been published, Jonathan Williams, Peter and Margaret Brittain, and all the patient staff at Mercier Press.

Thank you also to the staff at Beck n' Call Secretarial Services, Bill, Patricia and Ann at Millmount Avenue Secretarial Services,

Ann and Frances at Secretarial and Office Services, Br Tom of the O'Connell Schools Archives, and the staff of Reads in Nassau Street.

Special thanks go to All Hallows College: Don Moroney, who opened its hospitable doors for me each summer; the resident community lecturers, especially the history lecturer Fr Jim McCormack; the library staff, especially Geraldine O'Flanagan and John Murphy; all the administrative staff, including Chris Bellingham, Frank Lanigan and Celine Cleary; Fr John Hannon and his Accord team who had offices in All Hallows; and Aisling O'Loughlin. Without All Hallows' help this book would never have been finished.

I would like to thank the following who gave their time willingly in interviews: Father Moore of Rialto, Finian Czira, the Kelly family – Eddie and Kieran and their niece Aoife Duffy, who sent from Australia a copy of Grace's caricature of 'Rex' carrying the Kelly children over the Kilmainham Gaol gate – Eilís Dillon, Eoghan Plunkett, Colm Ó Laoghaire, Fr Dermot Brangan SJ, Molly Brohoon's grandson John Murphy, Frank Cleary, Terry O'Neill, Seoirse Plunkett, Denis Sexton and the staff at Taylor de Vere's Art Gallery.

Finally I would like to thank all my family and friends who have put up with my asocial behaviour. Thank you for your patience and forebearance.

INDEX

MERCIER PRESS
IRISH PUBLISHER - IRISH STORY

We hope you enjoyed this book.

Since 1944, Mercier Press has published books that have been critically important to Irish life and culture. Books that dealt with subjects that informed readers about Irish scholars, Irish writers, Irish history and Ireland's rich heritage.

We believe in the importance of providing accessible histories and cultural books for all readers and all who are interested in Irish cultural life.

Our website is the best place to find out more information about Mercier, our books, authors, news and the best deals on a wide variety of books. Mercier tracks the best prices for our books online and we seek to offer the best value to our customers, offering free delivery within Ireland.

Sign up on our website or complete and return the form below to receive updates and special offers.

www.mercierpress.ie
www.facebook.com/mercier.press
www.twitter.com/irishpublisher

Name: _____

Email: _____

Address: _____

Mercier Press, Unit 3b, Oak House, Bessboro Rd, Blackrock, Cork, Ireland

CPSIA information can be obtained
at www.ICGtesting.com
Printed in the USA
LVHW021653141120
671495LV00002B/143

9 781856 357128